INSPIRE / PLAN / DISCOVER / EXPERIENCE

# NORWAY

DK EYEWITNESS

# NORWAY

# CONTENTS

# DISCOVER 6

# EXPERIENCE OSLO 54

# EXPERIENCE NORWAY 132

# NEED TO KNOW 250

Left: Painted warehouses in Trondheim
Previous page: Morning in the Lofoten islands

# DISCOVER

The village of Loen, by Lovatnet Lake

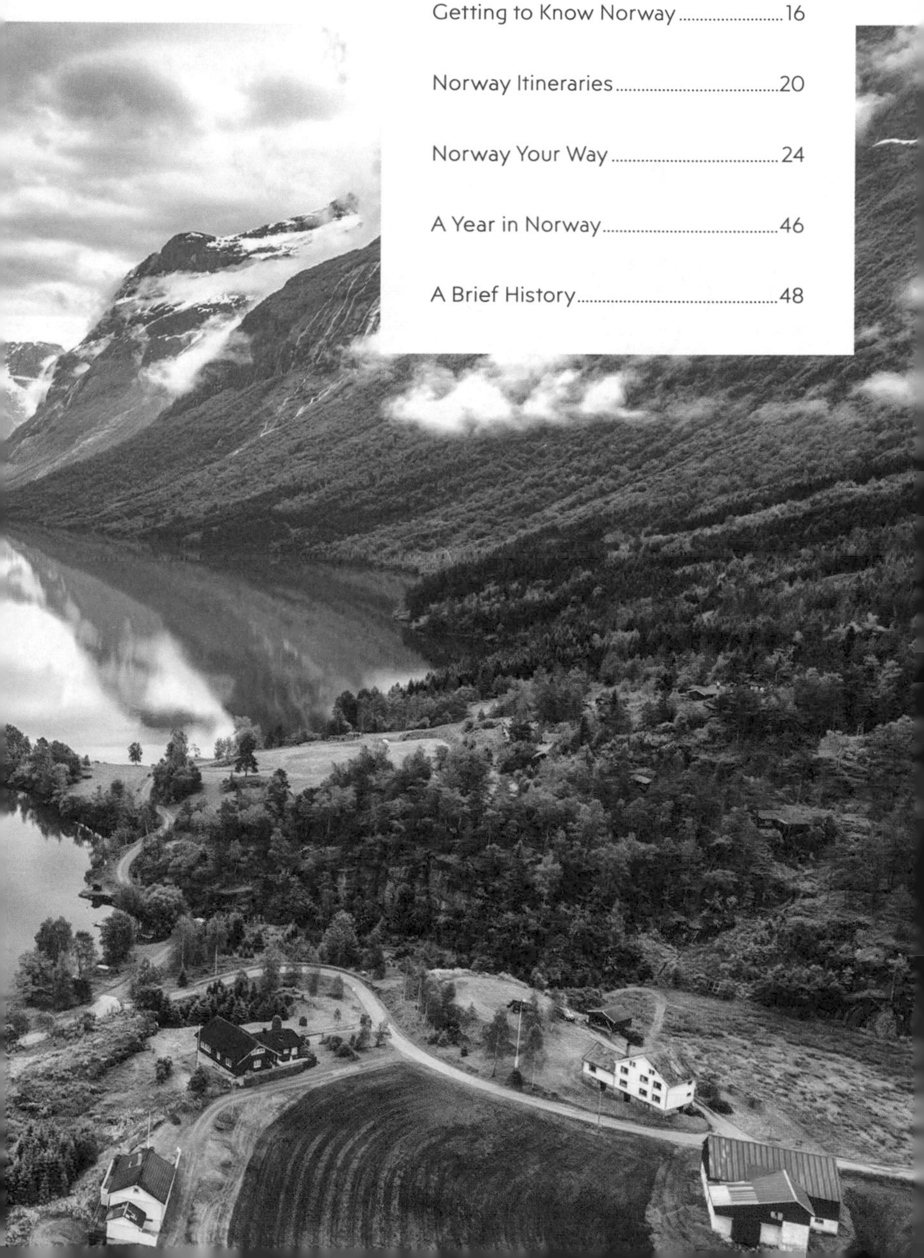

# WELCOME TO
# NORWAY

Epic and idyllic, Norway is home to some of Europe's most spectacularly beautiful landscapes. From its dramatic coastline and dazzling natural wonders, to its cosmopolitan cities and traditional towns, this is a country of contrasts. Whatever your dream trip to Norway includes, this DK Eyewitness Travel Guide is the perfect companion.

1 Colourful wooden warehouses on the waterfront of Bryggen, in Bergen.

2 A skier jumping from a snow ridge in Myrkdalen.

3 Trolltunga, a stunning scenic cliff overlooking Ringedalsvatnet Lake.

Follow in the footsteps of the Norse Vikings, who were prolific travellers themselves, as you explore this beguiling country – from the magical fjords of Vestlandet in the south to the frozen wilderness of the Arctic north. Adventure awaits you, whatever the season; hike around 'the Home of the Giants' in Jotunheimen, watch whales dance in the waters of Tysfjord or don your skis in the alpine resort of Hafjell. Alternatively, if you're after a more cosy trip, hunker down in a remote cabin and, if the time is right, you could find yourself beneath the mystical Northern Lights.

Craving the bustle of a city? Ultra-cool Oslo, Europe's fastest-growing capital, is home to superlative museums, world-class restaurants and cutting-edge architecture. On Bergen's waterfront, the city's maritime past remains evident in the attractive wooden warehouses, which now comprise buzzing bars and eateries. To the west, Ålesund's pastel-coloured fairy-tale turrets are quite unlike the clapboard and concrete of other Norwegian towns, while Trondheim counts picturesque waterways and an impressive cathedral among its attractions.

With so many different experiences and regions on offer, Norway can seem overwhelming. We've broken the country down into easily navigable chapters, with detailed itineraries and comprehensive maps to help plan the perfect adventure. Add insider tips, and a Need To Know guide that lists all the essentials to be aware of before and during your trip, and you've got an indispensable guidebook. Enjoy the book, and enjoy Norway.

# REASONS TO LOVE
# NORWAY

Its scenery is spectacular. It oozes history. It's a gourmet's delight.
Ask any Norwegian and you'll hear a different reason why they love
their country. Here, we pick some of our favourites.

### 1 HIKING IN THE WILDERNESS

Nature belongs to everyone in
Norway, and being in nature is
the nation's favourite pastime.
Vast, unspoiled wildernesses
– from mountain ranges to
glaciers – await exploration.

### THE NORTHERN LIGHTS 2

The most mesmerizing
phenomenon, the Northern
Lights (p24) shimmy across the
sky. To some they're a source of
mythology; to many, they're
the greatest show on earth.

### 3 OSLO'S CULINARY SCENE

There's a palpable excitement
around Oslo's restaurants (p62).
Upstart Oslo chefs are pushing
the boundaries of New Nordic
cuisine, showing off Norway's
abundance of irresistible
ingredients, spectacular
seafood and foraged fruits.

### MAGNIFICENT WILDLIFE 4

Norway is the last refuge for some of Europe's most beguiling wildlife – moose meander across highways and reindeer roam in national parks. Join a safari and see them for yourself.

### MUNCH'S BEACHES 5

A romantic and restless soul, Munch painted *The Scream* in Oslo and sought inspiration for *Three Girls on a Pier* in the idyllic beach towns of Hvitsten and Åsgårdstrand.

### THE NORWEGIAN ART OF *KOS* 6

Cosiness is a life skill in a climate as harsh as Norway's. Whether in a cabin or a café, being *koselig* means getting comfy, snuggling up and enjoying hearty food alone or with friends.

### NORWAY'S FJORDS 7

Carved into the coast by glaciers, the emerald fjords are the ultimate symbol of Norway *(p28)*. You can explore the breathtakingly scenery by boat, bike or on foot.

### SKIING 8

The word 'ski' comes from Old Norse, and Norwegians claim they were born with skis on their feet. Hit the powder during the winter months, or ski down a glacier in summer.

### 9 CRAFT BEER

Norwegians have been brewing since the Viking Age, so it's not surprising how enthusiastically they have embraced craft beer *(p44)*. In the last decade alone, over 200 microbreweries have bubbled up across the country.

## 10 WOODEN ARCHITECTURE

From stunning wooden cathedrals and charming turf-roof cabins to photogenic timber wharf buildings lining harbourfronts – you can't miss Norway's wealth of architecture (p40).

## 11 MIDNIGHT SUN OVER THE LOFOTEN

The red midnight sun hovers over the craggy Lofoten islands (p232) all night from May to July. A kayaking trip is an unforgettable way to experience this scene.

## 12 VIKING HERITAGE

There are many traces of the seafaring Vikings across Norway (p36) plus more modern monuments, from reconstructed longhouses to Fritz Røed's *Sverd i fjell* in Hafrsfjord.

# EXPLORE
# NORWAY

This guide divides Norway into seven colour-coded sightseeing areas: Oslo, Around Oslofjorden, Eastern Norway, Sørlandet and Telemark, Vestlandet, Trøndelag and Northern Norway and Svalbard, as shown on this map. Find out more about each area on the following pages.

SVALBARD

Nordaustlandet

Spitsbergen

Longyearbyen

Barents
Sea

0 km          100
0 miles        100

N

*Vesterålen*

*Lofoten*

*Vest-
fjorden*

Bodø

*Norwegian
Sea*

Mo i Rana

Trofors

Gäddede

Namsos

Steinkjer

**TRØNDELAG**
*p212*

Trondheim

Östersund

Kristiansund

Molde

Ålesund

Røros

Alvdal

Dombås

Florø

**EASTERN
NORWAY**
*p148*

Idre

Sveg

**VESTLANDET**
*p180*

Fagernes

Lillehammer

Mora

Hamar

Bergen

Odda

Rjukan

Drammen

**OSLO**
*p54*

**AROUND
OSLOFJORDEN**
*p134*

Karlstad

Örebro

Haugesund

*North
Sea*

Stavanger

**SØRLANDET
AND TELEMARK**
*p164*

Egersund

*Skagerrak*

Kristiansand

Linköping

0 km          100
0 miles        100

N

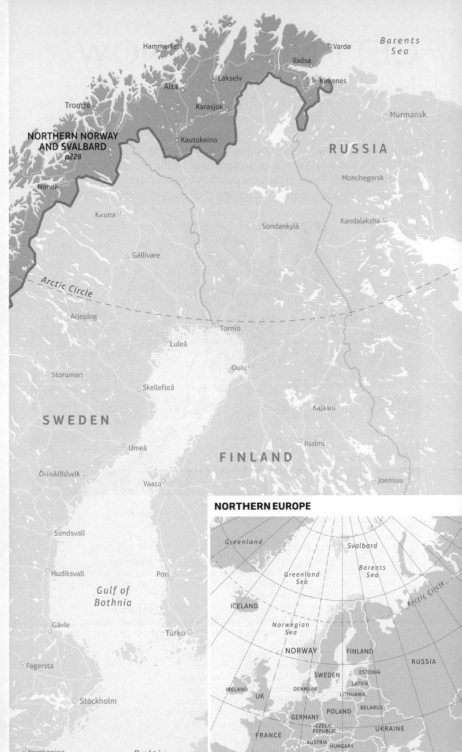

# GETTING TO KNOW
# NORWAY

Stretching up and around its Nordic neighbours, Norway's estimated 2,650 km (1,650 miles) of coastline is buffeted by the Arctic. The country's population of just 5 million reflects its often harsh landscape, but this hasn't stopped its various regions from having their own distinct personality.

## OSLO

PAGE 54

Tucked between Oslofjord and dense *marka* (forest), Europe's fastest-growing capital has reinvented itself as a destination to rival Copenhagen. Many of the city's top attractions have moved to the 9 km (6 mile) long harbour, dubbed Fjord City. This ongoing regeneration project attracts cyclists and pedestrians who promenade in harmony, overlooked by cultural hubs such as the Munch Museum, Astrup Fearnley Museum and the iconic iceberg Opera House. The harbour is also the spot for superlative restaurants and urban beaches, where the sounds of splashing and laughter ring out during the summer months. Central Oslo's grand Royal Palace and cobblestoned Karl Johans Gate are an architectural contrast to the harbourside, and offer a flavour of the past. Across the water in Bygdøy, a leafy peninsula with a rich maritime history, residential developments are punctuated by museums celebrating Norway's social and seafaring history.

**Best for**
*World-class art museums, modern architecture and New Nordic cuisine*

**Home to**
*Nasjonalmuseet, Nobel Peace Center, Akershus Festning, Norsk Folkemuseum*

**Experience**
*Twenty-one tempting courses at triple Michelin-starred Maaemo*

PAGE 134

## AROUND OSLOFJORDEN

It's easy to see why the sunlight-dappled towns, islands and beaches of Oslofjord have long inspired artists like Munch. Coastal towns such as Drøbak, Hvitsten and Son are characterized by wooden houses sloping towards the sea, waterfronts peppered with bobbing boats and seagulls shrieking as they wheel overhead. Inland, the counties of Akershus, Østfold and Vestfold are known for pretty, pastoral farmland, and history abounds here too; Fredrikstad is Norway's best-preserved fortress town, while Vestfold is home to Viking artifacts.

**Best for**
*Relaxing on beaches, Viking heritage and escaping the city*

**Home to**
*Fredrikstad, Jeløy, Verden's Ende lighthouse, Borre National Park*

**Experience**
*Stand-up paddle boarding at Hvitsten*

PAGE 148

## EASTERN NORWAY

With three of Norway's most beloved national parks, the appeal of Eastern Norway is simple: this is some of the most gorgeous, unspoiled wilderness you can find. Comprising one-fifth of Norway's land area, the parks' stirring landscapes include deep emerald valleys, Norway's longest river, Glomma, and massive Lake Mjøsa. Further north, Rondane, Jotunheimen and Dovrefjell national parks are famed for their snowcapped peaks and beautiful wildlife, with ancient herds roaming free. This is a nature lover and thrill-seeker's paradise, perfect for fishing, snowboarding and glacier-walking.

**Best for**
*Getting back to nature, mountaineering, hiking and skiing*

**Home to**
*Jotunheimen, Lillehammer, Rondane National Park*

**Experience**
*A musk oxen safari in Dovrefjell, or a summer hike across Besseggen Ridge*

→

PAGE 164

## SØRLANDET AND TELEMARK

The spectacular mountain plateau of Hardangervidda dominates Telemark. Hikers and skiers travel from one turf-roof *hytte* (cabin) to another as they scale the ravines, while fishermen wait for a catch in the rivers below. Sørlandet's coastline is the country's warmest and attracts holidaymakers in summer, while the port town of Kristiansand, idyllic settlement of Grimstad and historic island village of Lyngør all bustle with activity. The grand finale is photogenic Lindesnes lighthouse, Norway's southernmost point.

**Best for**
*Turf-roof cabins, hiking and cross-country skiing and a warmer climate*

**Home to**
*Hardangervidda, Kristiansand, Heddal Stavkirke*

**Experience**
*Hardangervidda with a* hytte-to-hytte *hike*

PAGE 180

## VESTLANDET

This is the land of the extraordinary fjords. Precipitous cliffs flank crystal-blue waters at the likes of the spectacular Geirangerfjord and Nærøyfjord. Waterfalls plunge down mountainsides, with onlookers stopping to reach out and taste the salty spray. Modern wood-and-steel viewpoints, such as Stegastein, allow enraptured visitors to pause and take in the awe-inspiring panoramas below, while fjord villages cling to the slopes overhead. Vestlandet is also home to historic Stavanger and Bergen, Norway's second city. Here you can expect a laid-back vibe, stunning art and architecture, and – famously – rain.

**Best for**
*Breathtaking fjords, traditional and Neo-Fjordic culinary scenes, and historic cities*

**Home to**
*Bergen, Stavanger, Borgrund Stavkirke, Geirangerfjord*

**Experience**
*Beautiful Bergen by catching the Fløibanen funicular to the top of Mount Fløyen and admiring the view below*

## TRØNDELAG

PAGE 212

Often overlooked in favour of Vestlandet and the Arctic North, Trøndelag is the Norway of the past. Pilgrims make for Trondheim, Norway's first capital city, where St Olav was laid to rest and independent shops and a competitive restaurant scene showcase the best crafts and cuisine in the region. To the north, the 1,000-year-old timber town of Røros is the equivalent of Norway's wild west. Quaint and picturesque, this mining town is perfect Instagram material.

**Best for**
*Historic Norway, pretty wooden towns, shopping and dining*

**Home to**
*Trondheim, Nidarosdomen, Røros*

**Experience**
*Snowy Røros by travelling through with a kicksled*

PAGE 228

## NORTHERN NORWAY AND SVALBARD

The primitive polar North is, perhaps, Norway at its most beautiful. The truly adventurous wrap up warm and travel here to experience the midnight sun over the craggy archipelagos of the Lofoten and Vesterålen islands. Continuing north, the Viking town of Tromsø is the mostly likely spot to witness the world's best show: the Northern Lights, which shimmy across the sky. At the northernmost tip, the Svalbard archipelago is a land of sub-zero temperatures, pristine snow and more polar bears than people.

**Best for**
*The Northern Lights, wild and untamed Norway, and natural wonders*

**Home to**
*Lofoten, Vesterålen, Tromsø, Svalbard*

**Experience**
*The amber midnight sun by kayaking around the Lofoton islands*

# 7 DAYS

## *In Summer*

**From lounging on urban beaches in Oslo and tucking into Neo-Fjordic cuisine in Bergen, to chasing waterfalls in Jotunheimen and watching the sun set in Ålesund, Norway in summer is unforgettable.**

### Day 1

Begin in the capital, starting at The Astrup Fearnley Museum *(p86)*, which has a lovely café terrace overlooking the fjord and sculpture park. Cross the canals en route to the striking white iceberg of Oslo Opera House *(p98)* and climb the sloping roof for stunning views of the fjord islands. As the path rolls east, grab a light lunch at cool Vippa food hall. Lose the afternoon lazing at the hip urban beach at Sørenga, but don't miss your dinner reservation at nearby Maaemo *(p98)*, Norway's best dining experience.

### Day 2

Cross the majestic Royal Palace Park on your way for a caffeine fix at nearby Fuglen *(p87)*, which is stylishly equipped with mid-century furniture. Take Ankerbrua *(p126)* to chic Grünerløkka *(p126)* and browse the funky boutiques along Markveien. If shopping isn't your bag, take a peek at Edvard Munch's childhood home. The Akerselva River path runs to Mathallen *(www.mathallenoslo.no)*, a reinvented warehouse with tempting drink and snack options, ideal for an imaginative taste of Norway. Watch the sun set from Akrobaten bridge, which swoops through Oslo's stand-out modern architecture.

### Day 3

From Oslo, take a 50-minute flight to Bergen *(p186)*. Begin by exploring the colourful timber wharf buildings at Bryggen. Enjoy a hearty meal of fish pie or reindeer and dumplings at central Pingvinen. Devote the afternoon to nearby KODE galleries, where great Norwegian

① Crossing Oslo Opera House.
② Bryggen in Bergen.
③ Bergen's fish market.
④ A ferry on Sognefjord.
⑤ Drinks atop Fjellstua.

landscape artists give their romantic interpretations of the wild. End at Lyseverket, a top spot for 'Neo-Fjordic'.

## Day 4

Begin your morning by ascending Mount Fløyen via the funicular, and marvel at the city-to-fjord panoramas. There are myriad opportunities for hikes here. Have a light bite at Fisketorget, a bustling market since the 1200s, with the freshest grab-a-snack seafood. Call in at the Bergen Sjøfartsmuseum and admire a Viking longship. Finally, head to Marg & Bein for a modern Scandi bistro meal followed by late cocktails at Apollon bar and record store.

## Day 5

Avoid the crowds on the fjord routes by driving out on the Aurlandsfjellet National Tourist Route, which provides spectacular views over Aurlandsfjord. The panoramic vista at Stegastein, a 30 m (98 ft) wood-and-steel platform, is a must. Motor to Flåm, where a Viking-style brew pub awaits, along with fjord-side, waterfall hikes. Alternatively, catch a ferry across

Sognefjorden (p194) and continue on Route 55, another wildly gorgeous drive through Jotunheimen (p152). Camp or lodge in the wilderness for the night.

## Day 6

Stretch your legs with a morning walk in Jotunheimen before getting back in the car. Drive the ruggedly beautiful route towards Ålesund along the UNESCO-listed Geirangerfjord (p198), where the Seven Sisters waterfalls cascade rainbows down the cliffs. Make it to Ålesund in time for sunset on the edge of Geirangerfjord.

## Day 7

Enjoy a more relaxed time in Ålesund (p210), which many Norwegians consider their loveliest city. If you do feel up to it, climb the 418 steps to Fjellstua, a famous viewpoint with great views of the city and sea – perfect for a preprandial drink. Finally, reserve ahead for dinner at Maki (www.brosundet.no), the town's best seafood restaurant, housed within Hotel Brosundet. If you feel like splashing out, book a room here for a final night's sleep.

1

3

# 10 DAYS

## *In Winter*

**Nowhere does winter like Norway. Don ice skates in Oslo, hit the slopes at Hafjell, sled through historic Røros and - if you're lucky - witness the Northern Lights in the sky above Tromsø.**

### Day 1

A cold winter morning in Oslo calls for a steaming beverage and *kanelsnurrer* (cinnamon twist) from Stockfleths *(p87)*. Stroll through the central cobblestoned Karl Johan retail area, checking out Scandinavian design at Paleet. If visiting between November and December, make your way to the Spikersuppa Julemarked (Christmas Market), and revel in the festive stalls and ice skating here. Warm up at the inspiring Nobel Peace Center *(p76)* before ending with a reimagined Norwegian Christmas meal at Brutus *(www.barbrutus.no)*.

### Day 2

Wrap up and catch a ferry from City Hall across the icy Oslofjord to Bygdøy. Meander through the open-air Folkemuseum *(p110)*, bedecked in twinkly lights at Christmas.

Lunch in the snug on-site café. Hop on a boat back to the waterfront in time for a glass of fizz at the Opera House bar before an evening performance there.

### Day 3

A 40-minute flight north takes you to Lillehammer *(p154)*, a serious ski city. With this in mind, keep the afternoon free for a visit to the Norwegian Olympic Museum and Flame Tower. Head for strong winter ale and a shot of Norwegian aquavit at cellar brewerBryggerikjelleren before trying an elk burger.

### Day 4

Avoid the crowds on the fjord routes and head out on the Aurlandsfjellet National Tourist Route, which provides spectacular

1 Ice skating in Oslo.
2 Skiing in Lillehammer.
3 Blackcurrant toddy.
4 Timber houses in Røros.
5 Northern Lights, Tromsø.

views over Aurlandsfjord. Magical, deep powder is just 15 km (9 miles) north at Hafjell ski resort. Check into a turf-roof, mountainside cabin for ski-in, ski-out conditions (running November to April) and wear yourself out on 32 easy to mid-level long runs. Unwind in your cabin sauna before a nightcap at Pelestova Hotel.

## Day 5

Slow down and glide along Hafjell's cross-country ski tracks, which pass through a forest of trees covered in a sparkling white blanket. Take time for a picnic with a blackcurrant toddy and *Kvikklunsj*, the crispy Norwegian chocolate bar invented for ski snacks.

## Day 6

Catch an early train due north to bleakly enchanting Røros *(p222)*. This former mining town has a maze of old, colourful wooden houses that are perfect Instagram material. Blend in by exploring on a wooden kicksled. Finally, warm up with a feast of local flavours at the snug Verthuset Inn.

## Day 7

Aim north again with an early train to Trondheim *(p216)* – once Norway's capital, now a cosmopolitan gem. Start at the soaring Gothic Nidaros cathedral *(p220)* before wandering through the independent boutiques in central Trondheim. Cross Gamle Bybro, with its photogenic view of painted wharf buildings – hopefully covered in snow – along the Nidelva river. Stroll through cobblestone Bakklandet for a meal at Skydsstasjon, a chic diner offering fish soup, reindeer casserole and a huge schnapps selection.

## Days 8-10

You might be hoping to see the Northern Lights or experience the winter wilderness with a team of huskies as your guide. If so, head to Tromsø, a 90-minute flight from Trondheim and 400 km (248 miles) north of the Arctic Circle. Allow a couple of days here to increase your chances of seeing the other-worldly *aurora borealis*. Turn over to p24 for more tips and information about the Northern Lights.

# THE MAGICAL NORTHERN LIGHTS

Possibly the world's most incredible natural phenomenon, no one forgets experiencing the dance of the celestial Northern Lights, and few places offer more opportunities and ways to experience the ethereal *aurora borealis* than Norway.

## WHERE AND WHEN

Ideally, give yourself a week for the weather and the timing to align. Increase your chances of witnessing this natural wonder by heading as far north of the Arctic Circle as possible - at least as far as Bodø. The Lofoten archipelago is situated just beneath the auroral oval and there's a strong chance of seeing the Northern Lights here *(p232)*. Tromsø is firmly in the middle of the aurora zone and also a good bet *(p236)*. Svalbard, far north and pitch dark, is another prime alternative *(p238)*. Once in place, keep an eye open from 8pm to 2am, September through to April, though the further into winter the better your chances. Many advocate 10pm to 11pm as the ultimate window.

← Watching the Northern Lights in Arctic Svalbard

## SCIENCE VERSUS MYTH

The Vikings believed the aurora was a bridge of fire built by the gods and connecting the earth to the heavens, while indigenous Samí culture says the Northern Lights are spirits of the dead. Science would have us believe the *aurora borealis* occurs when solar particles collide with the earth's atmosphere. Whatever the cause, it's up to the heavens to decide whether you'll be lucky enough to witness the Northern Lights.

↑ Tromsø illuminated by local lighting and the Northern Lights

## TO TOUR OR NOT TO TOUR?

You can see the Northern Lights in a city but the aurora is more vivid away from artificial light, so it's worth joining a tour. Websites Viator *(www. viator.com)* and Get Your Guide *(www.getyourguide.com)* both list reliable tours. Polar Adventures' 7-hour tour around Tromsø chases the lights *(www.polar adventures.no)*, while Svinøya Rorbuer in Lofoten offers a Lights 'hunt' *(www. svinoya.no)*. Tromsø's Arctic Guide Service teaches you how to photograph the Lights *(www.arcticguide service.com)*. Norwegian Coastal Ferries' 11-day Hurtigruten Classic Round Voyage operates between Bergen and Kirkenes and has a Lights guarantee *(www. hurtigruten.com)*. It's also worth picking a company that will take you elsewhere if the weather isn't cooperating.

**TOP 3 NORTHERN LIGHTS TIPS**

**Get online first**
Visit Norway's Northern Lights app *(p259)* forecasts the best conditions, time and place for a light show.

**What to wear**
Wool or fleece layers are a must, plus two pairs of woollen socks, lined boots and a woolly hat. Invest in a windproof coat and good gloves - the windchill is intense.

**If you miss them**
From husky sledding, reindeer sleighing or a local Samí meal, to skiing, snowmobiling and winter kayaking, the Arctic Circle has many rare and memorable experiences that won't disappoint.

↑ The Northern Lights dancing in the sky above Senja

### New Nordic in Norway

Norway registered as a foodie destination in 2016, when Oslo's Maaemo *(p98)* won three Michelin stars. Since then, a slew of like-minded chefs have opened New Nordic restaurants across the country. These include Christopher Haatuft at Lysverket in Bergen *(www. lysverket.no)* and Sven Erik Renaa at Re-naa in Stavanger *(p193)*. The common theme? Creative cooking that honours both Norway's rich cultural history and local ingredients to create minimal, nutritious, beautiful food.

→

Stunningly presented dishes at New Nordic powerhouse Maaemo

# NORWAY FOR
# FOODIES

Given geography's impact on food culture, it follows that Norway is a fascinating place to eat. Cuisine based on fishing, foraging and farming is irresistible – there really is something for everyone.

### Foraging for Food

Every Norwegian forages, and you can do the same. Norwegian cuisine relies on wild plants, from *ramsløk* (wild garlic), sorrel and elderflower to spruce and even birch trees. Vegetarians, vegans and meat-eaters alike should ask local tourist information offices about joining a foraging tour in August and September, when hedgerows are abundant. Look out for golden chanterelle and prized porcini mushrooms (though don't pick mushrooms without an expert guide), lingonberries and cloudberries, which are stunning amber-coloured berries that feature on many Norwegian menus. Rondane *(p160)* and Hardangervidda *(p168)* are both great for foraging.

←

Foraging for mushrooms in the wilderness

→ Chef Esben Holmboe Bang, Maaemo

# EAT

Don't miss Norway's New Nordic culinary scene, found throughout the country.

### Lyseverket
🅰A5 🏠Rasmus Meyers Allé 9, Bergen 🕐Mon, Sun D 🌐lysverket.no

Ⓚ Ⓚ Ⓚ

### Brutus
🅰D5 🏠Eiriks Gate 2, Oslo 🕐Lunch 🌐barbrutus.no

Ⓚ Ⓚ Ⓚ

### Sorrisniva
🅰F2 🏠Sorrisniva 20, Alta 🌐sorrisniva.no

Ⓚ Ⓚ Ⓚ

### Røst Teaterbistro
🅰C1 🏠Prinsens Gate 18/20, Trondheim 📞406 95 111 🕐Lunch, Mon & Sun

Ⓚ Ⓚ Ⓚ

### Restaurant Nyt
🅰E5 🏠Dronningens Gate 26, Bodø 🕐Lunch, Mon & Sun 🌐restaurant-nyt.no

Ⓚ Ⓚ Ⓚ

## Traditional *Husmanskost*

Norway's traditional cuisine - *husmanskost* - is hearty and comforting. Lunch typically entails *smørebrød* (open sandwiches) on rye or sourdough bread, topped with seafood, charcuterie and vegetables. Try for yourself at the likes of Havariet Bistro in Oslofjord *(p145)* and Inderøy Gårdsbryggeri in Trøndelag *(p225)*. Classic dinner dishes include *finnbiff* (reindeer stew) and elk meatballs, with places like Storgammen in Northern Norway *(p249)* and Elgstua Guesthouse in Eastern Norway *(p163)* both serving excellent evening meals.

↑ Open sandwich topped with smoked fish

### Sognefjorden

Want it all? Look no further than Sognefjorden. This is often called "King of the Fjords" because of its sheer size, but it deserves the title thanks to its spectacular scenery – from dramatic tumbling waterfalls to looming, snowcapped mountains (p194). At the heart of fjord country, it's easy to combine Sognefjorden with a hike across Nigardsbreen glacier and a visit to Jotunheimen National Park (p152). Balestrand is a top stop at Sognefjorden, and is sometimes referred to as the 'art village'. Stunning light, galleries and fruit farms make this a brilliant place to stop.

→

Sky reflected in the water of Lustrafjorden, an arm of Sognefjorden

# NORWAY'S
# EXTRAORDINARY FJORDS

Fjord country is perhaps the most legendary of Norway's astonishing landscapes. With some 1,000 fjords running throughout the country, it can be difficult to know where to begin. Here's a guide to picking the perfect fjord for your trip.

### Fjord Arms

Arguably the most high-impact fjords are, in fact, the side arms. Aurlandsfjord is a narrow, lush branch of Sognefjord, as is beautiful Nærøyfjord. Lysefjord is a 40 km (25 mile), mountain-flanked stunner that branches from Høgsfjorden and is famed for the viewpoint Pulpit Rock (p201). Lesser known beauties are Lusterfjord, Fjærlands-fjord and the Finnafjord.

←

Kayakers passing a waterfall on Nærøyfjord

### GLACIAL ORIGINS

Among the world's most spectacular geological formations, the Norwegian fjords are long, narrow inlets stretching deep into the surrounding mountains. At their innermost reaches, their depths often match the height of the cliffs above. They were created by a process of glacial erosion during the last Ice Age when enormous glaciers crept through the valleys, gouging steep-sided crevices into the landscape.

### Off the Beaten Track

Avoid the crowds and head for Hardangerfjorden *(p203)*, the country's second-longest fjord. Stretching from Bergen to the Hardangervidda mountain plateau, it's beautiful in springtime when hillside apple trees start to blossom. Its loveliest side arms are the Sørfjord and Eidfjord.

→

Fruit trees blooming in beautiful Hardanger

### UNESCO Fjords

The bucket list fjords of Geiranger and Nærøyfjord are worth the hype. Geiranger *(p198)* is a colossal 260 m (853 ft) deep and is famed for its impressive waterfalls. Nærøyfjord, an arm of the Sognefjord, is smaller but the Gudvangen-Aurland-Flåm boat passage along it makes for a truly unforgettable experience.

→

Ferry passing between Fodnes and Mannheller, Sognefjorden

### National and Urban Parks

Norway's cities have ample green spaces for budget-friendly days out. Bergen's Nordnes Park is perched on the tip of an urban archipelago (p184), while Trondheim has Marinen park, found between Nidaros Cathedral and the Nidelva River (p216). Then there are a whopping 46 national parks, including magnificent Jotunheimen (p152) and stunning Hardangervidda (p168).

↑ A family enjoying the urban beach at Bergen's Nordnes Park

### Did You Know?

*Allemannsretten* is the right to roam, a rule dating from ancient times. It means you can ramble nature for free.

# NORWAY ON A
# BUDGET

There's no denying that Norway can be pricey but there are ways to reduce the costs. Our best advice: head outdoors for awesome, affordable experiences. If you're on a city break, there's culture for the money-conscious. Whatever your trip entails, here are some savvy tips for saving those kroner.

### TOP 3 IDEAS FOR CHEAP SLEEPS

**Camping**
You can camp just about anywhere in Norway, and you're spoiled for choice for great spots.

**Cabins**
Norway's national trekking association, DNT, has cabins based in national parks. They contain provisions and cooking equipment.

**Airbnb**
Airbnb is well established here. While prices range massively, self-catering is where you'll really save.

### Spectacular Views

The most jaw-dropping sights in Norway are outdoors, public and free. Take Kjeragbolten, a boulder jammed into a crevasse 984 m (3,230 ft) above Lysefjorden (p200). There's also Preikestolen, a 604 m (1,980 ft) high viewpoint with a magical vantage point of the scene below (p201). Hovering 700 m (2,297 ft) above Ringedalsvatnet, Trolltunga is one of the most spectacular scenic cliffs.

↑ The iconic roof of Oslo Opera House and its interior *(inset)*

## Capital Savings

Oslo is a capital city packed with awesome, free attractions. Meander around sculpture parks Vigelandsparken *(p122)*, Ekebergparken *(p130)* and the Astrup Fearnley Museum *(p86)*, all of which are free to enter. The last even has an urban beach in summer. The historic Akershus Festning *(p94)* on the fjord is free to explore, and the Oslo Opera House is a top draw whether you're on a budget or splashing out on a performance *(p98)*.

## Cheap City Eats

From spots like Haralds Vaffel *(www.haralds vaffel.no)* in Oslo to Trekroneren *(Kong Oscars Gate 1)* in Bergen, Norway's cities offer excellent food without a hefty bill. Food halls offer great, varied food at good prices. Head to Vippa and Mathallen in Oslo and Fiske-torget in Bergen.

↑ Admiring the incredible cliff-side views from Preikestolen

→ Diners eating outside Vippa food hall in Oslo

### A Capital for Kids

City breaks can be challenging with kids in tow; not in Oslo. Climb the iceberg-shaped Opera House *(p98)* and the 200 sculptures at Vigelandsparken *(p122)*. Frogner Park has outdoor swimming pools and the largest playground in Norway *(p124)* while Det Internasjonale Barnekunstmuseet is the world's first full-scale museum dedicated to children's art *(p128)*.

→

Children interacting with sculptures at Vigelandsparken, Oslo

# NORWAY FOR
# FAMILIES

**Ranked one of the best countries to raise a family, Norway assumes you'll travel with the kids. There's something to thrill all ages – from Viking ships and archery lessons to interactive attractions and animal encounters.**

### Family-Friendly Hikes

Don some hiking boots and head outside. National parks such as Rondane *(p160)* and Hardangervidda *(p168)* have gentle hikes on moor plateaux – ideal for little legs. Look out for reindeer and sheep, and forage for cloudberries. When you need a proper energy boost, stop at a mountain lodge for waffles with jam.

←

Family hiking in the mountains near Bergen, Hordaland

## Time Travel

History comes to life at attractions across Norway. Oslo's Vikingskipshuset houses the world's best-preserved Viking ships (p113). Children can try their hand at archaeology, archery, axe throwing and farming at Midgard Historical Centre (p144) and Stiklestad Viking Centre (p226). Oslo's Norsk Folkemuseum (p110) and Lillehammer's Maihaugen (p154) are both vast open-air museums with with food and craft demos and animals.

← Incredible Viking ships at Vikingskipshuset in Oslo

## TOP 5 MONEY-SAVING IDEAS

**Free travel for kids**
Children aged 0–3 years can travel free on most public transport. Children aged 4–15 can get discounted tickets.

**Affordable accommodation**
Hotels in Norway have family room deals. DNT *hytte* (cabins) in national parks charge a fraction of hotel prices. Camping is nearly always free.

**Get outside**
Most coastal areas in Norway are free, as are national parks. Even Oslo has free outdoor parks, forests and beaches.

**Cheap city eats**
Mathallen and Vippa food halls in Oslo and Fisketorget in Bergen offer tempting treats at a fraction of city restaurant prices.

**Reduced entry fees**
Most attractions offer free admission for children up to 5 years of age and half-price admission for kids up to 16. Family tickets are available at many of Norway's sights. Check in advance.

## Animal Adventures

Whales, polar bears, reindeer, moose and more await at Europe's most exciting wildlife viewing destination. Little ones can feed moose, part of the Elgtun's Landeskogen Peace Center (*www.landes kogen.no*). In Karasjok, 60,000 reindeer graze in autumn and winter (p247). Northern Norway, particularly Vesterålen, is the top spot for a sperm whale safari, with bonus flocks of colourful puffins (p234).

← Children feeding a baby moose at Landeskogen Peace Center

### The Magic of Roald Dahl

It's impossible to estimate the global impact of Roald Dahl (1916-90). Born to Norwegian parents and named after polar explorer Roald Amundsen, Dahl wrote in English, his second language. His mother told him stories from Norwegian folklore and this undoubtedly inspired much of his own writing. He summered on the coast at Drøbak *(p142)* and Tjøme *(p146)*.

$\rightarrow$

Author of enduring children's books, Roald Dahl

# NORWAY FOR
# BOOKWORMS

Prolific playwrights, crime heavyweights, magical novelists and Nobel laureates – Norway has produced them all, and honours its literary giants with landmark attractions. Travel the literary trail for yourself.

### TOP 5 LITERARY WORKS

***The Bat*, Jo Nesbø (1997)** Officer Harry Hole heads Down Under to solve a murder.

***The BFG*, Roald Dahl (1982)** A little girl meets a Big Friendly Giant who catches dreams.

***Hunger*, Knut Hamsun (1890)** Set in 19th-century Oslo, this novel explores the dark side of city life.

***Peer Gynt*, Henrik Ibsen (1867)** This play is based around a famed Norwegian fairy tale.

***Kristin Lavransdatter*, Sigrid Undset (1920)** The life of a woman in medieval Norway.

### Pioneer Sigrid Undset

The 1928 Nobel Laureate for Literature, Sigrid Undset (1882-1949) wrote *Kristin Lavransdatter*, a trilogy set in Norway in the Middle Ages. Worthy of an HBO mini-series, it follows the dramatic life of one woman from birth until death. Undset's charming home, Bjerkebæk, is walkable from the centre of Lillehammer *(p154)*.

## King of Theatre, Henrik Ibsen

Playwright Ibsen (1828-1906) is regarded the master of realism, thanks to plays such as *A Doll's House*. You can visit his childhood home of Venstøp, which also has a café serving his favourite honey cake *(www.telemark museum.no)*. Oslo's Ibsen-museet is based in his flat *(p82)* and, in autumn, look out for the Nationaltheatret's International Ibsen Festival.

Statue of Henrik
↓ Ibsen by artist
Nina Sundbye

Knut Hamsun
↓ Centre, set in
stunning scenery

### Did You Know?

After Finland, Norway is the world's most literate country.

## Modern Heavyweight Knut Hamsun

Hamsun is the father of modern and postmodern literature. Born into a poor, rural family, Hamsun (1859-1952) won the Nobel Prize for Literature in 1920. The Knut Hamsun Centre – in Hamarøy, near where he grew up – honours his work with a library and exhibitions *(www.hamsunsenteret.no)*.

## Jo Nesbø and Harry Hole

One of the best-selling crime writers of the modern age, Nesbø has sold over 36 million books worldwide. You can follow the foot-steps of tormented police detective Harry Hole, the protagonist of Nesbø's dark Oslo crime series. Head to Hole's favourite bar, Schrøder's *(Waldemar Thranes Gate 8)*, and check out his address at Sofies Gate 5; his name is by the buzzer.

→

↑ Sigrid Undset's lovely
home of Bjerkebæk
in Lillehammer

Fictional Harry
Hole's apartment
buzzer, Oslo

### Oar-Some Ships

Viking ships were remarkable works of art and science, designed to travel speedily. Three of the world's best-preserved vessels rest in the Vikingskipshuset in Oslo *(p112)*, while Tønsberg has a replica Viking ship in its harbour *(p145)*. Look out for reconstructions of Viking ships on your travels in the likes of Lofoten *(p232)* and Vesterålen *(p234)*.

←

Replica Viking ship on the waters around the Lofoten islands

# NORWAY AND THE
# VIKING TRAIL

'Viking' comes from the Old Norse for 'to travel,' suggesting that the Vikings saw themselves as explorers. They left clues about their lives as they colonized and traded across the globe. Follow in their footsteps and learn more about their fascinating way of life.

### Life in the Longhouse

Used for feasting and sleeping, timber and turf longhouses were at the heart of Viking society. Lofotr Museum, on Vestvågøya, includes the archaeological excavation of a Viking chieftain's house, and the house has been reconstructed to the north of the site *(www.lofotr.no)*. There's a Viking farm in Avaldsnes *(www.opplevavaldsnes.no)* and Midgard also has a longhouse reconstruction *(p144)*.

### TOP 3 VIKING FESTIVALS

**Viking Festival Lofotr**
This August festival in Lofoten sees archery competitions, medieval markets, musical and combat performances and Viking ship sailing (*www.lofotr.no*).

**St Olav's Festival**
In July, Trondheim sees this open-air drama honouring St Olav, who died in battle when trying to convert Norway to Christianity in the 11th century (*www.stiklestad.no*).

**Viking Festival Avaldsnes**
Some 200 costumed Vikings set up craft and food tents as part of this large Viking party in June (*www. opplevavaldsnes.no*).

↑ Statue of Njård, Viking god of sailing and trade, in Gudvangen

### Did You Know?

In 2018, radar scans showed a possible 20-m- (65-ft-) long Viking ship just outside Oslo.

## Statues and Monuments

Viking monuments pepper Norway. Sverd i fjell (*p193*) in Stavanger comprises three mighty bronze swords planted in the earth. They honour the Battle of Hafrsfjord, when Norway was united under Harald Fair-Hair. In Bergen (*p184*), a 7-m (23-ft) sailor's monument at Torgallmenningen celebrates the country's seafaring history, starting with the Vikings. Not far from Voss (*p207*), in Gudvangen, a carved wooden Viking stands proudly beside the waters of Nærøydalselvi.

## Burial Mounds

When an important Viking died, their body would be placed in a ship alongside all their belongings. This would be set alight and pushed out to sea or covered with earth.

The country's largest site, Eidfjord in Vestlandet (*p206*), has 350 mounds (c 400–1000). The Borre Mounds at Midgard Historical Centre (*p144*) consist of both large and smaller mounds (c 600–900).

↑ Longhouse, Vestvågøy, and inside a longhouse (*inset*), Avaldsnes

→ Harald Fair-Hair's burial mound and grave in Haraldshaugen

### Kayaking and Climbing

Kayaking is an excellent way to soak up the majesty of the fjords while avoiding the throngs of hikers and boat passengers, especially in busy Vestlandet *(p180)*. A once-in-a-lifetime experience, kayaking under the midnight sun in Lofoten *(p232)* is an enthralling way to see this part of the world. Thrill seekers will relish rock climbing. The county of Romsdal is home to some of Norway's most famous climbs and Europe's tallest vertical rock face – Trolltindane, near Åndalsnes *(p211)*, which stands at over 1,000 m high (3,280 ft) and is a popular photo spot.

→

Kayaking on the emerald waters in Nordland, Northern Norway

# NORWEGIAN
# ADVENTURES

**Norway's untameable landscape and extreme climate have challenged humans to adventure here for millennia. Norwegians take great joy in exploring their jagged mountains and endless coastline, home to whales, polar bears and shaggy musk oxen. With a bit of planning, here are all the rugged adventures you can delight in.**

### Go Fish!

Norway's coastline is approximately 100,000 km (62,137 miles), although the precise figure isn't known. If laid out flat, it would circle the earth two and a half times. It's no surprise that the country's various waterways offer countless prime fishing spots. Fish for cod in the Lofoten islands *(p232)*, try to catch trout in the rivers of Hardangervidda *(p168)* and head for Guala River, close to Trondheim *(p216)*, for salmon fishing.

←

A fisherman hoping for a catch in Hardangervidda, in Telemark

INSIDER TIP
**Visiting ice caps**

Europe's largest ice caps are here in Norway, and they're best visited in summer (winter can be bitterly cold). You can join a hike, climb them, ski down them or just gaze in wonder. Experienced glacier walkers can join a guide and hike the formidable Jostedalsbreen glacier (p207) while, on Sogne-fjorden, Nigardsbreen is the most family-friendly option (p195).

## Wildlife Encounters

Whale safaris, polar bear safaris, reindeer experiences, birdwatching: there's plenty of ways to experience Norway's wildlife. Sperm whales frequent the waters near the Vesterålen islands, north of the Arctic Circle, and whale-safari operators guarantee a glimpse in summer (p234). Dovrefjell National Park (p160) offers safaris to spot the mighty musk ox, while Svalbard is home to 3,000 polar bears (p238).

→

Killer whale spyhopping in Northern Norway

## Did You Know?

The father of modern skiing, Sondre Norheim (1825–97) is the first recorded person to strap on skis.

## Hit the Slopes

The ideal way to get out into mighty Mother Nature during the winter months is by ski or snowboard. Unlike Europe's Alps, the ski resorts in Geilo (p162) and Lillehammer (p154) in Eastern Norway provide quieter pistes. Hemsedal is an excellent back-country destination (p162), and Lofoten also has back-country options (p232). For endlessly scenic, cross-country slopes, ski Hardangervidda's trail network (p168).

←

Peaceful cross-country skiing in Lofoten, Northern Norway

### Bergen's Timber Wharf Buildings

Bergen's UNESCO World Heritage wharf buildings were once a significant cultural and commercial settlement (p184). Used by the Hanseatic League for stockfish trade from the 12th to 16th centuries, these colourful buildings are today occupied by charming shops, bijou restaurants and artisan workshops, and the area pulses with activity.

←

Photogenic wharf buildings of Bryggen, in Bergen

# NORWAY'S BEAUTIFUL
# ARCHITECTURE

From Viking wood carvers to visionary modernists, Norwegian architects have long remained at the forefront of building design and continue to capture visitors' imaginations. Admire intricate medieval churches, picture-postcard cabins and concrete complexes while exploring Norway.

Charming turf-roofed cabins in Lofoten, Northern Norway ↓

### Traditional Dwellings

Norwegians have used turf as a means of insulation since the Viking Age, especially in the Arctic north. In Lofoten, fishermen's cabins (rorbuer) date back to c1120 (p232) and have turf roofs for warmth, while the roofs of Røros are frequently snowy (p222).

🔍 HIDDEN GEM
**Ureddplassen**

In the north, on the Fv17, is the world's most beautiful public toilet. This modern, glass, wave-shaped structure has stunning sea views. It's open all day.

## Trollstigen

This hairpin route – which translates as Troll's Road – zigzags for 100 km (62 miles) through the mighty nature of Fjord Norway. It can be viewed from a glass-and-steel viewpoint designed by Reiulf Ramstad Architects. Hovering at 200 m (656 ft), this viewing platform is an amazing feat of engineering *(p211)*.

→

Emerging from the mountainside, a viewpoint overlooking the Trollstigen

## Oslo Opera House

Visitors are encouraged to climb the roof at the marble and granite Oslo Opera House *(p98)*. Built by Snøhetta architects in 2008, the urban structure was designed to emulate Norway's celebrated mountains. Join a guided tour and learn about the acoustics and spacial symbolism inside.

←

Traversing the roof of Oslo's ultra-modern Opera House

## Stavkirke

While Europe used stone to build cathedrals, Norwegians used the natural resource at hand: the forest. Built from the 11th to the 13th centuries, these wooden churches are elaborately carved. The largest is Heddal Stavkirke *(p172)* and the oldest is Urnes Stavkirke *(p208)*.

→

The intricate spire of Urnes Stavkirke stretching into the sky

### Natural beauty at Nordre Isfjorden

Arctic foxes, kittiwakes, puffins and the occasional polar bear frequent this vast tundra on the north side of Isfjorden, the second-biggest fjord in Svalbard (p238). This place is particularly beautiful from late April to August when there's constant daylight.

↑ A puffin preparing for flight in Svalbard, Northern Norway

### Did You Know?

The snowy scenes in *Star Wars: The Empire Strikes Back* (1980) were filmed in Hardangervidda.

# NORWAY FOR
# NATIONAL PARKS

A once-in-a-lifetime wilderness destination, Norway is known for its untouched nature. Nowhere is better to experience its mountains, waterfalls, lakes, fjords, glaciers and wildlife than its national parks. Here we round up some of the best.

### INSIDER TIP
### DNT cabins

The Norwegian Trekking Association (DNT) runs over 550 cabins across Norway, providing comfortable and affordable stays for explorers. There are three types of DNT cabins: serviced, self-serviced and unserviced. If you go for unserviced, help yourself to the stocked food and leave a cash contribution when you leave.

### Glaciers at Jostedalsbreen National Park

Almost half of the Jostedalsbreen National Park is covered by the Jostedalsbreen glacier, one of the largest glaciers in mainland Europe. Ample glacial adventures await, from hiking and climbing to skiing; you can even spelunk in a blue ice cave (p207).

→ Mountaineers trek across Briksdal glacier, Jostedalsbreen

### Grandeur at Jotunheimen

Affectionately referred to as the 'Home of the Giants', this is Norway's most popular park (p152). Adventurers flock here for Galdhøpiggen (Norway's tallest peak) and Bøverbreen (Norway's largest glacier), while the busiest hiking route runs along the sharp Besseggen ridge, which straddles two aquamarine glacial lakes. It can get very cold at the park's sky-high summits, so be sure to pack appropriate clothing.

→

Besseggen ridge in Jotunheimen National Park

### Hiking in Hardangervidda

Reindeer herds roam free on Europe's largest mountain plateau, and the lakes below are popular with fishermen. A well-maintained trail system criss-crosses the relatively gentle slopes here, making this an excellent hiking destination for travellers who prefer easygoing beauty to an adrenaline rush (p168).

←

A backpacker hikes the wilderness in Hardangervidda

### Nature in Rondane

Founded in 1962, Rondane was Norway's first national park and boasts ten peaks at over 2,000 m (6,562 ft). Its mighty massifs range from gently rounded peaks in the south, ideal for family-friendly hiking, to steep summits for the intrepid in the north. Heather and reindeer moss cover its hills, and reindeer, bears, wolverines and lynx can be seen grazing (p160).

→

A waterfall cascading down a mountainside in Rondane National Park

### Capital Cocktails

A trip to Oslo isn't complete without a creative cocktail. From vintage-inspired Fuglen and indulgent Thief Bar in the west *(p87)* to award-winning Himkok and subtly stylish Justisen in the east *(p97)*, Oslo has cocktail bars to suit every taste. Culture vultures might like to enjoy a cocktail in the bar at the Opera House *(p98)* before watching a performance, or after an exhibition at Astrup Fearnley Museum's Vingen *(p87)*.

→

Prepping drinks at Thief Bar, home to cool cocktails *(inset)*

# NORWAY
# ON TAP

Norway's thirst has grown in the last decade. Brewers are tapping into their Viking roots to make hearty ales and celebrating their hoppy tipples at innovative craft beer festivals. As for craft cocktails, Oslo's expert bartenders won't let you down. Here, we toast Norway on tap.

### Season-ale Drinking

Norwegian ale isn't for the faint-hearted. While it's tricky to define strict categories, Scandi craft beer enthusiasts aim for memorable and unrestrained brews, often hitting double-figure ABVs. They take inspiration from the seasons and the landscape, from fjords to forests. In summer and around Christmas, brewers release limited edition seasonal beers so there's something different to try whenever you visit. Start your education at Ægir brewery (www.flamsbrygga. no) in Flåm *(p195)* and Austmann *(www.austmann. no)* in Trondheim *(p216)*.

←

Beers at Viking-style brewpub Ægir, in the heart of Ford Norway

## CRAFT BEER FESTIVALS

*Utepils* ('OOH-ta-pilz') is a tradition celebrating the first outdoor beer of the year. This is best embraced in May at Bergen Craft Beer Fest *(www.bergen craftbeerfest.no)* or at Fredrikstad Ølfestival *(www.fredrikstadolfestival. no)*. In June, Oslo welcomes Mikrobryggeri Festival *(www.brygghus.no)*. Trondheim holds Bryggeri Festivalen *(www.oimat. no/bryggerifestivalen)* in August.

## TOP 3 CRAFT BREWERIES

### Lervig Aktiebryggeri
The city's top brewery specializes in unusual flavours, including coconut and wild yeast. Must sip: Double Rye IPA. (Vierveien 1, Stavanger; www.lervig.no)

### Nøgne Ø
Founded in 2002, the first warrior in Norway's craft beer revolution is still going strong. Must sip: Imperial Brown Ale. (Lunde 8, Grimstad; www.nogne-o.com)

### Cervisiam
Award-winning upstart famous for punny brew names and cool, comic-style can art. Must sip: Satanic Panic Imperial Milk Stout (Torggata 18b, Oslo; www.cervisiam.no).

↑ Replica Viking drinking horns for holding beer and mead

## Drink like a Viking
The Vikings drank ale and mead, both of which were traditionally brewed by women, using hops, malted barley and rye, and juniper. According to Viking law, there were penalties for not partaking in the brewing of beer and public drinking rituals. Don't risk the penalty: take part in a feast night at Lofotr Museum and drink like a Viking *(www.lofotr.no)*.

# A YEAR IN
# NORWAY

## JANUARY

△ **Festival of Northern Lights** *(second half of Jan)*. A heady combination of an *aurora borealis* light show and live music in Tromsø.

## FEBRUARY

**Polar Jazz** *(early Feb)*. Hot jazz music in cool Longyearbyen, this is the most northerly jazz and blues festival.

△ **Røros Winter Fair** *(late Feb)*. A handicraft extravaganza celebrating traditional wool knit design and woodwork with a vendor fair, live folk music and dancing around blazing fires.

## MAY

△ **Norwegian National Day 'Sytennde Mai'** *(17 May)*. An important day on the calendar, Norway's National Day commemorates the signing of the constitution in 1814. Every town has a children's parade, speeches and vendors serving ice cream and sausages.

## JUNE

**Oslo Mikrobryggfest** *(mid-Jun)*. Twenty of Norway's best craft brewers present their tipples in ticketed tasting booths. Food stalls and live music add to the festivities.

**Norwegian Wood Rock Festival** *(mid- to late Jun)* Oslo welcomes a great line-up of indie singers, with past headliners including Bob Dylan, David Bowie and Patti Smith.

△ **Bergen Fest** *(second half of Jun)*. An intimate annual blues and Americana festival.

## SEPTEMBER

△ **International Ibsen Festival** *(early Sep)*. Celebrating the Norwegian playwright Henrik Ibsen, Oslo's International Ibsen Festival opens the autumn season at The National Theatre of Norway every even-numbered year.

**Matsreif** *(late Sep)*. More than 200 food stalls occupy the square outside Oslo's City Hall – the ultimate spot to discover Norwegian cuisine and fill your Instagram feed.

## OCTOBER

△ **Mushroom hunting** *(Sep–Oct)*. From September to October, Norwegians head to the woods to sniff out their favourite edible mushrooms, such as golden chanterelles and umami-rich porcini.

## MARCH

**Holmenkollen Ski Festival** *(first half of Mar)*. For more than a hundred years, Holmenkollen has hosted adrenaline-heavy ski-jumping events that draw thousands of spectators to Oslo.

△ **Birkebeiner Ski Race** *(mid-Mar)*. This long-distance cross-country ski race debuted in 1932, and sees participants glide 54 km (33.5 miles) across two mountains.

## APRIL

△ **Easter** *(late Apr)*. Easter symbolizes the end of winter, and is frequently celebrated with one last ski getaway and, strangely, many people reading Nordic Noir crime literature.

## JULY

**Molde Jazz Festival** *(mid-Jul)*. Thousands head to fjord-fronted Molde each summer for Europe's oldest jazz festival.

△ **Gladmat** *(mid-Jul)*. Stavanger's food festival is Norway's largest, celebrating regional and seasonal Nordic specialities.

## AUGUST

△ **Øyafestivalen** *(early Aug)*. Oslo's largest and coolest music festival spans three days and is packed with international stars, both up-and-coming and long established.

## DECEMBER

△ **Christmas Markets** *(throughout Dec)*. Folk museums such as the Norse Folkemuseum in Oslo and Maihaugen in Lillehammer arrange special concerts, crafts and gingerbread house workshops alongside traditional markets.

**Christmas concerts** *(throughout Dec)*. From Oslo Opera House to village churches, festive concerts are held across Norway.

**Saint Lucia Day** *(13 Dec)*. Norwegians combat the darkest day of the year with a parade of light featuring children dressed in white with candle crowns. Singing and saffron buns add to the warmth.

## NOVEMBER

△ **Lighting the Christmas tree** *(late Nov)*. With darkness comes the early preparation for Christmas, launching with the tree illumination festivities in large and small towns nationwide.

# A BRIEF
# HISTORY

This small country has a history of epic proportions. The mighty Viking Age famously saw Norwegians build a great empire. Conflict followed as Norway fought for independence from its Scandinavian neighbours and freedom during World War II, until it finally gained the prosperity it has today.

## Ancient Origins

Norway's first signs of human life date from the end of the Ice Age; the Komsa culture lived in the Arctic North and were sea-oriented people, while the Fosna people lived on the southwest coastline and used crude tools to hunt seals and reindeer. Rock carvings show the development of agriculture during the Bronze and Iron Ages. The expansion of the Roman Empire in the 1st century AD improved trading links, and the introduction of iron transformed Norway's agricultural abilities. Its people learnt to smelt and assemble new tools, allowing forests to be cleared and home-steads to be built, eventually creating a series of kingships.

1 Rock carvings in Alta, Northern Norway.

2 Woodcut showing a fleet of Viking ships at sea.

3 *Leif Erikson Discovers America* by Christian Krohg (1893).

4 The first King of Norway, Harald Hårfagre (c 850–932).

## Timeline of events

### 1800–500 BC
Bronze Age people build large burial mounds on ridges, roadsides and on the coast, such as in Jæren

### 9300 BC
The Komsa people, Norway's first inhabitants, live in Alta, Finnmark

### AD 793
Vikings raid the English monastery of Lindisfarne in Northumberland

### 799
Viking raids begin in France

### 870
Iceland is colonized by Vikings

## Viking Glory

As agriculture advanced, so the population grew and land became overcrowded. Expeditions were launched in search of new shores to conquer and plunder, with Sweden and Denmark joining the quest. Norwegian longboats arrived in the British Isles in the AD 780s, with other fleets making it as far as the Mediterranean and the Middle East. Leif Erikson even reached the Americas in 1,000. The Vikings murdered, enslaved and assimilated the peoples of their discovered lands, returning home with spoils of war and putting Scandinavia on the map as a powerful empire.

## Viking Unification

Norway's tribes battled under their various leaders until around 890, when Viking chieftain Harald Hårfagre – or Harald Fair-Hair – won a decisive victory at Hafrsfjord (Stavanger today). He gained control of a prominent swathe of coastline, making many minor kings flee. Harald united the country and became the first King of Norway, ruling for years. After his death, his son Erik Bloodaxe struggled to maintain unity and so his other son, Håkon the Good, returned from England to secure the allegiance of chieftains.

### VIKING WOMEN

Technically, women couldn't be Vikings; the name was only used for men. Like most civilizations of the time, the Viking Age was a patriarchy and women generally had domestic roles. They had some autonomy, however. Women could own property and run the family farm or business while the men were away. They could even request a divorce and reclaim their dowries.

### 876

Vikings permanently settle in England

### 890

The kingdom is united by Harald Hårfagre in the Battle of Hafrsfjord

### 948

Håkon the Good attempts to convert his countrymen to Christianity

### 985

Eric the Red, father of Leif Erikson, settles in Greenland

### c 1000

Leif Erikson discovers North America and calls it Vinland

## The Early Years of Independence

Conflict returned after Håkon the Good died, and it was the reigns of Viking chieftains Olav Tryggvason and Olaf Haraldsson, in 995 and 1015 respectively, that restored unity. Both sought to introduce Christianity, tearing down pagan statues and building stave churches. Norway then became a sovereign, Christian kingdom.

## Under Danish Rule

Independence ended when King Håkon VI married the Danish princess Margaret, in 1363. Their son Olav became king of Denmark in 1375, and he inherited the Norwegian throne on Håkon's death in 1380. When Olav died suddenly, Margaret was declared regent and she nominated Erik of Pomerania as king of all Scandinavian nations in 1397. This was the foundation of the Kalmar Union, which would last until 1523. Norway's political position weakened under King Christian III, who declared Norway a vassal state, but improved under King Christian IV, who took great interest in Norwegian affairs. His son, Frederik III, became absolute ruler in 1660 and the country was integrated into Denmark, giving lowlier Norwegians new jobs and simpler taxes.

↑ Borgund Stavkirke, Norway's oldest stave church

## Timeline of events

### 1349

The bubonic plague, or Black Death, arrives in Bergen and soon sweeps through Norway

### 1397

The Kalmar Union unites Norway, Denmark and Sweden under one king

### 1469

Norwegian expansion ends when the Orkney and Shetland islands are sold to the Scots

### 1523

The Kalmar Union ends, and Norway is affiliated with Denmark alone

4

## Under Swedish Rule

Norway's next defining moment came in 1807, when Frederik VI allied himself with Napoleon. Britain retaliated by blocking Norway's harbours. This, combined with a continuing war with Sweden, meant Norway was surrounded and isolated, triggering years of hunger and hardship. In Sweden, meanwhile, the crown prince Karl Johan convinced his allies that he could force Denmark to relinquish Norway. When Napoleon was defeated in 1813, Karl Johan marched towards Denmark. At the Treaty of Kiel, in January 1814, Norway was surrendered to Sweden after 400 years of a Danish-Norwegian union.

## The National Assembly at Eidsvoll

Christian Frederik, the Danish prince and governor-general of Norway, opposed the Treaty of Kiel. In April 1814, he and his supporters gathered at a country house in Eidsvoll to construct a Norwegian constitution, with Christian Frederik its king. Karl Johan rejected this and invaded Norway, demanding that the Treaty of Kiel be implemented. He eventually accepted the constitution, in November 1814, and became king of Norway in 1818.

1 Statue of Margaret I of Denmark (1353–1412). ↑

2 Christian IV of Denmark (1577–1648) with his wife.

3 The Kalmar Union.

4 The National Assembly at Eidsvoll, 1814.

### Did You Know?

Norway has a public holiday on 17 May to mark the signing of the Norwegian constitution in Eidsvoll.

### 1621

Vardø in Northern Norway's Finnmark sees one of the biggest witch trials in Scandinavia

### 1709

The Great Nordic War takes place between Denmark-Norway and Sweden

### 1769

Norway's population totals 723,000, of whom 65,000 live in towns

### 1814

Norway is ceded to Sweden, and Norwegians pen a constitution

1

2

## Growth and Freedom

Norway's economy boomed during the 19th century, thanks to the country's new sense of national identity. Industry grew, the arts flourished, and the country's population doubled in just 70 years. In 1905, 80 per cent of the people voted for independence from Sweden and so a constitutional monarchy was restored. Haakon VII was crowned king in 1906; his descendants rule today.

## The World Wars

Norway remained neutral during World War I, although half of its merchant fleet was sunk by the Germans, and again declared itself neutral when World War II broke out in 1939. Regardless, Germany invaded in 1940 and the royal family and cabinet fled to London. Military officer Vidkun Quisling became prime minister of an occupied Norway. With civil resistance mounting, an underground military organization was formed, controlled by the government in exile. They passed intelligence to the Allies and conducted covert operations against the occupying forces. The Germans retreated, burning everything in their path. King Haakon returned in 1945 and Quisling and other traitors were executed.

### WORLD HAPPINESS REPORT

Norway has been ranked one of the top four happiest countries for years and, in 2018, it was knocked off the number one spot by neighbouring Finland. Published by the UN, the in-depth report analyses all aspects of happiness, including wealth, ethics, health and psychology. Denmark, Iceland and Switzerland also rank highly year after year.

## Timeline of events

### 1905

Haakon VII, Queen Maud and Crown Prince Olav take up residence in the palace in Oslo

### 1911

Norwegian explorer Roald Amundsen leads the first expedition to the South Pole

### 1913

Norway introduces universal suffrage for women, one of the first European countries to do so

### 1940

German troops occupy Norway

### 1945

King Haakon returns home; Quisling is tried and executed

## Recovery and Reconstruction

The war brought Norway to its knees but national unity remained strong. Norway became a founding member of the UN, joined NATO and aligned with its neighbours to form the Nordic Council. The country rebuilt itself, but it was the discovery of a vast oil reserve in the North Sea, in 1969, that transformed Norway into one of the richest countries in Europe.

## Modern Norway

Today, oil and gas account for 20 per cent of the country's economy, and Norway continues to wield international influence. Its sense of independence remains strong and two referenda on EU membership have concluded with a 'no'. The Labour Party largely remained in power from 1945 to 1963 and created the welfare state that remains in place today, providing citizens access to education, health care and social benefits. The Conservative Party won the 2013 election and was re-elected in 2017. The party was extended to include the Liberal Party in 2018. Norway strives to be carbon-neutral by 2030, with Oslo winning Europe's Green Capital 2019 title, having previously been shortlisted three times.

1 King Haakon VII, Queen Maud and Crown Prince Olav in 1906. ↑

2 German troops disembark from navy destroyers in Oslo harbour, 1940.

3 Norwegian Prime Minister Erna Solberg celebrates Norway's national day in her home town of Bergen, 2018.

4 Cyclists in Oslo, Europe's Green Capital for 2019.

**1969**
Discovery of oil reserves in the North Sea, off the coast of Norway

**1994**
Norway hosts the Winter Olympics in Lillehammer

**2004**
*The Scream* is stolen from the Munch-museet in Oslo

**2017**
World Happiness Report ranks Norway as happiest country

**2019**
Oslo wins European Green Capital Award

# EXPERIENCE OSLO

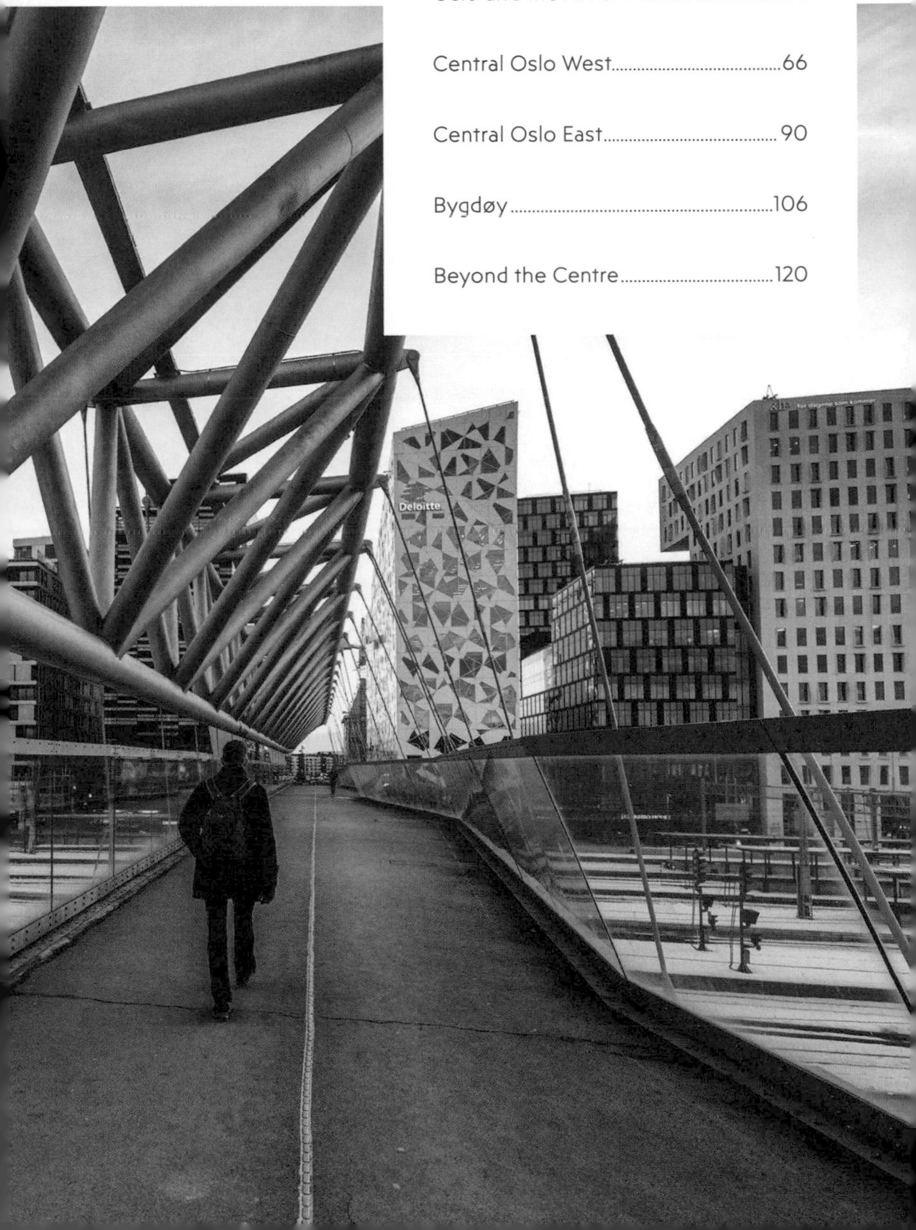
Deloitte

# EXPLORE
# OSLO

This guide divides Oslo into three sightseeing areas, as shown below, and an
area beyond the centre. Find out more
about each area on the following pages.

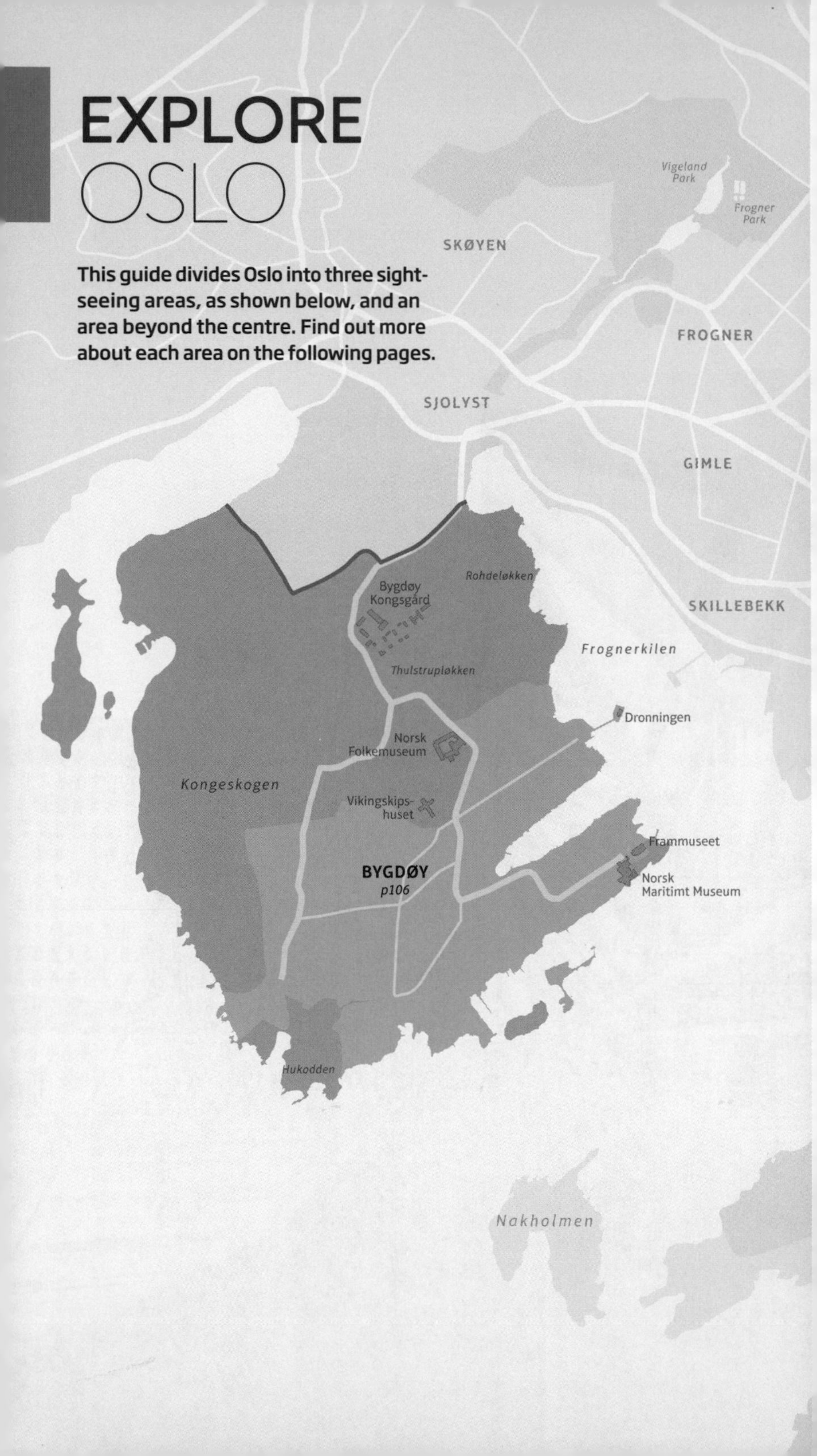

SKØYEN

Vigeland
Park

Frogner
Park

FROGNER

SJOLYST

GIMLE

Bygdøy
Kongsgård

Rohdeløkken

SKILLEBEKK

Frognerkilen

Thulstrupløkken

Dronningen

Norsk
Folkemuseum

Kongeskogen

Vikingskips-
huset

Frammuseet

Norsk
Maritimt Museum

**BYGDØY**
*p106*

Hukodden

Nakholmen

MAJORSTUEN

BOLTELØKKA

GRUNERLØKKA

VULKAN

SENTRUM

HOMANSBYEN

Vår Frelsers
Gravlund

FREDENSBORG

BRISKEBY

Slottsparken

Slottet

Historisk
Museum

**CENTRAL
OSLO WEST**
*p66*

National-
theatret

Youngs-
torget

Spikersuppa

Oslo
Konserthus

Rådhuset

Stortinget

Oslo
Domkirke

Oslo
Spektrum

Nasjonalmuseet

Rådhus-
Plassen

**CENTRAL
OSLO EAST**
*p90*

Jernbane-
torget

Aker
Brygge

Christian
Frederiks Pl.

Tjuvholmen

Pipervika

Norsk
Arkitekturmuseum

Astrup Fearnley
Museet

Akershus
Festning

The
Opera House

Lambda
Munch
Museum

Forsvars-
museet

Bjørvika

*Oslofjorden*

Sørenga
Sjøbad

**NORWAY**

*Hovedøya*

*Lindøya*

*Gressholmen*

→

1 Sun-seekers in Sørenga.

2 Barcode complex.

3 Soldier of the Norwegian Royal Guard outside Akershus Festning.

4 Astrup Fearnley Museum.

# 5 HOURS
## *In Fjord City*

### ▌ *Morning*

Oslo is undergoing an electrifying renaissance along Havnepromenaden, the city's pedestrianized harbour promenade and cultural epicentre, dubbed Fjord City *(p80)*. Oslo Sentralstasjon is the best gateway to this cosmopolitan hub. Disembark the train and walk across the Akrobaten Pedestrian Bridge *(p103)* to the cool new borough of Sørenga, where you can dip your toe in the seawater fjord pool here. Head west and you can't miss the Barcode buildings – a striking, monochrome line-up of high-rises. On the waterfront's first pier, Bispevika, you'll spy the lofty new Lambda Munch Museum as it nears completion, and the glacial Oslo Opera House *(p98)*, a much-loved landmark of the city. The architect designed this dramatic structure as a plaza so do walk across its roof and admire the views. Inside, the bar serves aperitifs – perfect for a pick-me-up. Continue on to Vaaghals *(p98)*, just across the path, for lunch. Housed in the modern Barcode, the kitchen produces small, delicious plates of Norwegian cuisine with a modern twist.

### ▌ *Afternoon*

After a leisurely lunch, continue to amble west until you reach Akershus Festning *(p94)*. You can't miss this – the medieval fortress is a dramatic contrast to the modern architecture of Fjord City. The castle's grounds are open for exploration and the hilltop position provides thrilling vistas of Oslo's half dozen fjord islands – but don't linger for too long! Follow Havnepromenaden as it unfurls, passing sailing boats and Rådhuset, until you reach Aker Brygge *(p83)*, a buzzy wharf with upscale shopping and dining. Walk through this complex and cross the tiny bridges to Tjuvholmen, or Thief Island, where you'll find the cutting-edge Astrup Fearnley Museum *(p86)*. With virtually no entry queues, a 30-minute wander is plenty to marvel at the mind-boggling artworks here. The museum has a lovely café or, alternatively, head back towards Sentralstasjon and stop at Vippa food hall *(p98)* and stock up on provisions for the rest of the day.

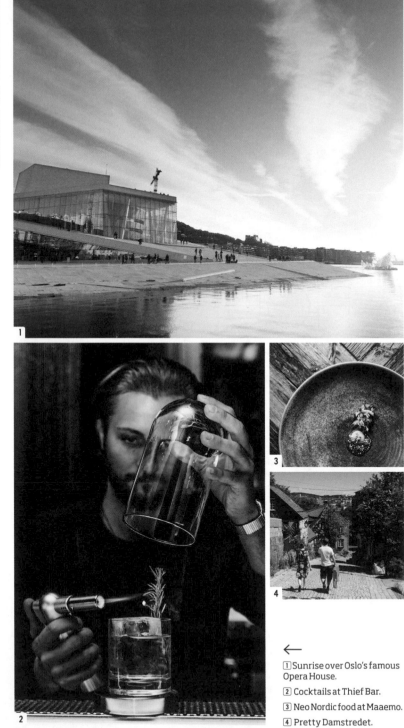

←

1 Sunrise over Oslo's famous Opera House.

2 Cocktails at Thief Bar.

3 Neo Nordic food at Maaemo.

4 Pretty Damstredet.

# 3 DAYS

## A Long Weekend in Oslo

### Day 1

**Morning** For a memorable start, get up early and get to Oslo Opera House (p98) before the crowds. Climb the gently sloping roof and watch the morning sun sparkle on the fjord. Aim westwards to Stockfleths Café (p87), where award-winning baristas will craft a perfect cup of light-roast coffee for you, and tuck into a hearty *kanelsnurrer* (Norwegian cinnamon roll). From here, a 5-minute walk past the Rådhuset (p74) will take you to the ferry stand for the Bygdøy peninsula. Continue the nautical theme and make for the Vikingskipshuset (p112) and marvel at the world's most spectacular Viking ships.

**Afternoon** Head next door to the Norsk Folkemuseum (p110) and lunch on traditional Norwegian fare at Arkadia Café before exploring this fascinating open-air museum. Feel free to interact with the staff there – they can show you traditional handicrafts such as wood-carving and weaving.

**Evening** Catch the return ferry back in time for a well-earned aperitif at the Thief Bar in the boutique Thief Hotel (p87). The cocktail menu theme changes; their thrillingly theatrical presentation does not. End the day at Lofoten Fiskebar (p81) with a harbour-side seafood dinner.

### Day 2

**Morning** Explore the heart of classic Oslo, kicking off with an amble around the elegant Slottsparken. The king's primary residence crowns the city's main thorough-fare of Karl Johans Gate (p78). Pick up a coffee at hip mid-century bar Fuglen (p87) before window-shopping for beautiful Scandinavian-designed souvenirs along Karl Johan, and at the likes of Paleet and Norway Designs (p83).

**Afternoon** The Grand Café (*www.grand cafeoslo.no*) makes for an elegant lunch spot. Stroll through Studenterlunden en route to the Nobel Peace Center (p76), where interactive exhibits will inspire you. The on-site café is ideal for reflection.

**Evening** Unforgettable flavours await discovery at Maaemo (p98), Norway's only three-starred Michelin restaurant – a temple to New Nordic cuisine.

### Day 3

**Morning** Travel back 250 years by visiting Damstredet, a narrow, cobblestone alley lined with vibrantly painted wooden houses and popular with Instagrammers. A 10-minute walk east is edgy Vulkan (p125) and here you'll find Mathallen food hall, which is bursting with tempting choices for breakfast. Stock up on supplies for a picnic while you're here, before crossing the forest-lined Akerselva River into Oslo's coolest borough.

**Afternoon** With an energy similar to Copenhagen's Nørrebro and Brooklyn's Williamsburg, Grünerløkka (p126) is home to Norwegian creatives. Explore the stylish independent boutiques and cosy cafés that line the side streets here and enjoy your picnic at the Botanisk Hage (p127).

**Evening** After a stroll in the botanical garden, make for an early dinner at Bass Oslo (p131) and savour the delicious New Nordic cuisine at bistro prices.

→

Patrons enjoying
New Nordic cuisine at
Bass Oslo.

**Did You Know?**

Norwegians drink more
cups of coffee per capita
than any other country,
except for Finland.

OSLO FOR
# FOODIES

**Move over Copenhagen; Oslo is the new Scandi capital of cuisine.
Here you'll find locally and ethically sourced inputs, New Nordic bistros
led by young, creative chefs, and dining options to suit all budgets.
The question is, where will you begin?**

### Food Halls and Pop-Ups

Oslo is shaking off its reputation
as expensive thanks to a influx
of exciting and affordable dining
spots. Mathallen food hall *(www.
mathallenoslo.no)* in Vulkan
*(p125)* has cafés, speciality shops
and restaurants galore, so you
can take a taste of Oslo home. In
the east, waterfront warehouse-
turned-food-hall Vippa's various
cuisines include Norwegian,
Syrian, Korean and much more
besides *(p99)*. At Maridalsveien
45, Syverkiosken is a hot dog
kiosk famous among locals
thanks to its high-quality
sausages, foraged toppings and
freshly made potato pancakes.
With prices starting at just 20Kr
per sausage, this is a brilliant
lunch option. Harald's Vaffel
*(p102)* and Fryd Doughnuts
*(www.talorjorgen.no)* serve
sweet and indulgent breakfasts.

↑ Stacked oysters at
Oslo's Mathallen
food hall

## Nucleus of New Nordic

Oslo rivals all other Scandinavian cities when it comes to New Nordic cuisine. Fyr Bistronomi & Bar (www.fyrbistronomi.no) excels at classic Norwegian dishes with a modern twist. Over in trendy Vulkan, Kontrast (p131) bears all the hallmarks of a New Nordic bistro – exposed brick, suspended lights and quality, primal fare. Icelandic chef Arnar Jakob Gudmundsson pushes the palate into new territory at Brutus (www.barbrutus.no) with delectable five-course tasting menus, while restaurant Bass Oslo (p131) is a great choice for small plates and expert wine advice.

← Simple, fresh ingredients dished up at Bass Oslo

## Raise a Glass

Oslo's pub and bar scene is as lively as its foodscape. Torggata Botaniske at Torggata 17B and Himkok (www.himkok.no) are both regarded as two of the world's best bars, with their cocktails using Norwegian spirits and herbs. Oslo has also a brilliantly creative craft beer scene – head to p44 for more.

→ Creatively presented cocktails at the Thief Bar

### The Scream

This is the artist's best known and most reproduced motif. Painted from 1892 to 1910, the ambiguous figure has its mouth wide open in a scream, amplified by the motion of the landscape. The Nasjonalmuseet *(p70)* and Munchmuseet *(p131)* hold versions of *The Scream*, and both were stolen in 1994 and 2004, respectively. Both paintings are moving to new spaces, so check ahead as to where they'll be on display.

→

*The Scream* at the National Gallery until 2020

# OSLO AND THE
# ART OF MUNCH

The most prominent Nordic painter and the pioneer of expressionism, Edvard Munch (1863-1944) painted intense and timeless artworks inspired by the urban and rural landscapes in and around Oslo. Explore these scenes and view the artist's masterpieces for yourself.

### TOP 3 HIDDEN MUNCH SIGHTS

#### University of Oslo's Aula Hall
The university's ceremonial concert hall features eleven large oil paintings by Munch.

#### Flats in Grünerløkka
Munch spent much of his childhood in the now-trendy neighbourhood of Grünerløkka. Visit Olso has a map of all the flats he lived in here.

#### Studio at Ekely
In 1916 Munch bought the estate of Ekely, on the outskirts of the city. Here he finally had enough space for his work.

### Munch-museet and Lambda
The Munch collection has outgrown its home in Tøyen, beyond the centre of Oslo *(p131)*. As many top cultural institutions relocate to the rapidly transforming Oslo waterfront, the Munch-museet will join them. A sensational modern building beside the iconic Opera House, Lambda Munch Museum *(p99)* is set to open in 2020 and will house a spectacular number of artworks by the artist.

→

Lambda Munch Museum, currently under construction and opening in 2020

## Inspired by Ekebergparken

How did *The Scream* come to be? Munch took a walk in Oslo's Ekebergparken *(p130)*, where a vibrantly red sky – combined with his own internal torment – inspired him to paint the famous work of art. Today, the park's 'Munch Spot' marks the scene immortalized in the artist's most famous work, so visitors can paint their own version. From here, you can see all the way to Grünerløkka *(p126)*, where Munch largely lived.

← Ekebergparken, the scene that inspired Munch's most famous piece

### EDVARD MUNCH BEYOND OSLO

Munch was a restless soul. When Oslo overwhelmed, he sought peace in the idyllic archipelagos of the Oslofjord and the stately mansions in the countryside. He painted the peaceful night scene *The Girls on the Bridge* (1899) at his beach house in lovely Åsgårdstrand, which has since been converted into a museum about the artist *(www. munchshus.no)*. He later purchased Nedre Ramme at Hvitsten *(p142)* before residing at the manor house Grimsrød in Jeløya from 1913 to 1916.

## Grand Café, Oslo

This charmingly old-fashioned, opulent café *(www.grandcafeoslo.no)* opened its doors in 1874 and swiftly became a hangout for artists and writers. Among its patrons were Edvard Munch and his contemporary Henrik Ibsen. Munch famously offered his painting *Sick Girl* in exchange for 100 steak dinners here.

↑ The interior of Oslo's old-world Grand Café, a haunt of creatives in times gone by

# CENTRAL OSLO WEST

Tucked between the Slottet (the Royal Palace) and the beguiling fjord front, Oslo's compact centre charms. Many of the capital's most important institutions, such as the Nasjonalmuseet and Nobel Peace Center, are situated here. Central Oslo West became the capital's core in the second half of the 19th century, after the Royal Palace was completed and Karl Johans Gate, the cobblestoned main thoroughfare, was laid out. Today it includes Oslo's most popular swathe of green: delightful Studenterlunden and the bucolic Slottsparken (Castle Park). Karl Johans Gate and side streets buzz with shoppers and diners; summer or winter, cafés and open-air markets spill onto the streets. The appeal culminates at the waterfront, where Rådhuset (City Hall) links to the regenerated Aker Brygge and Tjuvholmen boroughs along Havnepromenade, a scenic fjord-side path. Here, this capital city really shows off, with its vintage wooden sailing boats and cute canals, stylish shops, modern restaurants and stunning new architecture, such as the Renzo Piano-designed Astrup Fearnley Museum.

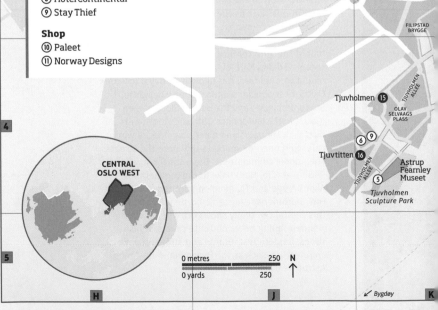

# CENTRAL OSLO WEST

**Must Sees**
1. Nasjonalmuseet
2. Historisk Museum
3. Rådhuset
4. Nobel Peace Center

**Experience More**
5. Karl Johans Gate
6. Universitetet
7. Slottet
8. Nationaltheatret
9. Det Norske Teatret
10. Rådhusbrygge 2
11. Studenterlunden and Spikersuppa
12. Oslo Konserthus
13. Ibsenmuseet
14. Aker Brygge
15. Tjuvholmen
16. Tjuvtitten

**Eat**
1. Theatercafeen
2. Ling Ling
3. Lofoten Fiskerestaurant

**Drink**
4. Fuglen
5. Vingen
6. Thief Bar
7. Stockfleths

**Stay**
8. Hotel Continental
9. Stay Thief

**Shop**
10. Paleet
11. Norway Designs

BRISKEBY

RUSELØKKA

FILIPSTAD BRYGGE

Tjuvholmen 15
OLAV SELVAAGS PLASS
6 9
Tjuvtitten 16
Astrup Fearnley Museet
5
Tjuvholmen Sculpture Park

CENTRAL OSLO WEST

0 metres 250
0 yards 250

N

Bygdøy

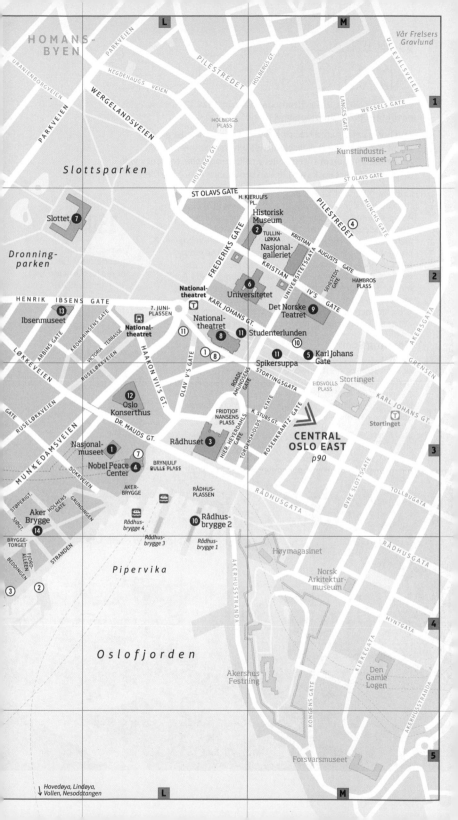

**1** 🗝️ 🚫 🍴 💻 🎒

# NASJONALMUSEET

📍L3 🏠Bodestrasse 1-3 🚇Nationaltheatret 🚌12 🕐Currently closed; opening in 2020 🌐nasjonalmuseet.no

The hotly anticipated Nasjonalmuseet will be the largest art museum in the Nordic countries when it opens in 2020. An amalgamation of three gallery collections, this treasury will display 6,000 artworks and house thousands more besides.

This powerhouse of art will bring together the National Gallery, the Museum of Contemporary Art and the Museum of Decorative Arts and Design under one roof. The new Nasjonalmuseet is a sleek, modern building that celebrates Oslo's evolving architectural scene, from its waterfront projects to the brown-brick Rådhuset, which stands near the site (p74). The ground and first floors will house the permanent collection, with further exhibition spaces on the lower and upper levels. A terrace is being constructed on the roof, providing stunning views towards the harbour and the fjord. A tree-lined square and outdoor seating, 200-capacity auditorium and restaurant will provide public spaces for visitors to linger and reflect.

## 130,000

pieces of art are being documented and packed for the museum move in 2020.

### Opening Soon

The National Gallery will be the last of the three museums to close its doors before its artworks are transferred to the Nasjonalmuseet, opening in early 2020. Check online to learn more about this project, or visit Mellomstasjonen (Brynjulf Bulls Plass 2), next to the Nobel Peace Center (p76), which provides more information about the new museum and offers guided tours of the site.

## NORWEGIAN ARTISTS

When it comes to Norwegian artists, most think of Edvard Munch and *The Scream* and his more optimistic works, such as *The Girls on the Pier*. You will be able to see these and much more at the Nasjonalmuseet. *Larvik by Moonlight* (1839), by J C Dahl, is a peaceful depiction of a sea town just south of Oslo. Harald Sohlberg's Neo-Romantic *Winter Night in the Mountains* (1914) portrays a dreamy, snow-covered massif in Rondane rising towards a starry sky.

↑ Artworks will be displayed in light, airy spaces

→ The Nasjonalmuseet will be found next to the Nobel Peace Center

↑ The expansive Nasjonalmuseet lit up as night falls

### Museum Timeline

**2016–2017**

The Museum of Contemporary Art and the Museum of Decorative Arts and Design closed. You will be able to see these collections in the new building from 2020.

**2018–2019**

Some National Gallery collections are on view at Universitetsgata 13, open 10am–6pm Tue–Fri (until 7pm Thu), 11am–5pm Sat & Sun. Check online for closures.

**2020**

The Nasjonalmuseet – which combines three existing museum collections – is set to open in a purpose-built space, designed by architects Kleihues + Schuwerk.

② ⊛ ⊛ 🏛

# HISTORISK MUSEUM

📍 M2 🏛 Frederiks Gate 2 🚇 Nationaltheatret 🚋 11, 13, 17, 18, 19 🚌 30, 31, 32, 45, 81, 83 🕐 Mid-May–mid-Sep: 10am–5pm Tue–Sun; mid-Sep–mid-May: 11am–4pm Tue–Sun 🚫 Public hols 🌐 khm.uio.no

**Viking treasures, ancient coins and medieval art galore – this encyclopedic menagerie of curiosities comprises three separate collections, and provides a detailed understanding of Norway's early history.**

The Historisk Museum is part of the Kulturhistorisk Museum (Museum of Cultural History) of the University of Oslo, and it houses the Oldsaksamlingen (National Antiquities Collection), Etnografisk Museum (Ethnographic Museum) and Myntkabinettet (Collection of Coins and Medals). Together they document Norwegian and international history, from the first settlements to the present day, while the Collapse exhibition explores the impact of natural forces on civilizations. Rare objects from Viking and medieval times, along with a rich collection from the Arctic cultures, are displayed throughout the building, which was designed by Henrik Bull and completed in 1902.

↑ Exterior of the Historisk Museum, on leafy Frederiks Gate

### The Viking Age Exhibition

Of all Viking graves exhumed in Scandinavia, few can rival the finds at Gjermundbu farm near Haugsbygd, and specifically the Gjermundbu helmet – the only completely intact Viking helmet ever found. In 1943, a Norwegian farmer accidentally stumbled upon a burial mound and uncovered a chainmail shirt, weaponry and the prized iron helmet, all of which are displayed in the museum's exhibition.

---

**GALLERY GUIDE**

The museum covers four floors. The National Antiquities Collection is on the ground floor, as is the Collapse exhibit. The first floor houses the Collection of Coins and Medals and the Ethnographic Museum, which also occupies the second and third floors. English and German information is available.

---

St Olav is the patron saint of Norway

*Shaman's Robe*

▽ This robe (c 1900) was brought by Roald Amundsen from the Northwest Passage.

*Highlights*

*St Olav*

▲ This weathered statue (c 1250) of St Olav is from Fresvik church in Leikanger, Vestlandet.

*Viking helmet*

▲ The Gjermundbu helmet (c 920) is the world's only known intact Viking helmet.

## Did You Know?

The museum holds the world's first coins, minted 2,600 years ago by King Alyattes (c 591–560 BC).

The Hoen treasure, the greatest find ↑ of gold jewellery from the Viking Age

3 M3

# RÅDHUSET

📍 L3 🏛 Fridtjof Nansens Plass Ⓣ Nationaltheatret, Stortinget
🚋 12, 13, 19 🚌 30, 31, 32, 45, 81, 83 🕐 Jul–Aug: 9am–6pm daily;
Sep–Jun: 9am–4pm daily 🚫 Public hols and during special events
🌐 oslo.kommune.no

Oslo's twin-towered city hall has become a landmark since it opened in 1950, despite many locals initially disliking the building's design. Behind its grandiose façade Rådhuset is a treasure trove of vibrant artworks, and it's free to step inside and take a look.

In 1918, architects Arnstein Arneberg and Magnus Poulsson won a competition to design a new civic centre that reflected city pride. The City Hall opened in 1950 to mark Oslo's 900th anniversary, but it has taken many years for the city to come to terms with this dark-brown-brick building. Today, Rådhuset remains the administrative heart of Oslo. Most visitors head for the richly adorned hall known as Rådhushallen, where important ceremonies take place. Norwegian artists were invited to decorate its interior, including Henrik Sørensen, whose dazzling painting *Work, Art and Celebration* fills an entire wall and took a decade to complete. Other highlights include the Viking friezes on the building's exterior and, at the back of Rådhuset, six statues representing the labourers who built it.

🔍 HIDDEN GEM
**Mythological friezes**

The courtyard features 16 wooden friezes made by Norwegian painter and sculptor Dagfin Werenskiold (1892–1977). These intricate, vibrant artworks unfold like a storybook, and show figures and motifs from Norse mythology. They're free to view.

Crown Princess Martha Square is a garden and pedestrian area.

← Axel Revold's *Fishing and Agriculture* on the east wall of Festival Hall

The Munch Hall

← Henrik Sørensen's *Work, Art and Celebration* mural

## Did You Know?

The Nobel Peace Prize is awarded here every December, on the anniversary of Alfred Nobel's death.

*Handmade bricks known as "monkstone" were used in construction.*

*The Hall of the City Council (Bystyresalen) lies at the heart of Rådhuset. The council's 59 representatives have regular meetings here.*

*The Eastern Tower is 66 m (212 ft) tall.*

*The ceremonial main hall, Rådhushallen, covers 1,519 sq m (16,350 sq ft). Henrik Sørensen's oil painting on the rear wall is the largest in Europe.*

*The venue for grand dinners, the Banqueting Hall – or Bankettsalen – is a light, airy room richly decorated and embellished with royal portraits.*

*St Hallvard, the patron saint of Oslo, was killed and thrown into a fjord when he tried to save a woman from robbers but floated to the surface and was hailed a martyr.*

*Axel Julius Revold's fresco in the Feast Gallery shows the industrial and consumer society of the 1950s.*

↑ Brown-brick exterior of Rådhuset, Oslo's City Hall

**④** 🖼️ 💻 🛍️

# NOBEL PEACE CENTER

📍L3 🏛️Vestbanebygningen, Rådhusplassen 🚇Nationaltheatret 🚌12
🕐Mid-May-Aug: 10am-6pm daily (to 8pm Thu); Sep-mid-May: 10am-6pm
Tue-Sun 🌐nobelpeacecenter.org

**Norwegians take huge pride in their prestigious, humanitarian Nobel Peace Prize, awarded annually by a five-person committee. Step inside Oslo's stylish Nobel Peace Center and come face to face with award-winning trailblazers via films, photographs and high-tech exhibits.**

The Nobel Peace Prize is arguably the world's most famous accolade and has been awarded to over 100 individuals and organisations. This centre, in the heart of Oslo, aims to show the work of prizewinners and offer a forum for discussions around issues of war, peace and conflict resolution. The Nobel Peace Center is one of the most popular museums in Norway, with 250,000 annual visitors. Housed in an attractive former train station, this is not a museum in the traditional sense. Multimedia exhibits enable visitors to connect with prizewinners, while children can take part in discovery trails. The centre has a rich programme of events and exhibitions, plus a fjord-fronted café – the ideal spot to reflect after spending time in this enlightening and inspiring museum.

←

The Nobel Peace Center, housed in Oslo's old Vestbanen train station

*Alva Myrdal (1982)*
From Sweden, she worked towards nuclear weapons-free zones in Europe

*Malala Yousafzai (2014)*
▽ The youngest winner champions women's and girls' rights to education

*Notable prizewinners*

*Martin Luther King, Jr (1964)*
▲ Honoured for non-violent resistance to racial prejudice in America

*14th Dalai Llama, Tenzin Gyatso (1989)*
The Buddhist leader and peaceful campaigner has supported numerous international causes

*Nelson Mandela (1993)*
▲ Ended apartheid and laid the foundations for a newly democratic South Africa

**Did You Know?**

Gandhi never won the prize; he was nominated five times, including a few days before his assassination.

The Nobel Field, an interactive display of prizewinners ↑

### ALFRED NOBEL (1833-96)

During his career, Nobel was an engineer, scientist, inventor, chemist, business leader and non-profit founder. Born in Stockholm, when Norway and Sweden were under common rule, Nobel worked first at his father's arms factory, where he invented dynamite in spite of his pacifism. He accrued much wealth from his work and posthumously left his fortune to found the five Nobel Prizes (for chemistry, literature, medicine, peace and physics). It is believed he did this as an act of atonement.

# EXPERIENCE MORE

**5** 🍴 🖥 🛍

## Karl Johans Gate

📍 M2 🚇 Stortinget, Nationaltheatret 🚃 11, 13, 17, 18, 19 🚌 31, 32, 34

Norway's best-known and busiest thoroughfare is Karl Johans Gate. Named after the king of Norway and Sweden, Karl Johan (r 1818–44), it is locally referred to simply as Karl Johan, and is flanked by stately, Neo-Classical buildings as is befitting of a central city boulevard.

The upper section is the most imposing. Stortinget (the Norwegian parliament) is situated here and Slottet (the Royal Palace) takes pride of place at the western end of the street. Between these two buildings lie the university and Nationaltheatret, a park known as Studenterlunden, and a skating rink that is open

↑ The wide, bustling Karl Johans Gate on a crisp afternoon

to the public in winter (skates are available for hire). The lower part of Karl Johans Gate terminates at Central Station. Basarhallene (the market halls) at Kirkeristen can be found in this section.

In addition to the many public buildings, the street is lined with department stores, specialist shops and places to eat. A popular meeting place since the 19th century, the citizens of Oslo used to stroll along Studenterlunden to see and be seen. Today, young people continue to meet on the "Strip". Each evening, as darkness falls, lights switch on automatically and illuminate the façades along Karl Johans Gate. The street continues to teem with life until the early hours. Visitors are often surprised by the vibrancy of the nightlife in this area, which is more on a par with some of the larger capitals of Europe.

Karl Johan is also the focal point for royal occasions, state visits and national holidays, most notably Norway's National Day, 17 May, when thousands of children, singers and musicians parade towards the palace to be greeted by the royal family from the grand balcony.

## STAY

**Hotel Continental**
An elegant, five-star hotel, ideally located across the street from the National Theatre.

📍 L2 🚪 Stortingsgata 24/26 🌐 hotel continental.no

Ⓚ Ⓚ Ⓚ

---

**Stay Thief**
Oslo's swankiest design hotel is perched at the edge of Tjuvholmen island and boasts a killer rooftop bar.

📍 K4 🚪 Landgangen 1 🌐 thethief.com

Ⓚ Ⓚ Ⓚ

**6**

## Universitetet

📍 M2 🚪 Karl Johans Gate 47 🚇 National-theatret 🚃 11, 13, 17, 18, 19 🚌 31, 32, 34 🌐 uio.no

The university dominates the northeast side of Karl Johans Gate. The Neo-Classical building was completed in 1852, 41 years after Frederik VI decreed that Norway could finally have its very own university. He gave it his name, the "Royal Frederik University in Oslo", by which it was known until 1939.

Over the years, most of the teaching, other than the Faculty of Law, has moved to Blindern on the outskirts of Oslo. The university complex is directly opposite the Nationaltheatret and comprises three buildings that encircle University Square. To mark its centenary in 1911, the university built a new auditorium, the Aula. This extension is renowned for its murals by Edvard Munch, installed in 1916 and regarded by the Norwegian artist as his major work. The main canvas

→ An equestrian statue of King Karl Johan outside the Royal Palace

on the right, *Alma Mater*, depicts a nursing mother representing the university, while that on the left, *History*, represents knowledge and wisdom. Note that the Aula is not open to the public outside of events.

Over the years, politicians and humanitarians from all over the world have visited the Aula. It was the venue for the presentation of the Nobel Peace Prize until 1990, when the award ceremony was moved to Rådhuset (Oslo City Hall).

On one day in mid-August every year, some 3,000 students descend upon University Square to register for a university place.

**7** ⊘ Ⓜ 🛍️

## Slottet

📍 K2 🏛️ Slottsplassen 1 🚇 Nationaltheatret 🚃 11, 13, 17, 18, 19 🚌 32, 34 🕐 End Jun–mid-Aug: daily (tours only) 🌐 royalcourt.no

Det Kongelige Slottet (the Royal Palace) overlooks Oslo city centre and forms a natural focal point on Karl Johans Gate.

On ascending to the Swedish-Norwegian throne, in 1818, King Karl Johan decided to build a royal residence in Oslo. He commissioned Danish-born architect Lieutenant H D F Linstow to design the project and Linstow went on to plan Karl Johans Gate. Work on the palace interior began in 1836 under the supervision of architects H E Schirmer and J H Nebelon. The palace wasn't completed until 1848, by which time Karl Johan had died. It was inaugurated by Oscar I amid great festivities.

The grand buildings did not become a permanent residence until 1905, when Norway finally became an independent nation. The newly crowned King Haakon and Queen Maud moved into what was then a poorly maintained palace. It has been gradually restored and upgraded over time and underwent a further comprehensive restoration at the end of the 20th century.

The brick and plaster palace has two wings and beautiful gardens to the south and east. These gardens, or Slottsparken, aren't fenced off and are open to the public. Dronningsparken, to the west, is private property and is not open to visitors.

The palace has a particularly splendid collection of fine art. The public were first able to view the collection (and some of the interior) in the summer of 2000, as part of a guided tour. These tours are now a regular feature every year, from the end of June until mid-August. Book tickets online in advance, as only a handful are available at the door on the day.

**8** (🏃) (🍴) (🛍️)

# Nationaltheatret

📍 L2 🏛️ Johannes Dybwads Plass 1 Ⓣ Nationaltheatret 🚋 11, 13, 17, 18, 19 🚌 32, 34 ⏰ Box Office: 11am–6:30pm Mon–Fri (to 5pm Sat) 🚫 Public hols 🌐 nationaltheatret.no

It was no coincidence that a play by the illustrious Norwegian dramatist Henrik Ibsen was on the programme when the National Theatre opened its doors in 1899. The theatre's first production was the socially critical drama *An Enemy of the People* and Ibsen's work remains a central part of the theatre's repertoire. The National Theatre even hosts a biennial International Ibsen Festival, allowing his powerful plays to inspire new audiences.

The Baroque-style building was designed by Henrik Bull. It is regarded as Norway's most significant expression of the 19th-century renaissance of brickwork, with a design

→

Locals congregating on bench-lined paths in Studenterlunden park

typical of theatre architecture throughout Europe during this period. A fire caused extensive damage to the building in 1980 and the subsequent restoration work took five years to complete.

A ticket for a play here also gives access to one of Norway's finest art collections. Throughout the building are paintings by the likes of Erik Werenskiold, Karl Fjell, Christian Krohg, and busts by Gustav Vigeland, Per Palle Storm and other great Norwegian artists. In front of the theatre stand sculptures of two of Norway's most renowned writers – Henrik Ibsen and Bjørnstjerne Bjørnson. Their names (along with Dano-Norwegian playwright Ludvig Holberg) are also engraved on the theatre's façade like badges of honour.

---

**9** (🏃) (🍴) (💻)

# Det Norske Teatret

📍 M2 🏛️ Kristian IVs Gate 8 Ⓣ Nationaltheatret 🚋 13, 19 🚌 30, 31, 32, 45, 81, 83 ⏰ Box office: 11am–5pm Mon, 11am–7:30pm Tue–Fri, 11am–5:30pm Sat 🌐 detnorsketeatret.no

Norway's 'second National Theatre', Det Norske Teatret, opened in 1913, but had no permanent location until September 1985, when it was finally able to welcome audiences to its own ultra-modern, glass-fronted home.

The theatre has two stages. Hovedscenen has 757 seats, advanced technical equipment and movable units, meaning stage layouts and sets can be changed quickly. Biscenen is a more intimate space with just 200 seats. Stages aside, the theatre boasts rehearsal rooms, beautifully decorated foyers and a bistro.

Det Norske Teatret is the main venue for works in the *nynorsk* language, or 'new Norwegian'. Its principal repertoire features Norwegian and Nordic drama, but both modern and classical plays are performed on a regular basis.

---

## FJORD CITY

Oslo's waterfront was an industrial port zone until an urban renewal project began in 2008. Estimated to finish in 2030, this regeneration aims to reinvent the Oslofjord into a beautiful, dynamic city space. The innovative plans sprawl across 10 km (6 miles), transforming shipyards and roads into ultra-modern museums and imaginative public spaces. The key to experiencing Fjord City is to follow the Havnepromenade (harbour promenade) pedestrian and cycle path, signposted in orange. Highlights in the west include the iconic Oslo Opera House, creative, budget-friendly Vippa Food Hall and the Nasjonalmuseet, which will relocate to stunning new premises by the fjord in 2020. In the east is the fjord-fed saltwater swimming pool and Munch museum Lambda, again opening in 2020. For more ideas about what to see here, check out our Fjord City itinerary on p60.

## ⑩

### Rådhusbrygge 2

**📍 L3**

This 100-year-old pier, right outside the Rådhuset (p74), has been restored to its original beauty and function. Cobblestones and wooden masts recall the old structure, while modern additions include picnic benches and the glass-bottomed jetty to view marine life.

Visited by international artists for over a decade, Oslo's waterfront has a vibrant art scene. The pair of murals by Norwegian artist Martin Whatson on the Rådhusbrygge 2 building are exceptional. On one side there is *Zebra* (2015), a life-size, rainbow-coloured grazing zebra, and on the opposite side, *All White* (2015) features a man painting over graffiti. Visit Oslo (www.visit oslo.com) provides a map of where to find the city's best street art.

Ferries to the islands leave from the pier next door. In summer the ferries take advantage of the long daylight hours and operate from early morning till late at night; in winter there are only 7–8 departures per day.

## ⑪ ⊙

### Studenterlunden and Spikersuppa

**📍 L2 🚏 Johannes Dybwads Plass 🚇 Stortinget, Nationaltheatret 🚋 11, 13, 17, 18, 19 🚌 32, 34 🌐 visitoslo.com**

The unofficial heart of central Oslo is the pretty 'students grove' park. Built for the University of Oslo when the downtown campus opened in the mid-19th century, the green stripe swiftly became a popular place for students, workers and shoppers to relax in. The park is flanked by Oslo's key thoroughfares, Karl Johans Gate and Stortingsgata, home to the city's royal and political powerhouses.

A number of charming statues can be found here, including works by Norwegian sculptor Arne Durban, depicting children gazing at one another across the park's pond. There are also pieces by city favourite Gustav Vigeland. In summer, cultural events and concerts are held here, while winter welcomes a cosy Christmas market and Spikersuppa, the free open-air ice-skating rink (usually opening in late November).

# EAT

### Theatercafeen

Oslo's buzziest bohemian meeting spot has a skilfull New Nordic menu. Afternoon tea is also available.

**📍 M2 🚏 Stortingsgata 24-26 🌐 theater cafeen.com**

Ⓚ Ⓚ Ⓚ

---

### Ling Ling

Cantonese small plates are reimagined with Norwegian inputs, alongside an inventive cocktail menu.

**📍 K4 🚏 Stranden 30 🚫 Sun 🌐 lingling. hakkasan.com/oslo**

Ⓚ Ⓚ Ⓚ

---

### Lofoten Fiskerestaurant

Named for the seafood-rich northern archipelago, this harbourfront restaurant has floor-to-ceiling windows and elegant regional dishes.

**📍 K4 🚏 Stranden 75 🚫 Fri 🌐 lofoten-fiskerestaurant.no**

Ⓚ Ⓚ Ⓚ

## ⑫ 🖵

# Oslo Konserthus

📍L3 🏛Munkedamsveien 14 🚇Nationaltheatret 🚋13, 19 🚌30, 31, 32, 45, 81, 83 🕐Box office: 11am–5pm Mon-Fri (to 2pm Sat) and 2 hrs before a performance 📅Jul 🌐oslokonserthus.no

Oslo's concert hall, which is situated in the area of Vika, has been a leading venue for Norwegian cultural and musical life since its opening in 1977. Famed artists and orchestras from across the globe have performed at the Konserthus, and more than 300 events are held here annually, with audiences totalling more than 200,000 over the year.

In the 1960s, the Swedish architect Gösta Åberg won a competition to design the new building. The result was a dramatic exterior clad in polished granite, while the internal floors and walls are of white marble. The hall has been specially designed to stage orchestral works, and features a massive podium large enough to accommodate 120 musicians. It can be transformed into a theatre for shows and musical productions, with seating for

↑ *Heptakord* by Turid Angell Eng, standing outside the Koncerthus

an audience of 1,400. Outside the hall's main entrance stands *Heptakord* (1984), or 'The Listening Seven', a group statue by the Norwegian artist Turid Angell Eng. Cast in bronze, it shows seven intent figures gathered in a circle.

The concert hall is the home of Oslo-Filharmonien – the Oslo Symphony Orchestra – which plays a central role in the musical life of the city, and gives around 65 concerts every year (mostly in the Koncerthus). The orchestra is regarded as one of the world's leading symphony ensembles, its recordings having gained international acclaim.

## ⑬ ♿ Ⓜ 🖵 🏛

# Ibsenmuseet

📍K2 🏛Arbins Gate 1 🚇Nationaltheatret 🚋13, 19 🚌30, 31, 32, 45, 81, 83 🔧For renovation until 2021 🌐ibsenmuseet.no

Henrik Ibsen, Norway's revered playwright, produced the major part of his work between 1864 and 1891, while living in Munich.

After his return to Oslo in 1891, Ibsen and his wife took an apartment in Arbins Gate, on the first floor on the corner facing Drammensveien. This was where he wrote his last plays, *John Gabriel Borkman* (1896) and *When We Dead Awaken* (1899). It was also here that Ibsen suffered a stroke, which prevented him from writing. He subsequently died here in 1906, aged 78 years.

The museum was founded in 1990, and great attention has been paid to the restoration and redecoration of the couple's large apartment. Even the colour scheme resembles that of Ibsen's day, while his study, the highlight of the museum, contains the playwright's original furniture.

→

The painstakingly restored interior of Ibsen's study, Ibsenmuseet

---

## HENRIK IBSEN

Henrik Ibsen (1828–1906) is Norway's most famous writer. He was born in southerly Skien, and began writing while working as a chemist's assistant. From 1857–63 he was director of the Norwegian Theatre in Oslo, but moved abroad when the theatre went bankrupt. Over the next 30 years he wrote numerous dramas, such as *Hedda Gabler* and *Peer Gynt*, focusing on social issues and the pettiness of Norwegian society. His plays won him literary fame and in 1891 he returned to Oslo a national hero. This statue of Henrik Ibsen *(inset)* is by artist Nina Sundbye.

Every day, Ibsen would set off from here to walk to the opulent Grand Café in Karl Johans Gate, where he held court until illhealth confined him to the apartment.

The museum houses a permanent exhibition entitled 'On the Contrary', a nod to both the playwright's final words and his famously sceptical personality. There is a gift shop on site that stocks a good range of literature by and about Ibsen, as well as other souvenirs.

Note that the museum, which is usually open for tours, is undergoing renovation work from 2019 and is expected to reopen 2021.

---

**14** 🍴 🖥 🛍

## Aker Brygge

📍 K3 🚇 Nationaltheatret 🚋 12 🌐 akerbrygge.no

In 1982 the historic shipyard Akers Mekaniske Verksted – which had been in operation for over a century – closed down, freeing up Oslo's harbourfront. Seeing the potential, developers set out to create a new public space. Many of the old shipyard warehouses have been restored, and Aker Brygge has been transformed to provide a major shopping and entertainment centre with residential apartments and the city's biggest concentration of restaurants. Bold new architecture blends with the old, and the site has attracted international acclaim as a brilliant example of inner-city redevelopment. A delightful setting, this is a great spot in which to enjoy a beer or glass of wine at the quayside. From the development's harbourside location there is a panoramic view across the water to the fortress of Akershus (p94). There are also enough stores to satisfy the most seasoned shopper.

The Aker Brygge was also the inspiration behind Oslo City Council's ambitious reclamation project at Fjord City's waterfront (p80), which began in 2008 and should finish in 2030.

(p94) ... (p80)

# SHOP

**Paleet**
The stylish set flock to this conglomeration of 30 Norwegian concept boutiques for fashion and interior design. APHRU, Follestad and Svean stock top fashions, while YME offers edgy homeware.

📍 M2 🚇 Karl Johans Gate 37-43 🕐 Sun 🌐 paleet.no

---

**Norway Designs**
A one-stop shop for the finest Scandi design products, from glass and ceramics, through wooden homewares and kitchen utensils, to jewellery and fashion accessories.

📍 L2 🚇 Stortingsgata 28 🌐 norwaydesigns.no

Sunset over Aker Brygge, home to the Astrup Fearnley Museum

## 15 Ⓨ 🍴 🛍 Tjuvholmen

📍 K4 🚇 Nationalt Theatret
🚋 12, 19 🚌 21, 30, 31, 32, 54
🌐 tjuvholmen.no/en

**Elegant pedestrian bridges span canals, leading from the smart shops and restaurants of Aker Brygge to the lovely islet of Tjuvholmen.**

Once notoriously seedy, today Tjuvholmen is an attractive, modern waterfront borough known for its contemporary art, architecture and urban beaches. Elegant pedestrian bridges span canals, leading from the smart shops and restaurants of Aker Brygge to the lovely islet of Tjuvholmen. More exclusive destination restaurants, cafés and galleries are clustered here, including Pushwagner, a gallery dedicated to one of Norway's most important contemporary artists.

The must-visit sight in Tjuvholmen is the **Astrup Fearnley Museum**. This private art museum was inaugurated in 1993, but was relocated to this fabulous premises in 2012. Designed by renowned architect Renzo Piano to resemble a boat, the building seems ready to set sail from its position, where the city meets the fjord. The stunning building, which seems to blend into the surrounding seascape, makes as much of a state-ment as the fascinating collection inside.

The museum's permanent exhibitions include inter-national artists from post-World War II to the present day, with a significant focus on conceptual American work from the 1980s. The most famous piece in the museum is *Michael Jackson and Bubbles*, a gold ceramic sculpture by Jeff Koons that depicts the singer and his beloved pet chimp. Other contemporary international artists include Damien Hirst and Cindy Sherman. Norwegian art is represented with pieces by the likes of Sigmar Polke and Anselm Kiefer. An exciting schedule of well-curated temporary exhibitions explores provocative themes, and these often debut with buzzy events. Weekly Sunday tours are a worthwhile way to engage more deeply with the collection. Vingen, an on-site café and bar, is a popular hangout for visitors as well as the general public, thanks to its New Nordic menu, first-rate cocktails and gorgeous beach-side views. There is also a museum shop, which has an excellent range of books to purchase, alongside jewellery and other design items.

Located just outside the museum is the vibrant **Tjuvholmen Sculpture Park**, which is free to access and open 24 hours a day. Here, seven contemporary and thought-provoking pieces – from Louise Bourgeois' cheeky *Eyes* to a colourful anchor, *Spalt*, by Franz West – share a striking fjord backdrop. Like the Astrup Fearnley Museum, the park was also designed by Renzo Piano, and flows smoothly into one of Oslo's most popular urban bathing spots. Some people swim directly off the park pier, and there are two family-friendly sandy beaches on the canal.

## Astrup Fearnley Museum

⊛ ⊗ ⊜ ⬛ Strand-promenaden 2 ◯ Noon-5pm Tue-Fri (to 7pm Thu), 11am-5pm Sat & Sun
ⓦ afmuseet.no

## Tjuvholmen Sculpture Park

⬛ Strandpromenaden 2
◯ 24 hours daily

Modern artworks on display at the Astrup Fearnley Museum

---

**16** ⊗

## Tjuvtitten

◉ K4 ⬛ Albert Nordengens Plass 🄲 23 11 88 90
Ⓜ Nationaltheatret
🚃 12, 19 🚌 21, 30, 31, 32, 54
◯ May-Sep: Sat & Sun

Not far from the Astrup Fearnley Museum is the Tjuvtitten tower, which opened in 2012. Its name

### Did You Know?

Tjuvholmen means 'Thief Island', thanks to unsavoury 18th-century characters who met here.

translates literally as 'sneak peek', and the lift in this mind-boggling, clear-glass tower whisks its occupants 54 m (177 ft) into the air to offer them just that. From this birds-eye position, you'll be able to take in panoramic views of the urban cityscape, the harbour, the deep blue sea and the ferries taking visitors to the verdant fjord islands. Note that there are often queues to board the lift.

The closest island you'll spy is Høvedoya, a forested nature reserve with pretty beaches and a gastropub. Høvedoya is also home to the ruins of a Cistercian monastery that dates from 1147. The island once belonged to the Norwegian military and two 19th-century gunpowder depots from this period can still be viewed here today. One of the former military buildings, Lavetthuset, now houses art exhibitions.

Oslo appears to have something of a taste for spectacular viewpoints, with a further addition to this category – the meandering Stovnertårnet pathway, which opened in 2017. This winding, elevated platform is lit as night falls.

←

Locals enjoying the sunshine in the waterfront borough of Tjuvholmen

---

# DRINK

### Fuglen
A hip café and bar with a twist: all of the furniture is for sale.
◉ M2
⬛ Universitetsgata 2
ⓦ fuglen.no

---

### Vingen
Linger over coffee or cocktails on Vingen's waterfront patio.
◉ K4 ⬛ Strandpromen-aden 2 ⓦ vingenbar.no

---

### Thief Bar
A notoriously lavish cocktail bar with high standards of presentation.
◉ K4 ⬛ Landgangen 1, Tjuvholmen
ⓦ thethief.com

---

### Stockfleths
Founded in 1895, this is the heart of speciality coffee in Oslo.
◉ L3 ⬛ Brynjulf Bulls Plass 1 ⓦ stockfleths.as

# A SHORT WALK
# KARL JOHANS GATE

**Distance** 1.5 km (1 mile) **Time** 20 minutes
**Nearest T-banen** Stortinget

In the heart of Oslo, Karl Johans Gate – or simply Karl Johan to locals – is the city's busiest thoroughfare and connects the west side of the city to the east. Every day, some 100,000 Osloites pound the pavements here, passing many of Norway's foremost institutions as they go about their business. The Royal Palace (Slottet), Stortinget (the Norwegian Parliament), Historisk Museum and university are grand reminders of the city's rich cultural heritage. This area is also a commercial hub; department stores, specialist shops and places to eat line the bustling street and offer locals and explorers alike a chance to grab refreshments.

## Did You Know?

King Harald V (1937-) secretly dated Queen Sonja for nine years before they were permitted to marry.

**START**

The **Royal Palace** – or Slottet – is on a hill at the end of Karl Johans Gate. It forms a natural and imposing focal point (p79).

**Dronningparken** is an enclosed part of the large and open Slottsparken.

Queen Maud's statue was designed by Ada Madssen in 1959.

This statue of King Karl Johan on his horse is by Brynjulf Bergslien and dates from 1875. Karl Johan built the Royal Palace and gave Oslo's main street its name.

**Karl Johans Gate** (p78) is Oslo's main thoroughfare, and is the focal point for both city life and national events such as the 17 May parades. It was planned by the palace architect, H D F Linstow, in 1840 and named after King Karl Johan.

← People strolling around Karl Johans Gate as evening falls

↑ Grand exterior of the National Theatre

Housed in an Art Nouveau building dating from 1902, the **Historisk Museum** (p72) features an Ethnographic collection, coins and the National Antiquities – comprising 36,000 archaeological finds.

**Locator Map**
*For more detail see p68*

The Nasjonalgalleriet's collection is in the process of being moved into the Nasjonalmuseet (p70), alongside two other institutions. The gallery will be open until the Nasjonalmuseet opens in 2020.

BERGS GATE

KRISTIAN IVS GATE

FREDERIKS GATE

UNIVERSITETSGT

The **Universitetet** (p78) faces Karl Johans Gate and Universitetsplassen. Together with the Royal Palace and the National Theatre, it contributes to the imposing and historic character of the street.

KARL JOHANS GATE

| 0 metres | | 100 |
| 0 yards | | 100 |

N ↑

R AMUNDSENS GT

☐ **FINISH**

The National Theatre – or **Nationaltheatret** (p80) – is the main stage for Norwegian drama. Designed by Henrik Bull, it was completed in 1899.

Statue of Bjørnstjerne Bjørnson

Statue of Henrik Ibsen

Statue of Henrik Wergeland

# CENTRAL OSLO EAST

Eastern was founded by King Harald Hardrade in around 1049. Bjørvika, once home to the city's first market and a commercial port, is now at the heart of the dynamic Fjord City project *(p80)*. Here, the iconic Oslo Opera House crowns the waterfront promenade and has inspired a spate of ultra-modern buildings, such as the Lambda Munch Museum, Deichman Biblioteket and Barcode complex, many of which are still under construction. Old and new converge in the east. Alongside the chic, concrete powerhouses of the arts is Akershus Festning, a medieval fortress built to protect the city from foreign invasion. Under the auspices of Christian IV, the area of Kvadraturen (Quadrangle) developed to the north of the fortress, and the king renamed the new city Christiania in 1624. Many of its historic buildings remain, alongside places of interest such as museums dedicated to Norwegian resistance and the history of Christiania. As if culture and history aren't enough, this part of the city is home to multicultural communities and a cosmopolitan mix of fashionable and revered restaurants and ethnic shops.

# CENTRAL OSLO EAST

**Must See**

1. Akershus Festning

**Experience More**

2. Norges Hjemmefrontmuseum
3. Old Town Hall
4. Høymagasinet
5. Christiania Torv
6. Norsk Arkitekturmuseum
7. Den Gamle Logen
8. Forsvarsmuseet
9. Oslo Opera House
10. Lambda Munch Museum
11. Børsen
12. Oslo Domkirke
13. Basarhallene
14. Deichman Biblioteket
15. Sørenga Sjøbad
16. Stortinget
17. Youngstorget
18. Akrobaten Pedestrian Bridge
19. Oslo Spektrum

**Eat**

1. Vaaghals
2. Maaemo
3. Vippa

**Drink**

4. Himkok
5. Sentralen
6. Justisen

# ①  AKERSHUS FESTNING

📍M4  🏛Akershus Fortress area  📞23 09 35 53  🚇Stortinget  🚊12 & short walk from 13, 19  🚌60 & short walk from 30, 31, 32, 45, 81, 83  🕐Castle: May–Aug: 10am–4pm Mon–Sat, noon–4pm Sun; Sep–Apr: noon–5pm Sat & Sun  🚫Public hols

This medieval fortress is a dramatic contrast to the modern complexes found further along Oslo's waterfront. Built in 1299 to safeguard the city from foreign invasion, Akershus has seen battles, housed criminals and witnessed executions.

Akershus has a long history as a strategic stronghold. For more than 700 years the fortress has been standing guard over Oslo to ward off all attempts to invade the city from the sea. The *slott* (castle) occupies a spectacular setting on a hill at the head of Oslofjorden. King Håkon V began building in 1299, and since then the fortifications have undergone numerous improvements and reconstructions. One of the fortress's greatest moments was to resist the siege of the Swedish king, Karl XII, in 1716 – one of eight occasions in which the Swedish attacked the fortress without success. In the 19th century, the castle's defensive role declined in significance and it became an administrative centre for the armed forces, before Nazi collaborators were executed here in 1945. Today, Akershus Festning is the government's main venue for state functions. It is open to the public, and comprises historic buildings, museums and defence installations. Tours take place daily in summer and on weekends throughout the year.

*Olav's Hall was renovated in 1976 and named after King Olav V (1903–91).*

*The grand fireplace (1634–42) in Romeriks Hall shows the coat of arms of Governor-General Christopher Urne and his wife.*

← Akershus Festning, overlooking the water and illuminated at night

## Timeline

### 1299
▽ King Håkon V begins building the fortress to protect the city from invasion

### 1827–45
Akershus serves as a dungeon for notorious criminals, including outlaw Gest Bårdsen

### 2018
▽ The fortress becomes the Norwegian Ministry of Defence Headquarters

### 1945
▲ Eight Norwegians, including Vidkun Quisling, are executed here for war crimes

---

The impressive exterior of Akershus Festning, a medieval fortress
↓

INSIDER TIP
**Cheap eats**
A short walk along the harbour promenade from Akershus Fortress is Vippa food hall, which specialises in creative and affordable snacks *(p98)*. Stock up on treats and tuck in on the pier by the fortress.

Remains of Vågehalsen, the medieval tower which once divided the courtyard.

The Blue Tower (Blåtårnet) stands opposite Romeriks Tower.

In the 17th century, Christian IV's Hall formed part of the Danish king and queen's private apartments before becoming a military arsenal. It is used by the government for receptions.

Known as Skrivestuene, these rooms were named after the Scribes Rooms House that once stood here. It was used by court administrators.

The Royal Mausoleum contains the remains of Håkon VII and his wife Maud, Olav V and Crown Princess Märtha, among others.

← Night falling over
Oslo's historic
Old Town Hall

The museum exhibition, on the first and second floors, gives an excellent overview of Oslo's history. It also explores the city's urban development and theatre history.

### 4 Høymagasinet

**♥M4 ♠Akershus fortress area ⓘ ⓣStortinget 🚋12, 13, 19 🚌60 ⊙Jun-Aug: noon-5pm Sat & Sun**

A former hay barn at Akershus Festning is the location for Høymagasinet, a museum devoted to the history of Christiania from 1624 to 1840.

The year 1624 saw the devastating fire that left most of the old city of Oslo in ashes. The Danish-Norwegian king, Christian IV, decided to rebuild the city further west and named it Christiania. Reconstruction was slow during the first 100 years, but it gathered speed in the 18th century. The city's history is illustrated here with the help of models and a variety of other displays, including a 25-minute multimedia

# EXPERIENCE MORE

### 2 Norges Hjemme-frontmuseum

**♥M4 ♠Akershus fortress area ⓣStortinget 🚋10, 12, 13, 19 🚌 30, 31, 32, 45, 60, 81, 83 ⊙Jun-Aug: 10am-5pm Mon-Sat, 11am-5pm Sun; Sep-May: 10am-4pm Mon-Sat ⊗Public hols 🌐forsvaretsmuseer.no**

On 9 April 1940, German forces occupied Norway. While the Norwegians made a valiant attempt at halting their advance, the country succumbed 62 days later. For the next five years the Norwegian Resistance conducted a heroic campaign against the occupying German army, and their exploits are well documented in Norway's Resistance Museum. Taped speeches and film clips recreate the World War II years, and bring to life the comprehensive collection of documents, posters and memorabilia from that time.

The museum is situated in a 17th-century stone vault, 200 m (656 ft) long, in Bindingsverkshuset (Half-Timbered House), at the top of Akershus Festning. It opened on 8 May 1970, which was the 25th anniversary of the liberation. Alongside the museum, there is a memorial to the Norwegians who were shot here during the war.

The museum has a small bookshop that offers a fine collection of reference books on the Norwegian war effort.

### 3 Old Town Hall

**♥M4 ♠Christiania Torv 1 ⓣStortinget 🚋12, 13, 19 🚌 30, 31, 32, 45, 60, 81, 83 ⊙Jun-Aug: 11am-4pm Tue-Sun ⊗Public hols 🌐gamleraadhus.no**

Built in 1641, Oslo's first town hall is imbued with urban history, having served variously as a fire station, a church and even a prison. Today, it houses a small museum and, more famously, one of the city's oldest restaurants, Gamle Raadhus (it predates the Engebret Café by a year). In operation since 1856, the ground-floor restaurant's longevity is echoed in its charming, historic decor and traditional Norwegian cuisine.

→ Oslo's national monument to victims of World War II

> **The Danish-Norwegian king, Christian IV, decided to rebuild the city further west and named it Christiania.**

programme. The museum also offers visitors short guided walks through the streets of Kvadraturen *(p104)*, the original Christiania.

---

**5**
## Christiania Torv

📍M3 🚇Stortinget 🚊12, 13, 19

The square is old, but the name is rather new. It was decided in 1958 that this part of Oslo's original market square *(torv)* should be called Christiania, after the old name for Oslo. For many years the square was plagued by heavy traffic. It underwent extensive renovation in the 1990s when traffic was diverted through a tunnel. Now pedestrianized, Christiania Torv is once more a pleasant

place to visit. In 1997, a fountain created by the artist Wenche Gulbransen was erected in the square. It is also home to several popular restaurants and historic buildings, among them the Garnison Hospital, the oldest building in the capital.

---

**6** 🍽 🛍
## Norsk Arkitektur-museum

📍M4 🏛Kongens Gate 2
🚇Stortinget 🚊12, 15, 19
🚌30, 31, 32, 60 🕐11am-
5pm Tue, Wed & Fri, 11am-
7pm Thu, noon-5pm Sat &
Sun 🚫Public hols
🌐nasjonalmuseet.no

Founded in 1975, the Museum of Norwegian Architecture features drawings, photos and models covering 1,000 years of the nation's building history. It also arranges touring exhibitions of past and present architectural projects.

Norsk Arkitekturmuseum is based in old Christiania. The oldest part of the house dates from 1830. The building underwent renovation to accommodate the museum in 2008.

# DRINK

### Himkok
Ranked 20th on the World's 50 Best Bars list, this trendy speakeasy offers tempting cocktails and seasonal varieties of aquavit, gin and vodka.

📍P2 🏛Storgata 27
🌐himkok.no

---

### Sentralen
Once a bank building, this hipster hangout has an excellent wine and cocktail menu. There's also a formal restaurant (reservations required).

📍M3 🏛Øvre Slottsgate 3 🚫Sun 🌐sentralen.no

---

### Justisen
Dripping with atmosphere, this traditional central bar has stylish interiors and a buzzing back garden.

📍N2 🏛Møllergata 15
🚫Sun & Mon
🌐justisen.no

Striking fountain by Wenche Gulbransen, in Christiania Torv →

### 7

## Den Gamle Logen

M4 · Grev Wedels Plass 2 · Jernbanetorget · 12, 13, 19 · 30, 31, 32, 41, 45, 60, 81, 83 · gamlelogen.no

If walls could talk, those of Den Gamle Logen (The Old Lodge) would have a fascinating story to tell. The city council held its meetings here from the end of the 19th century until 1947, and the lodge was used as a court room during the legal proceedings against Vidkun Quisling, who was sentenced to death for treason at the end of World War II (*p52*).

The lodge opened in 1839, and is based on drawings by Christian H Malling and Jens S Seidelin. Its central feature is the vast Neo-Classical banqueting hall. Noted for its excellent acoustics, it was the city's foremost concert hall for many years. It fell from grace after World War II, however, when the lodge was taken over by the Oslo Port Labour Office and the banqueting hall became a canteen. It reverted to its first use in the 1980s, when Oslo Summer Opera moved in, and has since undergone restoration.

---

# EAT

### Vaaghals
A sleek restaurant with an excellent mix of traditional and modern Norwegian dishes.

P4 · Dronning Eufemias Gate 8 · Sat L, Sun · vaaghals.com

Ⓚ Ⓚ Ⓚ

---

### Maaemo
Norway's pride and joy holds three Michelin stars. Advance booking is a must, as diners wait months to revel in chef Esben Holmboe Bang's artfully plated menu.

Q3 · Schweigaards Gate 15B · Sun · maaemo.no

Ⓚ Ⓚ Ⓚ

---

### Vippa
Sip craft beer and sample budget-friendly food options, such as pulled duck burgers or tasty dumplings, at this bustling food hall.

M5 · Akershus- stranda · vippa.no

Ⓚ Ⓚ Ⓚ

---

### 8

## Forsvarsmuseet

M5 · Akershus Festning, Building 62 · 23 09 35 82 · 10, 12, 13, 15, 19 · 60 · May–Aug: 10am–5pm daily; Sep–Apr: 10am–4pm Tue–Sun · Public hols

The history of the Norwegian armed forces, from Viking times to the present day, is represented in Forsvarsmuseet – the Armed Forces Museum – at Akershus Slott. Two large brick buildings from the 1860s, once used as military arsenals, provide an appropriate historical setting.

Military items on display include a collection from the 16th-century union with Denmark and the subsequent Nordic wars, through to the struggle for independence during the union with Sweden. Exhibits are arranged in time blocks, and include a number of lifelike models and objects, such as a German tank and a V-1 bomb from World War II, and dioramas. There are also temporary exhibitions.

---

### 9

## Oslo Opera House

P4 · Kirsten Flagstads Plass 1 · Bjørvika · 34, 70, 504 · Times vary, check website · operaen.no

Inaugurated in 2008, the Opera House is the home of the Norwegian National Opera and Ballet. On the waterfront at Bjørvika, it has a

spectacular sloping roof, which is covered in white marble and granite. It creates the illusion of glistening ice, like a glacier rising from the Oslofjord. Buildings in Norway are not held to European Union safety codes, so visitors can stroll up the roof's incline and enjoy views of Oslo and the fjord.

The Opera House has a total area of about 38,500 sq m (415,000 sq ft). It has three main performance spaces for opera, ballet and concerts, though concerts are also held in the foyer and on the roof.

The principal entrance is through a crevasse beneath the lowest portion of the roof. The interior, which is mostly wood, creates a stark contrast to the glacial exterior, and the sense of height is breathtaking. Slim white columns branch towards the vaulted ceiling, and light floods in through windows that soar as high as 15 m (49 ft).

At the heart of the theatre is the majestic *Wave Wall*. Designed by Norwegian boat builders, strips of golden oak curve around the auditorium and flow seamlessly into timber stairways. *She Lies* is a floating steel-and-glass sculpture permanently installed on a platform in the adjacent fjord. In winter, visitors can walk onto the frozen fjord and explore the sculpture.

The Opera House presents both classic and contemporary pieces. In addition to its two resident companies, its programme includes work by visiting groups. It also plays host to music festivals, including the Oslo Chamber Music Festival and the Oslo World Music Festival.

---

### Lambda Munch Museum

📍P4 🏛Kirsten Flagstads Plass 🚇Jernbanetorget/ Oslo S 🚌34, 37, 54 🚋11, 12, 13, 17, 28, 29 🔒Currently closed; opening in 2020 🌐munchmuseet.no

A Norwegian icon and forerunner of Expressionism, artist Edvard Munch

(1863–1944; *p64*) bequeathed the works in his possession to the city of Oslo. In 1963 the Munch-museet opened in Tøyen with the largest collection of Munch artwork in the world. It became clear, however, that the donation – over 28,000 works – exceeded its home. As Oslo reinvents itself as a Fjord City, the Munchmuseet will move to a grand new building in Bjørvika next to the Opera House.

Lambda is due open in June 2020 and its bold 16-storey glass tower, designed by architect Juan Herreros, will be a striking sight in keeping with Oslo's regeneration. The museum will contain works from every aspect of Munch's life, from versions of *The Scream* to the sensuous *Kiss* (1897). The Munch-museet in Tøyen (*p129*) will remain open with limited artworks and capacity during the transition.

The unusual sloping roof and dramatic oak interior *(inset)* of Oslo Opera House ↓

**11**

# Børsen

**N4** **Tollbugata 2**
**Jernbanetorget** 🚋 11,
13, 19 🚌 30, 31, 32, 45, 60,
81, 83 🌐 oslobors.no

One of the oldest institutional
buildings in Oslo is Børsen
(the Stock Exchange). Long
before the construction of
the Royal Palace and the
parliament building, it was
decided that commodity
trading should take place on
a site of its own. Børsen, the
first of Oslo's grand buildings,
was consequently opened
in 1828. The Neo-Classical
façade with its Doric columns
contrasts strongly with the
more modern buildings
nearby. The two side wings
and a southern wing were
added in 1910. Originally the
site included an enclosed
courtyard, but this was
redesigned to house the new
Stock Exchange hall in 1988.

The entrance hall is dominated by Gerhard Munthe's
mural from 1912, *Handelen og
Sjøfarten* (*Trade and Shipping*).
Børsen also has its own

↑ Børsen, fronted by a
statue of Mercury, the
Roman god of commerce

library, reading room and
antique trade museum,
as well as a portrait gallery.

---

**12**

# Oslo Domkirke

**N3** **Karl Johans Gate 11**
**Jernbanetorget,**
**Stortinget** 🚋 11, 17, 18 🚌 37
**Daily** 🌐 oslodomkirke.no

Oslo Domkirke is the principal
church for the diocese of Oslo.
The foundation stone was laid
in 1694, and the church was

built in several stages; the
altarpiece and pulpit date
from 1699, and the interior
was completed in the 1720s.
Countless reconstructions
and renovations followed;
in the mid-1850s the Baroque
interior was remodelled in
Neo-Gothic style. Some 100
years later, the baptismal font,
altarpiece and pulpit were restored to the pre-1850s style.

Among the cathedral's
adornments are stained-
glass windows by Emanuel
Vigeland, a silver sculpture
with a Lord's Supper motif
by Arrigo Minerbi and bronze
doors by Dagfin Werenskiold.
The modern painted ceiling,
which depicts scenes from
the Bible, was created by
Hugo Lous Mohr between
1936 and 1950. During the
course of this work the
original ceiling paintings were
destroyed, an act that has
since attracted much criticism.

The cathedral has 900
seats and hosted the wedding
ceremony of Norway's Crown
Prince Haakon and Mette-
Marit in 2001.

In the church tower hangs a
great bell, weighing 1,600 kg
(3,527 lb), and three smaller
bells. Below the ground floor
of the cathedral is a crypt.

↑ The light stone façade
and church tower of
Oslo Domkirke

## TOP 5 INSTAGRAM HOTSPOTS

**Oslo Opera House**
Climb the roof for enviable views across the fjord (*p98*).

**Sørenga Sjøbad**
Snap a friend mid-dive at this open-air pool.

**Akrobaten Pedestrian Bridge**
This striking bridge is best when it's lit at night (*p103*).

**Vippa**
Graffiti, fjord views and creative eats – ideal for Instagram (*p98*).

**Barcode**
Beautifully designed high rises make for dynamic shots (*p103*).

↑ A café tucked under the 19th-century arches of Oslo's Basarhallene

---

**13** 🖥 🏛

## Basarhallene

📍N3 🚇Kirkeristen
🚆Jernbanetorget, Stortinget 🚋11, 17, 18 🚌37

Just behind Oslo Domkirke, these Romanesque brick arcades were designed in the mid-19th century by Christian H Gross. Once housing chiefly butchers, today the arcade shelters small boutiques and terraced cafés. It's also used for *bonden marked* (farmers' markets) and *jul marked* (Christmas markets).

---

**14** 🍴 🖥 🏛

## Deichman Biblioteket

📍N2 🚇Kirsten Flagstads Plass 🚆Jernbanetorget 🚋11, 12, 13, 17, 28, 29 🚌34, 37, 54 🕐Currently closed; opening in 2020 🌐deichman.no

Europe's most modern library will open on the Oslo waterfront in early 2020.

Lund Hagem Architects have designed a dynamic building space to hold the collection of Norwegian businessman and book hoarder Carl Deichman (1705–80), alongside a media lounge, restaurant and cinema. The library's goal is accessibility, creating a welcoming central hub where tourists and locals can linger to nourish both the mind and the body. The project is part of Oslo's push for a new urban scene with the concentration of creative, cultural attractions and public spaces being moved to the waterfront.

From a buzzy restaurant and lounge zone with fjord views on the ground floor, visitors can journey to the children's centre on the first floor, which will offer a storytelling circle and family-friendly café. On the second floor, the media centre will house gaming zones, comics, music and more. Those seeking more traditional reading spaces can continue on to the 'knowledge universe' on the third floor, which will have ensconced reading rooms, while the top floor will house a collection of books covering Oslo's history, and the original, historic Deichman collection. Like much of Oslo, this new space will celebrate the old with the new.

---

**15**

## Sørenga Sjøbad

📍P6 🚇Sørengkaia 69
🚆Jernbanetorget/Oslo S
🚌81, 83 🕐24 hours daily
🌐sorenga.no

A floating, water-based urban park, Sørenga Sjøbad is completely unique. This sea pool is one of the most successful ideas in Oslo's unrolling Fjord City plan. The Sørenga pier has been transformed into a water play area with a sandy beach, a floating wooden jetty with diving boards, a seawater swimming pool and a children's pool The beach and the large seawater pool are exposed to the fjord, offering wide vistas out to Hovedøya island. There are also excellent views back towards the city, which take in the new Barcode area, Lambda and Oslo Opera House.

The sea pool is particularly popular in summer, although it remains in use when the cold weather arrives, at which point the sauna becomes a sought-after facility. Alongside the pool is Sørenga, Oslo's harbourfront neighbourhood, which is lined with cafés and restaurants – perfect for a post-swim snack.

←
People relaxing in front of Stortinget, Norway's parliament building

**17** 🍴 🍺 🛍️

## Youngstorget

📍N2 🚇Jernbanetorget
🚋11, 12, 13, 17 🚌30, 31, 32, 34, 38, 56

This large public square has long-established political affiliations. Many of the Labour movement's most important institutions, including the Norwegian Labour Party, have their headquarters around Youngstorget, and other political parties, such as *Fremskrittspartiet* (Progress Party) and *Venstre* (Liberals), also have offices in the area.

Youngstorget was laid out in 1846, and was for many years a cattle and vegetable market, as well as a place for political demonstrations. Today local farmers continue to sell fresh produce here, and there are also clothes and exotic handicrafts on sale. In summer, concerts and events for all ages are held here.

**16**

## Stortinget

📍M3 🏛️Karl Johans Gate 22
🚇Stortinget 🚋13, 19 🚌30, 31, 32, 41, 45, 81, 83
🌐stortinget.no

Norway's National Assembly has its seat in the grand Stortinget (Norwegian parliament building). It was designed by the Swedish architect Emil Victor Langlet, after a series of different proposals. The foundation stone was laid on 10 October 1861. Construction took five years and in 1866 the assembly met for the first time in its own building.

Stortinget is built of yellow brick on a reddish granite base, in a blend of Norwegian and Italian building traditions. It has been expanded and partly reconstructed on several occasions; the wing towards Akersgata, for example, was added in the 1950s.

The assembly chamber, which seats the 165 members of parliament, resembles an amphitheatre. The speaker's chair is positioned below Oscar Wergeland's painting of the 1814 Eidsvoll assembly, which ratified the Norwegian constitution. The painting dates from 1885 and depicts many of the men who helped to shape Norway's constitution.

The building has been richly decorated by Norwegian artists, including the painter Else Hagen, who embellished the stairwell. A colourful tapestry by Karen Holtsmark, *Solens Gang*, hangs in the central hall, while the sculptures in the stair hall are by Nils Flakstad.

Public entry is by guided tour only; tours in English take place on Saturday mornings, except during summer.

> 🔍 HIDDEN GEM
> **Waffling on**
>
> Duck behind the Youngstorget to visit Harald's Vaffel, which sells waffles to rival any from Belgium thanks to its inventive flavour range. Reasonable prices make this a brilliant snack spot.

→
Akrobaten Pedestrian Bridge leading to the Barcode Complex

The square is named after the merchant Jørgen Young, who originally owned the area. In 1990 it underwent substantial renovation. A copy of an original fountain from 1880 was installed and market kiosks from 1876 were restored. There are shops, workshops and various places to eat and drink in the bazaar halls at the back of the market square, as well as in the market itself.

## 18
### Akrobaten Pedestrian Bridge

**Q4** Jernbanetorget **18, 19**

Akrobaten, or "the acrobat", is an impressive steel-and-glass bridge that connects Bjørvika in the south with Grønland in the north. This near-futuristic construction was designed by the Oslo-based firm L2 Architects, and the bridge was awarded first place in the European Award for Steel Bridges in 2012. Installed in 20 phases, Akrobaten is a remarkable feat of engineering; it stretches 206 m (676 ft) and crosses 19 of the central station's railway tracks. The bridge is pedestrianized and is particularly popular with visitors to the city thanks to its

excellent views and proximity to the imposing Barcode development (where high-rise buildings of varying heights and widths resemble a barcode from afar). If possible, visit Akrobaten at night, when the bridge is colourfully lit and makes for great photos.

## 19
### Oslo Spektrum

**P3** Sonja Henies Plass 2 Jernbanetorget **12, 13, 18, 19** **30, 31, 32, 34, 38, 41, 45, 46** Box office: 9am–4pm Mon–Fri oslospektrum.no

The 10,800-capacity Oslo Spektrum is the main venue for large-scale sporting and cultural events. Designed by Lars Haukland, the complex was completed in 1991. It was planned and constructed as part of a scheme to revitalize the Grønland/Vaterland area, and has created a bridge between Oslo's city centre and the eastern part of the city. The façade is clad with a massive mosaic designed by Rolf Nesch and crafted by

### OSLO'S STREET ART

In the last decade, local and international artists have turned the streets of East Oslo into one of the city's liveliest art scenes. Check out Martin Whatson's *High Up* (2015), located near Akershusstranda 3, and *Zebra* (2015), near Rådhusbrygge 2. If you're enjoying a bit to eat at Vippa, don't miss the Octopus and Giraffe (2017) murals, and *Sleeper* (2014), which is close to Barcode at Schweigaards Gate 48.

artist Guttorm Guttormsgaard and ceramicist Søren Ubsisch.

A number of major events, such as the Nobel Peace Prize concert (December), are held here, along with shows such as *Disney on Ice*. International pop stars, such as Josh Groban, Elton John and Rhianna, regularly perform at the stadium. It is also the venue for national handball matches. Tickets can be purchased online or through the box office.

# A SHORT WALK
# KVADRATUREN

**Distance** 1.5 km (1 mile) **Time** 20 minutes
**Nearest T-banen** Stortinget

Oslo has been ravaged by fire on a number of occasions, but the most devastating was in 1624, when almost the entire city was destroyed. The king, Christian IV, decided to build a new city to be known as Christiania. Development started at the foot of the Akershus fortress. The area of Kvadraturen (the Quadrangle) took the form of a rectangular grid. Although few of the original buildings remain, Kvadraturen is still characterized by its historic architecture. It has old market squares and museums, picturesque sights and traditional eating places that still pulse with life today. The fortress bordering the harbour is the focal point, and contrasts with the modern architecture that has sprung up from Oslo's waterfront.

The city's first market square, **Christiania Torv** (p97) has been renovated and is now home to several eateries. The fountain, Christian IV's Glove, is by Wenche Gulbransen (1997).

**FINISH**

CHRISTIANIA TORV

AKERSGATA

RÅDHUSGATA

Originally a hay barn, the half-timbered **Høymagasinet** (p96) dates from 1845. It houses models illustrating the history of the city's buildings.

**START**

### Did You Know?

Apparently, after the 1624 fire Christian IV pointed at Christiania square and said "The new town will lie here!"

↑ The impressive sailing ship *Christian Radich*, moored in Oslo's waters

**Hjemmefrontmuseum** (p96) is Norway's Resistance Museum. Situated at the top of the Akershus fortress, it provides a picture of the years of German occupation in 1940–45.

Christian Radich, 1937, is often moored at Akershus. The sailing ship achieved worldwide fame for its part in the film Windjammer (1957).

**Norsk Arkitekturmuseum**
(p97) – or the Museum of
Norwegian Architecture – is
filled with models of buildings
old and new, such as the Law
Courts, 1994.

*Engebret Café,
established in 1857,
is Oslo's oldest
existing restaurant.*

RÅDHUSGATA

KONGENS GATE

REVIERSTREDET

NEDRE SLOTTSGT.

MYNTGATA

**Locator Map**
*For more detail see p92*

0 metres                    100

0 yards                     100

↑ Medieval fortress Akershus Festning,
sprinkled with snow

The King's Battery

*One of Oslo's top attractions is the
**Akershus Festning** (p94). Begun in
1299, its stout walls and historic
interiors bear the scars of many a
battle. The complex is strategically
situated on a rocky outcrop with
excellent views over Oslofjorden.*

*Oslo has built a harbour
promenade to make the
city harbour accessible to
pedestrians and cyclists.
The path stretches across
Sørenga, past the Opera
House, Aker Brygge and
Tjuvholmen, over Bygdøy.
The route is marked by
orange information towers
and shouldn't be missed;
there's lots to see and do
along the way (p58).*

AKERS HUSSTRANDA

*Munketårnet*

# BYGDØY

Situated on the innermost reaches of Oslofjorden, Bygdøy is just a short distance from Oslo's centre. Its name means "the inhabited island", and it was an island until the end of the 19th century, when the sound between Frognerkilen and Bestumkilen was filled in, conveniently providing more land for Osloites. It is one of the city's most exclusive residential areas and a popular tourist destination, with its select group of museums that collectively reflect Norway's cultural history, seafaring traditions and intrepid voyages of discovery. A sign-posted walking route links the museums, making this a pleasant place to stroll. The area's connections with royalty go back to the 16th century, when the Danish-Norwegian kings came here to hunt. Much of Bygdøy is still forested. There are groves, meadows and parkland, and a wealth of different plant species. Several of Oslo's most popular bathing beaches, including Huk and Paradisbukta, which means "Paradise Bay", are on Bygdøy.

A B C

3

HENGSENGVEIEN

HENGSENGVEIEN

Bygdøy sjøbad

*CHRISTIAN FREDERIKS VEI*

*Bygdøy Kongsgård*

**BYGDØY**

*Kaffeskjær*

*Killingen*

4

*Kongeskogen*

*Lysakerfjorden*

5

LOVISENLUND

JACOB FAYES VEI

S.H. LUNDHS VEI

Christian August-
monumentet

*Paradis-
bukta*

STRØMSBORGVEIEN

6

# BYGDØY

**Must Sees**
① Norsk Folkemuseum
② Vikingskipshuset

**Experience More**
③ Dronningen
④ Kon-Tiki Museet
⑤ Norsk Maritimt Museum
⑥ Frammuseet
⑦ Sjømannskirken
⑧ Hukodden Beach
⑨ Bygdø Kongsgård
⑩ Oscarshall Slott

Holocaustsenteret

*Hukodden*

7

*Huk
nudiststrand*

*Hukodden
Beach*
⑧

C

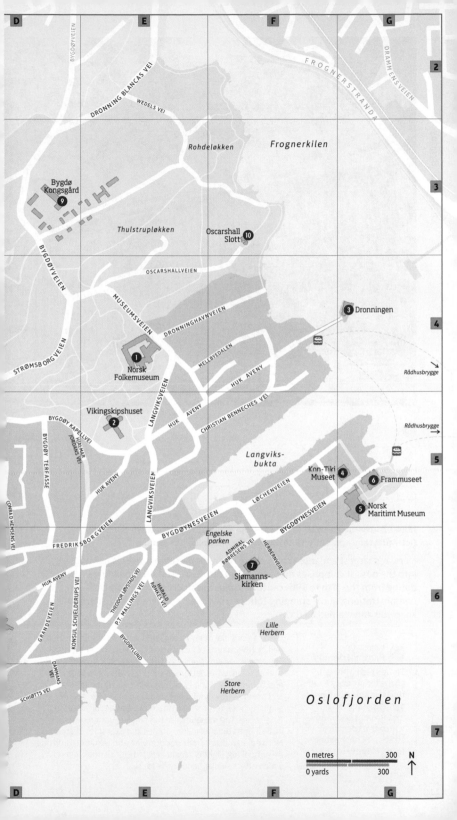

❶ 🎨 Ⓜ 🖥 🛍

# NORSK FOLKEMUSEUM

📍E4 🏛Museumsveien 10 🚌91 (Apr-Sep) 🚌30 🕐May-Sep: 10am-5pm daily; Oct-Apr: 11am-4pm daily 🚫24-25 Dec 🌐norskfolkemuseum.no

Norway's largest and most compelling open-air museum provides a window into the past. It comprises more than 150 reconstructed rural buildings dating from the 17th to 19th centuries, plus livestock, cooking and craft demonstrations, and a stunning folk art collection, so there's plenty here to keep you entertained all day.

💬 INSIDER TIP
**Family-friendly**

There's plenty to keep all the family busy. Feed the farm animals, have a go at flipping *lefse* (potato pancakes) and watch craft demonstrations. Check online for weekly events.

Europe's original open-air museum was established by Hans Aall in 1894, a time of widespread nationalist enthusiasm. The Norsk Folkemusuem – or Norwegian Folk Museum – seeks to evoke the pattern of everyday life in the valley, fjord and fishing communities of bygone times by recreating farm settlements. Town buildings from all parts of the country have similarly been reconstructed to represent a typical Gamlebyen (Old Town). The museum also has smaller, undercover exhibits, including traditional folk costumes and examples of stunning Norwegian folk art, from woodcarving and textiles to knitting. An annual highlight is *Julemarkedet*, the Christmas market, which offers similar handicrafts for sale.

## TOP 5 — FOLKEMUSEUM BUILDINGS

**Gol Stav Church**
A medieval church (c 1200) moved here from Hallingdal in 1880.

**Sámi *goahti***
The Sámi used these turf and log cabins as houses and barns.

**Åmlid Farmhouse**
A quaint turf-roof farmhouse (c 1650-1700).

**Storehouse from Søndre Berdal**
Gorgeously carved storehouse (c. 1750s) on wooden posts.

**Wessels Gate 15**
Charming 19th-century apartment building.

←
Traditional wooden turf-roof cabins at the Norsk Folkemuseum

### SÁMI CULTURE

The Sámi are Europe's northernmost indigenous people, and some 45,000 live in Norway's Arctic tundra. One of the world's oldest cultures, the Sámi are traditionally reindeer herders. The Sámi Culture exhibit examines their way of life and the turf cabins - *goahti* or *gamme* (plural) - give a sense of how they lived.

1 Visitors can peer through windows and touch exhibits as they explore this fascinating open-air museum.

2 History is brought to life with traditional handicraft demonstrations. Here, a woman weaves using a hand-held loom.

3 Buildings from Old Christiania (Oslo), such as the Town House, have been reconstructed at the museum.

↑ The Oseberg longship, one of the star attractions at Oslo's Vikingskipshuset

**② ⊗ Ⓜ 🛍**

# VIKINGSKIPSHUSET

📍E5 🚌Huk Aveny 35 🚌91 (Apr–Sep) 🚌30 🕐May–Sep:
9am–6pm daily; Oct–Apr: 10am–4pm daily 🚫Public hols
Ⓦkhm.uio.no

Don't be fooled by the modest exterior of this museum
on Bygdøy. Inside is a trilogy of Norway's most prized
cultural treasures – the Oseberg, Gokstad and Tune
ships. These vessels are three of the world's best-
preserved Viking ships, dating from the 9th century,
and the Vikingskipshuset tells their story.

The Oseberg and Gokstad vessels were discovered in Vestfold,
and the Tune ship at Haugen in Tune, Østfold, in the 19th
century. The Vikings repurposed their sturdy, seafaring
longships as burial chambers to transport the bodies of high-
ranking chieftains on their last journey to the kingdom of the
dead. The oak Oseberg ship is understood to be the oldest of
the trio and was used as a burial chamber for two wealthy
women, while the Gokstad held the remains of a 60-year-old
man. Smaller than the other ships, the Tune was found with the
remains of one man and three horses. The museum itself forms
part of the Museum of Cultural History, University of Oslo, and
was designed by Arnstein Arneberg. Head for the museum's
*Vikings Alive* film to learn more about the Viking Age.

↑ Visitors approaching the
entrance to the museum

**GALLERY GUIDE**

The main attractions
are arranged in the
form of a cross. Near
the entrance hall
stands the Oseberg
ship and on the far
side is the Oseberg
Collection. The
Gokstad ship stands
alone in the left
wing. The Tune ship
is housed in the right
wing. In the gallery
above the entrance
there are rotating
exhibits.

## Excavating the Ships

Unearthing the 1,000-year-old Viking ships from the burial
mounds proved a difficult task. The Oseberg ship was buried
in blue clay and covered with stones beneath a 6-m (20-ft)
high burial mound. The grave was almost hermetically sealed.
Ground movement had partly compressed the ship and caused
it to break up. The Gokstad ship was also buried in blue clay but
the forces of nature had allowed it to lie in peace, and the ship
and its contents were well preserved. Robbers had plundered
some of the grave furnishings, meaning not all of the original
treasures are displayed at the Vikingskipshuset today.

↑ Excavation of the Oseberg Viking ship
in Vestfold, 1904

↑ Detailed animal-head
post from the Oseberg

# EXPERIENCE MORE

**3**

## Dronningen

📍G4 🏠Huk Aveny 1 🚌91
(Apr-Oct) 🚌30 🕐9am-4pm
Mon-Fri 🚫Jul 🌐knw.no

Before and after World War II,
Dronningen ("the Queen") was
one of Oslo's most popular
summer restaurants. The building, constructed in 1930 and
situated on Dronningskjæret
in Frognerkilen, was one of
the first to be designed in the
Functionalist style in Norway.
A similar restaurant, Kongen
("the King"), stood on the
opposite bank. In 1983,
however, Dronningen was
converted to offices. The
Royal Norwegian Yacht Club
and the Norwegian Students'
Rowing Club are based here.

Frognerkilen is a major
sailing centre dotted with
large yachting marinas.

**4** 🍽️🛍️

## Kon-Tiki Museet

📍G5 🏠Bygdøynesveien
36 🚌91 (Apr-Oct) 🚌30
🕐Jan-Feb & Nov-Dec: 10am-
4pm daily; Mar-May & Sep-
Oct: 10am-5pm daily; Jun-
Aug: 9:30am-6pm daily
🚫Public hols 🌐kon-tiki.no

The world watched with
interest when Thor Heyerdahl
(1914–2002) and his five-man
crew sailed across the Pacific
in the fragile balsa-wood raft
*Kon-Tiki* in 1947. Over the
course of 101 days the raft
covered 8,000 km (4,970 miles)
from Peru to Polynesia. The
voyage proved that it would
have been possible for South
Americans to have reached
Polynesia in bygone days on
balsa rafts. Heyerdahl's raft
is the main attraction in the
Kon-Tiki Museet, though there
are a number of other objects
connected with the voyage
also on show. Text and

montages in Norwegian and
English give a graphic account
of how close those on board
were to marine life. They
describe how on one occasion
the crew felt a massive whale
shark pushing against the raft.

Heyerdahl embarked on a
new expedition in 1970. He
sailed a papyrus boat, *Ra II*,
across the Atlantic from
Morocco to Barbados to prove
a theory that it was possible
for West African explorers
to have landed in the West
Indies before Columbus. The
boat's predecessor, *Ra I*, had
broken up during a previous
attempt due to a design fault,
but *Ra II* survived and is on
display in the museum.

Seven years later, Heyerdahl
steered a reed boat, *Tigris*,
across the Indian Ocean to
prove that the ancient civilizations of the Indus Valley and
Egypt could have had contact
with each other.

The museum's exhibits
include archaeological finds
from Heyerdahl's expeditions
to places such as Easter Island
and Peru. Its 8,000-volume
library is based around his
private library and contains
the world's largest collection
of literature about Polynesia.

> ### Did You Know?
>
> Thor Heyerdahl's book,
> *Kon-Tiki*, has sold over
> 50 million copies and
> been translated into
> 65 languages.

**5** 🍷🛍️

## Norsk Maritimt Museum

📍G5 🏠Bygdøynesveien
37 🚌91 (Apr-Oct) 🚌30
🕐May-Sep: 10am-5pm
daily; Oct-Apr 11am-4pm
daily 🚫Some public hols
🌐marmuseum.no

The most southerly of the
museums on the idyllic
Bygdøy peninsula is Norsk
Maritimt Museum (the
Norwegian Maritime Museum).
Located near the Frammuseet
and Kon-Tiki Museet, it has its
own quay and a marvellous
view over Oslo's harbour and
its approach from the fjord.

Norwegian maritime
traditions, including the fishing industry, the country's
1,500-year-old history of
boat-building, shipping and
marine archaeology, form the
focal point of the collection.

← *Krigseilermonument*, a
statue standing outside
the Norsk Maritimt Museum

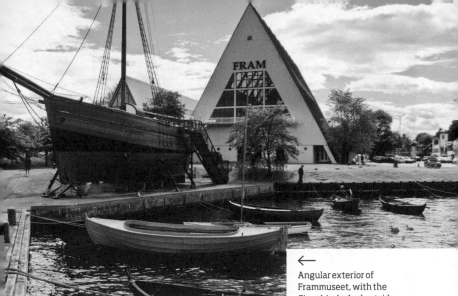

← Angular exterior of Frammuseet, with the Gjøa ship docked outside

> No other sailing vessel has been further north or south in the world than the polar ship *Fram*, used for three polar expeditions and now proudly on display.

The museum traces the development of shipping from the Middle Ages to present-day supertankers. The main theme linking the exhibits is man's use of the sea through the ages, and how the challenges and dangers of this mighty element have been faced.

From the museum's main entrance visitors enter the Central Hall, which contains a model of the Norwegian Navy's steam frigate *Kong Sverre*, one of three of the largest and most powerful warships ever built in Nordic lands. Christian Krohg's painting *Leiv Eiriksson Discovers America* hangs on one of the walls. The exhibition halls feature an abundance of model ships, in addition to relics from various maritime activities.

In the Boat Hall, traditional fishing craft and working vessels are on show, and there is a display on the diversity of coastal culture. The schooner *Svanen* is often moored at the quayside when it is not at sea as a training ship. Also standing outside the museum is the *Krigseilermonument*, which commemorates sailors killed in World War II.

The museum is the centre for a marine archaeological department, which protects finds discovered along the Norwegian coast. There is also a well-stocked museum library that contains drawings, marine literature, archives and photos.

---

**⑥** ✍️ 🅼 🏛️

## Frammuseet

📍G5 🏠Bygdøynesveien 36 🚌91 (Apr–Oct) 🚌30 🕐Jan–Apr & Oct–Dec: 10am–5pm daily; May & Sep: 10am–6pm daily; Jun–Aug: 9am–6pm daily 🔒Public hols 🌐frammuseum.no

No other sailing vessel has been further north or south in the world than the polar ship *Fram*, used for three polar expeditions and now proudly

on display. Explorers Fridtjof Nansen, Otto Sverdrup and Roald Amundsen all sailed on the *Fram*. Expeditions took place in 1893–96, 1898–1902 and 1910–12. On the third, in 1911, Amundsen became the first person to raise a flag on the South Pole.

The schooner was built by naval architect Colin Archer, and was specially constructed to prevent it from being crushed by pack ice. On its first commission with Nansen's expedition to the North Pole, it was frozen in at 78° 50'N. The vessel's rounded form allowed it to be pressed up on to the ice, where it remained undamaged until the ice thawed. The *Fram* also proved to be extremely seaworthy in the stormy Antarctic Ocean on Amundsen's historic expedition to the South Pole.

The museum opened in 1936, with the restored ship – which can be explored – as its centrepiece. Expedition equipment, paintings, busts and photographs of the polar explorers are on show. An extension was built in 2013 to house Amundsen's first polar exploration vessel, *Gjøa*. This was the first ship to cross the Northwest Passage (1903–06).

↑ The rear façade of Sjømannskirken, with its shaded porch

## 7
### Sjømannskirken

**♀F6** **⌂ Admiral Børresens Vei 4** **🚌91 (Apr-Oct)** **🚌30** **🕐 Noon-5pm Fri-Sun** **🌐 sjomannskirken.no**

In 1954 Oslo Sjømannsmisjon (the Seamen's Mission) acquired a building on Bygdøy as a centre to help sailors and harbour workers. Originally a private residence, the house was built by Arnstein Arneberg, who designed the Vikingskipshuset (p112), in 1915. It was consecrated as a church, and an assembly hall and a sacristy were added in 1962. Until then, the Mission's preachers used to conduct their sermons standing on fishing crates.

The church was taken over in 1985 by Den Indre Sjømannsmisjon (Internal Seamen's Mission). A 1966 memorial commemorates Norwegian sailors who died at sea.

> 🔍 HIDDEN GEM
> **Lille Herbern, Lanternen**
>
> Catch a ferry to reach this pearl of a restaurant, located on a tiny island just off shore. Guests have been enjoying the seafood, cocktails and stunning view here since 1929.

## 8
### Hukodden Beach

**♀D7** **🚌91 (Apr-Oct)** **🚌30**

Most of Bygdøy's south side facing the fjord is public land, with tranquil walkways along the shore and through the woods. On the southernmost tip of the peninsula lies Hukodden Beach, which teems with bathers on fine days thanks to the water quality (in spite of the proximity to the city). It is easily accessible from the city by boat or bus, and there is a beach restaurant during the summer.

From the furthest point on Huk there is a splendid view over Oslofjord, from Dyna lighthouse to Nesoddlandet in the south and to the islands in the west. The popular waterway bustles with ships and pleasure craft.

In the park area there are two modern sculptures: *Large Arch*, by Henry Moore, dating from 1969, and *Ikaros* (1965) by Anne Sofie Døhlen. On a stretch of land to the north of Huk there is a naturist beach, and beyond this is the popular bathing spot of Paradisbukta (Paradise Bay).

→ Bygdøy Peninsula, part of the royal country estate

## 9 🏞
### Bygdø Kongsgård

**♀D3** **🚌91 (to Dronningen)** **🚌30** **🚫 Closed to the public (walking trails accessible to all)** **🌐 bygdokongsgard.no**

The royal estate of Bygdø Kongsgård was used as a summer residence by King Olav V (r 1957-91), who treasured the tranquillity and idyllic surroundings of the royal farm.

King Håkon V Magnusson acquired the farm and gave it to Queen Eufemia in 1305. It became a monastic estate in 1352, but was taken back by the crown in 1532. During the 1536 Reformation it became a

royal *ladegård* (working estate). King Karl Johan bought it from the state in 1837. Here King Christian Frederik received his farewell deputation on 10 October 1814; he had expected to become king of Norway but was forced to make way for Karl Johan. Bygdø Konsgård's building, a stately wooden mansion painted in brilliant white, makes a lovely sight in summer when surrounded by green foliage.

Oscar II took an interest in the estate, and in 1881 he set up an open-air museum of old Norwegian wooden houses in the grounds. This collection later became the foundation of the Norsk Folkemuseum (*p110*). King Oscar also built the Kongvillaene in Swiss Alps chalet-style for employees of the court. Today only one of these villas remains (Villa Gjøa).

Bygdø Kongsgård covers a large area of northwestern Bygdøy. It comprises 200 hectares (500 acres) of forest and agricultural land. The area facing the sea is known as Kongeskogen (King's Wood), and there are 9.5 km (6 miles) of public walking tracks here. The grounds around the main house are part of the Norsk Folkemuseum, which now runs the farm (whose animals can be visited during spring and autumn). The manor house is still used by Norway's royal family, and is not open to the public.

> **Bygdø Kongsgård's building, a stately wooden mansion painted in brilliant white, makes a lovely sight in summer when surrounded by green foliage.**

## Oscarshall Slott

**⬚F3** ⬚Oscarshallveien 805 ⬚30 ⬚Mid-May-Aug: 11am-5pm Wed-Sun; 1-15 Sep: 11am-5pm Sat & Sun ⬚**royalcourt.no**

King Oscar I of Sweden and Norway (1799–1859) built a pleasure palace on a headland in Frognerkilen between 1847 and 1852. He named it Oscarshall and it became a favourite party venue for the kings of the Bernadotte dynasty. In 1863 it was sold to the state, and has been at the disposal of the ruling monarch ever since. It was never intended to be a residence, but rather a showcase for the architecture, handicrafts and fine art of the time, and for many years it was open to the public.

After the dissolution of the union in 1905, Oscarshall was closed, and large parts of its artistic decoration were placed in the Norsk Folkemuseum. Plans in the 1920s to refurbish the palace for the crown prince were abandoned,

and instead the building was extensively restored and reopened to the public.

Oscarshall is built in the style of an English castle. A Classical influence is evident in the proportions of the palace and in the strictly geometric shape of the rooms.

The drawing room is the largest room in the palace, with elegant windows and glazed doors opening on to the park. The entrance hall was inspired by a chapel from the Middle Ages and has a circular stained-glass window on one of its end walls. The dining room is noted for its decorations by Adolph Tidemand (1814–76), a popular artist known for his portrayals of everyday life in Norway. The king invited him to decorate the dining room with a series of 10 paintings inlaid in friezes around the upper walls. These panels depict peasant life, from childhood to old age. In the king's living room there are Gothic-style carved and moulded decorations, as well as paintings based on old Norwegian legends.

# A SHORT WALK
# AROUND BYGDØY

**Distance** 2.5 km (1.5 miles) **Time** 30 minutes
**Nearest ferry** Dronningen, Bygdøynes

A visit to Oslo wouldn't be complete without a trip to bucolic Bygdøy, easily accessible by car, bus and ferry. Here, locals and tourists alike enjoy the beautiful outdoors away from the hubbub of central Oslo. What's more, here are some of the most remarkable museums in Europe. Viking ships, polar expeditions and daring voyages across the Pacific Ocean on rafts such as the Kon-Tiki form the focal points for three of the collections. As well as a taste of adventure, here visitors can discover a sense of the past, as stave churches and rural buildings have been reassembled to create the open-air Norsk Folkemuseum.

*Set in an idyllic landscape, the open-air exhibits of the **Norsk Folkemuseum** (p110) feature 160 reconstructed townhouses, farm buildings and churches from Norway's past. Inside there are exhibitions of folk art and costumes.*

*Gamlebyen, at the Norsk Folkemuseum, is a collection of old restored townhouses.*

```
0 metres        150    N
0 yards         150    ↑
```

*The **Vikingshipshuset** (p112) contains Norway's most prized treasures – three Viking ships discovered not far from here.*

LANGVIKSVEIEN

LANGVIKSVEIEN

BYGDØYNESVEIEN

*Stately private homes and embassies are situated in the area along Bygdøynesveien.*

← A stave church at the open-air Norsk Folkemuseum

Locator Map
For more detail see p108

↑ The exterior of the Royal Norwegian
Yacht Club on Oslo's waterfront

START ▶

*The headquarters of the Royal Norwegian Yacht Club, Kongelig Norsk Seilforning, is a prominent landmark on the fjord's shoreline.*

HUK AVENY

*The main attractions at the Kon-Tiki Museet (p114) are the balsa-wood raft, Kon-Tiki (1947), and the reed boat, Ra II (1970). Thor Heyerdahl won worldwide acclaim when he set sail across the oceans in these craft.*

BENNECHES VEI

*The Frammuseet (p115) is dedicated to the polar ship Fram (1892) and the intrepid expeditions made by Fridtjof Nansen and Roald Amundsen to the Arctic and Antarctic. Their heroic exploits are captured in the museum's various displays.*

 FINISH

Boat Hall

BYGDØYNESVEIEN

HERBERNVEIEN

*Norway's proud seafaring history is showcased in the award-winning Norsk Maritimt Museum (p114). The Boat Hall contains a variety of craft.*

# BEYOND THE CENTRE

Some of Oslo's most interesting attractions and stunning green spaces are a short distance outside the city centre. In the west, Vigelandsparken comprises numerous expressive sculptures and is one of Oslo's most-visited attractions. To the east, trendy neighbourhoods Vulkan and Grünerløkka sandwich the Akerselva River with their ultra-creative communities, stylish restaurants and buzzy nightlife. The river and the area surrounding it is Oslo's green lung and provides opportunities for swimming, strolling and café-hopping. To the north, you'll meet *marka*, or the Oslo forest, where passing elk might be spotted.

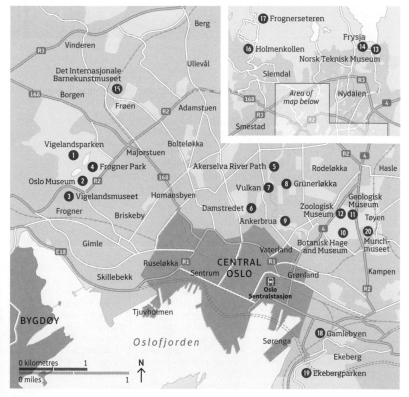

## TOP 5 UNMISSABLE SCULPTURES

**Sinnataggen**
Translating as 'Little Hot-Head', this statue shows a little boy throwing a tantrum.

**Triangle**
Beautifully balanced, two airborne women are depicted grasping on to a standing man.

**Man Chasing Four Geniuses**
More commonly referred to as 'man attacked by four babies'.

**Wheel of Life**
This circle represents man's journey from the cradle to the grave.

**Dancing Girl**
A top photo spot, this playful, prancing lady holds up her serpent-like locks of hair.

## ❶
# VIGELANDSPARKEN

🚇 Kirkeveien 🚋 Majorstuen 🚌 12 🚌 20 🕐 Park: 24 hours daily; Museum: May-Aug: 10am-5pm Tue-Sun; Sep-Apr: noon-4pm Tue-Sun
🌐 vigeland.museum.no

This remarkable sculpture park celebrates humanity in all its forms, as seen through the eyes of Norway's much-loved sculptor Gustav Vigeland. Free to enter, and with more than 200 emotive artworks, this is among Norway's most visited attractions.

Entwined lovers, angry children, doting parents: these are just some of the 212 sculptures representing humanity dotted throughout this public park. The focal point is the soaring obelisk on a stepped plinth, surrounded by groups of figures. Oslo's largest park is named after sculptor Gustav Vigeland (1869–1943) who created the park's expressive pieces in bronze, granite and cast iron. Originally a woodcarver, Vigeland started work on the park in 1924. By 1950, seven years after his death, most of the pieces were in place. The sculptures were modelled in full size in clay by Vigeland himself, but the carving in stone and casting in bronze were carried out by others. The interplay between the sculptures, the green areas and the architecture is a breathtaking sight. At the southern end of the park is a small museum based in Vigeland's studio *(p124)*. He was so invested in the park's artworks that his ashes were interred in the tower here.

💬 INSIDER TIP
**Get Climbing**

Don't panic if you see someone scrambling over a sculpture, or climbing up to take a selfie. You're meant to get involved – it's welcomed. Much like the stone figures, visitors of all ages can interact by climbing and clutching.

↑ Entrance to Vigelandsparken, one of Norway's most popular tourist attractions

↑ These statues are intended as mirrors, reflecting the cycles of relationships

↑ A mass of figures, the park's central obelisk represents life's upward struggle

*This particular piece is bronze; other statues are granite.*

*One of the more cheerful statues, here a young mother joyfully lifts up her baby.*

→

*Mother and Child* sculpture, Vigeland Park

# EXPERIENCE MORE

## Oslo Museum

**⌂ Frognerveien 67** 🚃 **12**
🚌 **20** 🕐 **11am-6pm Tue-Sun**
🚫 **1-15 Jan & some public
hols** 🌐 **oslomuseum.no**

The Oslo Museum is housed
in the Frogner Hovedgård, a
well-preserved 18th-century
manor house located in
Gustav Vigeland's park (p122).
This museum of cultural
history has one of the largest
collections of paintings in
Norway. The history of Oslo is
illustrated by thematic exhibitions on the development
of the city and its cultural and
commercial activities. A presentation entitled "Oslo During
the Past 1,000 Years" offers
an informative overview.

Also within the museum
is the Teatermuseet, which
explores Oslo's dramatic arts
from the early 19th century
onwards. Theatre, ballet, opera,
music revues and the circus
are all represented through
paintings, photographs,
posters, cartoons, costumes
and other memorabilia. The
original building dates from

the Middle Ages, and the
former farm is laid out in
traditional style, with three
buildings set around a square
yard behind the museum.

---

## Vigelandsmuseet

**⌂ Nobelsgate 32** 🚃 **12** 🚌 **20**
🕐 **May-Aug: 10am-5pm Tue-
Sun; Sep-Apr: noon-4pm
Tue-Sun** 🚫 **Some public hols**
🌐 **vigeland.museum.no**

A major part of Gustav
Vigeland's (1869–1943)
artistic output can be seen in
Vigelandsmuseet, located just
outside the vast Vigelandsparken (p122). Vigelandsmuseet
contains around 2,000 sculptures cast in plaster, bronze,
granite and marble, 12,000
drawings and around 400
woodcuts and carvings. The
original models for the
Vigeland Park sculptures, as
well as casts for busts and
other monuments, are on
display, and old photographs
chronicle the making of the
sculpture park. The museum is
the result of a contract drawn

up in 1921 between the artist
and Oslo City Council. Vigeland
donated all his existing and
future works to the city. In
return, the council built him a
studio (later converted into a
museum to exhibit his work).
The studio-turned-museum,
which dates from the 1920s, is
considered one of the finest
examples of Norwegian Neo-
Classicism. Vigeland chose the
interior colour scheme.

Visitors follow the artist's
development – from his
expressive and thin-figure
style in the 1890s to the
heavier expression adopted in
the years between the two
world wars. The artist's living
quarters are also on view.

After Vigeland's death in
1943, his ashes were placed in
the tower at his own request.

---

## Frogner Park

**⌂ Kirkeveien** 📞 **23 49 37 00**
🚇 **Majorstuen**
🚃 **20** 🚌 **12**

Once a pleasure garden,
Oslo's largest park remains an
especially lovely and popular
recreational spot. Visitors
flock here both for Vigelandsparken and the Oslo City
Museum, which is housed in
the grand estate office,
Frogner Manor. There's
also Frogner Stadium and
Frognerbadet – a 50-m (164-ft)
open-air pool. Here you'll also
find a children's playground
plus an outdoor café and a
pub during the summer.

---

## Akerselva River Path

**⌂ Sandakerveien 2** 📞 **23
28 41 78** 🚃 **12, 13**

The Akerselva River
runs for some 8 km
(5 miles) through the

---

### MUNCH & VIGELAND

Both monumental figures in the art history of Norway,
Expressionist painter Edvard Munch (1863-1944) and
Gustav Vigeland (1869-1943) moved in the
same bohemian circles, and even lived and
worked in adjoining rooms in Berlin. Both
artists depicted psychologically fraught
individuals, love motifs and the drama
of the human condition, and both
attempted to render an entangled
pile of human bodies through
different media; Munch
painted *The Human Mountain*
(1927-29), while Vigeland
constructed *The Monolith*
(1936), found in Vigelandsparken. The pair were never
friends, nor were they enemies.
Their rivalry was perhaps born
as a result of Munch's sculptures
never receiving acclaim.

heart of Oslo, winding north to south from Maridalsvannet lake to the Oslofjord. Akerselva was the country's cradle of industrialism, from 1800 to 1850, leaving behind brick factory buildings as a reminder.

Aside from the path that winds alongside the river, among the loveliest sections of this area is the red Hønse-Lovisas hus. This former saw-miller's house, which crosses into the neighbourhood of Grünerløkka, dates from 1800 and houses a gallery, craft shop and charming café. At the front, the Akerselva's highest waterfall, Mølla, cascades beneath Åmot suspension bridge.

---

**6**

## Damstredet

🏠 Damstredet 🚋 1, 2, 3, 4, 5 🚌 37, 54

The narrow cobblestone alleys of Damstredet are lined with charming, pastel-hued wooden houses, built from the late 1700s to the mid-19th century. It's unsurprising that these picture-perfect streets are

beloved by Instagrammers, while locals use them as shortcuts to and from the Grünerløkka neighbourhood. The most scenic patch on tiny Damstredet runs between Akersveien and Fredens-borgveien. Further north from Damstredet, the Telthusbakken is another pretty street, found between Maridalsveien and Akersveien. One side of the street is lined with small wooden houses; the other is dominated by a garden area, Egeberggløkka. This is the oldest and largest plot of allotments in the city, having been in use since 1915. Alongside the gardens runs the romantic Kjærlighetsstien, which translates as the Love Trail.

---

**7** 🍴 🖥 🛍

## Vulkan

📍 1 km (0.5 miles) N of city centre 🚋 11, 12, 13 🚌 34, 54 🌐 vulkanoslo.no

Sandwiched between hip Grünerløkka (p126) and central Oslo on the west side of the Akerselva River is

↑ Traditional houses lining Oslo's picturesque Damstredet

Vulkan, one of the city's emerging neighbourhoods. Since 2013, Vulkan has transformed from a largely abandoned industrial zone to an eco-friendly borough, promoting green energy and modern architecture.

In a city once dominated by fish markets, there was great excitement when International food hall Mathallen opened here in 2015, offering more than 30 shops and restaurants. On the same street, Dansens Hus is Norway's national stage for dance and houses innovative beehives on its roof. These stunning, Snøhetta-designed hexagonal beehives were built and installed to bring more bees to the city: 160,000 in total. In this area, you'll also find Hendrix Ibsen, a fun record store-cum-coffee shop, and Kontrast, an ultra-cool Michelin-starred restaurant dishing up New Nordic.

> **Since 2013, Vulkan has transformed from a largely abandoned industrial zone to an eco-friendly borough, promoting green energy and modern architecture.**

A colourful street mural in hipster haven Grünerløkka →

### TOP 5 CRAFT BREWERS

**Schouskjelleren Mikrobryggeri**
Just six beers (Trondheimsveien 2; www.schouskjelleren.no).

**Crow Bar & Brewery**
Brews with fun names (Torggata 32; www.crowbryggeri.com).

**Grünerløkka Brygghus**
Brewing pioneer (Thorvald Meyers Gate 30B; www.brygghus.no).

**Cervisiam**
Five rotating taps (Torggata 18b; www.cervisiam.no).

**Siste Sang**
Bizarre brews and tacos (Grønlandsleiret 27; www.sistesang.no).

## Grünerløkka

🏠 1 km (0.5 miles) N of city centre 🚊 11, 12, 13 🚌 30, 58

Often compared to New York's Williamsburg, Nørrebro in Copenhagen and Hoxton in London, Grünerløkka is among Oslo's coolest postcodes. *Vogue* agrees, ranking it among the world's chicest neighbourhoods from 2014 to 2017. Known simply as Løkka to locals, the rectangular block of streets, bordered roughly by the Akerselva River to the west and Sofienbergparken to the east, was once a working-class neighbourhood. The Labour Museum still shows the dwellings of its 19th-century residents. Gradually, however, artists, designers and other creatives claimed it as their own (Edvard Munch was an early convert). Løkka remains a hub for small, edgy galleries such as Young Artists' Society, Galleri TM51, Purenkel and Standard.

The district's narrow side streets are made for strolling. Independent shops ranging from eclectic vintage to Scandinavian design cluster on Markveien and Thorvald Meyers Gate, and you're spoiled for choice when it comes to restaurants, cafés and bars. At night, Grünerløkka is a buzzing hotspot, attracting those in the know to live music venues such as Blå nightclub and Parkteatret.

The neighbourhood has a special relationship with the Akerselva River. In the northern part of the district, the river path winds past Akerselva's highest waterfall, Mølla, while in the south the forested trail is especially lovely around Ankerbrua.

## Ankerbrua

🚊 11, 12, 13 🚌 30, 58

Also known as the Fairy Tale Bridge, Ankerbrua is among the most memorable of bridges spanning the Akerselva. Built in 1926, the corners are topped by four bronze sculptures inspired by Norwegian folk and fairy-tale heroes. Artist Dyra Vick chose the well-known Peer Gynt, Ibsen's legendary deer hunter, for his addition. Lesser-known characters include Veslefrikk, a youth granted three wishes by a troll; Kvitebjørn, a man cursed to remain a polar bear when he refused to wed a witch; and Kari Trestakk, who escaped her evil stepmother on the back of a musk ox.

← A statue of Peer Gynt, by Dyra Vick, adorning Ankerbrua bridge

**10** ⬡ ⬡ ⬡ ⬡

## Botanisk Hage and Museum

📍 Sars' Gate 1 🚇 Tøyen/
Munch-museet 🚊 17
🚌 20, 31, 32, 60 ⏰ Museum
and greenhouses: 10am–
8pm daily; Botanisk Hage:
7am–9pm daily ⏰ Some
public hols 🌐 nhm.uio.no

Across from Munch-museet
*(p131)* is the Botanisk Hage,
Norway's largest botanical
garden. Oslo's residents come
both to admire the thousands
of Norwegian and interna-
tional plants and to escape
the bustle of the city.

One of the highlights is the
Alpine Garden, which features
a waterfall and 1,450 species of
mountain flora from Norway
and abroad. The Aromatic
Garden is a particularly special
attraction. Here, fragrant
plants grow in raised beds
and are accompanied by texts
in Braille. In the Victoria House
and Palm House are plants
from tropical and temperate
regions, including rare orchids,
carnivorous pitcher plants and
cocoa trees.

The Botanisk Hage is part of
the Natural History Museum,
and has formed the basis

for botanical research and
education at the University
of Oslo since 1814.

A manor house, Tøyen
Hovedgård, which dates from
1780, stands in the middle
of the garden. It's home to
an extensive herbarium
containing 1.7 million examples
of herbs and provides an
important resource for
research into Norwegian flora.

**11** ⬡ ⬡ ⬡ ⬡

## Geologisk Museum

📍 Sars' Gate 1 🚇 Tøyen/
Munch-museet 🚌 20, 31, 32,
60 ⏰ 11am–4pm Tue–Sun
⏰ Some public hols
🌐 nhm.uio.no

A showcase of Norwegian
gemstones is the first eye-
catching exhibit upon entering
the Geologisk Museum. The
ground floor of the museum is
devoted to a presentation of
the geological processes at
work in the earth. Norway as an
oil-producing nation is the subject of a separate exhibition.

The serene Botanisk
Hage, home to rare
orchids *(inset)* ↓

**SHOPPING IN GRÜNERLØKKA**

Head to Oslo's most
stylish neighbourhood
to browse independent
boutiques. Markveien
and Thorvald Meyers
Gate are made for win-
dow shopping, with
standout shops includ-
ing Velouria Vintage
(Thorvald Meyers Gate
34) and Fransk Bazaar
(Grüners Gate 5). For
modern Scandi design,
head to Ensemble for
womenswear (Nordre
Gate 15) and, next door,
Dapper for menswear.

In a display about Oslofeltet
(the Oslo Field), fossil-bearing
rocks are on show alongside
other geological items that
would normally lie deep below
the earth's crust or in the
depths of the North Sea.
Exhibits include fossils such
as weird-looking trilobites and
various microscopic creatures.

## ⑫ 🚲 Ⓜ 🏛
### Zoologisk Museum

📍 Sars' Gate 1 🚇 Tøyen/Munch-museet 🚊 17 🚌 20, 31, 32, 60 🕐 11am–4pm Tue–Sun 🚫 Some public hols 🌐 nhm.uio.no

Completed in 1908, the Zoologisk Museum was the first of three natural science museums to be built in Oslo's botanical garden (p127). Throughout its exhibits, animals from Norway and the rest of the world are on show. The Norwegian Hall features displays of stuffed native animals in re-creations of their various habitats, including fish and marine creatures, mammals and birds. Ptarmigan and reindeer can be observed against a mountain backdrop and the pre-mating antics of the wood grouse are demonstrated. There are beaver dams and a display of the bird colonies that nest on sea cliffs.

In the Svalbard Hall, exhibits feature Arctic animals, such as polar bears. The Animal Geography Hall presents large and small creatures in different world zones, while in the Systematic Hall there are displays of Norway's animal life, from single-celled amoebas to the largest mammals. A "sound bar" provides recordings of animal noises from the wild.

## ⑬ 🚲 Ⓜ 🍴 🏛
### Norsk Teknisk Museum

📍 Kjelsåsveien 143 🚂 To Kjelsås 🚊 11, 12 🚌 54 🕐 Mid-Jun–mid-Aug: 11am–6pm daily; mid-Aug–mid-Jun: 9am–4pm Tue–Fri, 11am–6pm Sat & Sun 🚫 Some public hols 🌐 tekniskmuseum.no

The Norsk Teknisk Museum (Norwegian Museum of Science and Technology), founded in 1914 in Kjelsås, displays both past and present technology.

> **The bucolic meadow of Frysja, north of Oslo, is set in a lovely forested area where the Akerselva River flows from its source at serene Maridalsvannet lake.**

Exhibits include Norway's first steam engine, car and plane, as well as early sewing machines, and other everyday objects.

The ground floor is dedicated to industry, and the first floor covers transport and communications. Here it is possible to follow the development of steam power, while telecommunication is traced from the first warnings sent via beacons to the wide usage of the telegraph and telephones, mobile phones and the internet.

An exhibition illustrates oil and gas exploration in the North Sea, showing how raw materials are pumped to the surface and refined. In a display titled *The Forest as a Resource*, the importance of cellulose in revolutionizing the production of paper 150 years ago is also highlighted.

There are educational exhibits and a science centre with hands-on activities. Family events are held at weekends.

## ⑭
### Frysja

🚊 L3, R30 🚌 54

The bucolic meadow of Frysja, north of Oslo, is set in a lovely forested area where the Akerselva River flows from its source at serene Maridalsvannet lake. A great spot for swimming, it's a popular place to start off on the 8-km (5-mile) walk to central Oslo along the Akerselva River trail. Idyllic Frysja is perfect for a relaxing picnic and a swim. The freshwater swimming area ends at the Brekkefossen waterfall, which is 6 m (20 ft) high.

## ⑮ 🚲 Ⓜ 🏛
### Det Internasjonale Barnekunstmuseet

📍 Lille Frøens Vei 4 🚇 Frøen 🚌 46 🕐 Jul–mid-Aug: 11am–4pm Tue–Thu; mid-Sep–Jun: 9:30am–2pm Tue–Thu, 11am–4pm Sun 🚫 Public hols 🌐 barnekunst.no

Children's art from over 180 countries has been assembled in the Barnekunstmuseet (International Museum of Children's Art). This pioneering institution is the world's first full-scale museum displaying children's art. Exhibits include

↑ Brekkefossen waterfall, surrounded by the lush greenery of Frysja

Skiers gather in front of the Holmenkollen ski jump

paintings, sculptures, ceramics and textiles. Although the museum is designed to give space specifically to children's works, the pieces are still selected based on quality.

The museum was set up in 1986 in collaboration with the SOS Children's Villages, an international organization for children in need. Visiting children can express themselves in a variety of ways: in the Music and Dance Room, the Doll Room, and the Painting and Drawing Studio. Films on children's art are shown on weekdays. Other events include face painting, live shows, various sports or workshops and more.

---

**16** Ⓜ Ⓨ Ⓓ

## Holmenkollen

⬛ 6 km (4 miles) N of city centre Ⓣ Holmenkollen Ⓢ Skimuseet & Ski Jump: Jan-Apr & Oct-Dec: 10am-4pm daily; May & Sep: 10am-5pm daily; Jun-Aug: 9am-8pm daily
Ⓦ holmenkollen.com

Ski-jumping is guaranteed to attract the crowds in Norway, and the impressive jump at Holmenkollen, rebuilt in 2011, is no exception. The venue for the annual Holmenkollen Races and ski-jumping events

is Norway's biggest tourist attraction, drawing more than 1 million visitors a year. The races have been held here since 1892, when the ski jump was created from branches covered in snow. Crown Prince Olav participated in the jumping competitions in 1923 and 1924. The world championships have been held here on four occasions (most recently in 2011), as were many of the skiing events for the 1952 Winter Olympics. It has also become the main arena for the Biathlon, an event that involves both cross-country skiing and marksmanship.

The public can visit both the ski jump and the jump tower all year round. There are splendid views over Oslo and the inner Oslofjord from the tower's outdoor viewing platform, while in summer intrepid visitors can zipline down from the top for a fee.

The Skimuseet, at the base of the ski jump, focuses on more than 4,000 years of skiing history, with displays on various types of skis from different eras and regions of Norway. The 1952 and 1994 Olympics are covered, as is Norway's prominent role in polar history, with the now antique-looking equipment used by Nansen and Amundsen *(p115)* on display.

---

# DRINK

**Territoriet**
Join locals and linger at Oslo's favourite wine bar, which serves 400 wines by the glass – the second-largest selection in the world. Choose an exclusive Bordeaux or a unique Italian orange wine, and relax in the golden wood and leather lounge.

⬛ Markveien 58
Ⓦ territoriet.no

**Tim Wendelboe**
World Barista Champion Tim Wendelboe – the pioneer of Norway's signature single-origin, light-roast coffee – is often credited with brewing the world's best cup. See for yourself at his micro-roastery, coffee training centre and espresso bar, which is run with the precision of a Michelin-starred restaurant.

⬛ Grüners Gate 1
Ⓦ timwendelboe.no

**17**

## Frognerseteren

📍 7 km (4 miles) N of city centre 🚇 Frognerseteren 🌐 frognerseteren.no

Only a short walk from the station that bears its name is Frognerseteren, a popular excursion spot and a surprising pasture in a capital city. Located just 15 minutes via train from the city centre, Frognerseteren is the last station on the Holmenkollen Tunnelbane line. It is a favoured starting point for walks in the Nordmarka woods throughout the year, and gives access to the network of footpaths and ski trails.

The road northwards from Holmenkollen to Frognerseteren was opened in 1890 in the presence of Oscar II and the German Emperor Wilhelm II, and was named Keiser Wilhelms Vei. After World War II it was renamed Holmenkollveien.

The wooden lodge at Frognerseteren is one of Oslo's most unusual buildings. Designed by the architect Holm Munthe (1848–98) and built by the municipality, it was completed in 1892. The structure is built in the traditional Scandinavian "dragon style", so called because of the carvings of dragon heads located at the peak of the gables.

The terrace – with its spectacular panoramic view over Oslo, the fjord and surrounding areas – stands at 435 m (1,427 ft) above sea level. Below the lodge visitors will find a stone monument

### Did You Know?

The capital of Norway since 1814, Oslo occupies 454 sq km (175 sq miles), over half of which is forest.

↑ *Marilyn Monroe* sculpture by British artist Richard Hudson, Ekebergparken

commemorating the 1814 Constitutional Assembly, plus a number of traditional houses with grass-topped roofs.

The building also houses two eateries: Restaurant Finstua and Kafe Seterstua. Guests at the restaurant can sample traditional Norwegian food. The café offers hot and cold dishes from self-service counters, as well as delicious homemade treats from the Frognerseteren pastry shop.

**18**

## Gamlebyen

📍 2 km (1 mile) E of city centre 🚉 18, 19 🚌 34, 70

In the Middle Ages, Oslo was centred on Gamlebyen, or the Old Town. From the 12th century until the great fire of 1624, nearly all development in this area lay between Ekebergåsen, Bjørvika, Grønland and Galgeberg. Many of the medieval ruins have been preserved, including those of Mariakirken (Maria Church), Kongsgården (the Royal Manor) and Clemenskirken (Clemens Church). Excavations have revealed the remains of timber town houses, and a medieval park has been re-created next to the ruins of St Hallvard Cathedral. Other reminders of the Middle Ages

include Oslo Ladegård og Bispegården (Oslo Manor and the Bishops' Residence).

**19**

## Ekebergparken

📍 Kongsveien 23 🚇 Oslo S 🚉 18, 19 🚌 34, 74 🌐 ekebergparken.com

Southeast of Gamlebyen is Ekebergparken, where visitors can easily spend half a day exploring the vast forested space, dotted with modern sculptures, overlooking Oslofjord. The park is perhaps most famous for being the inspiration for Munch's anxiety-drenched *The Scream*. The park's history dates back further, however, with Iron Age and Viking burial mounds found in the park. This was also the scene of a decisive battle in the Seven Years' War in 1567, and comprised part of the King's road to Copenhagen at the beginning of the 18th century. In 1889, the City of Oslo designated the area as a public park, so that factory workers could head here for some outdoor exercise. After a number of tumultuous years as a German minefield in World War II, the area fell out of use and it was finally reborn as a world-class sculpture park in 2013.

Ekebergparken's impressive sculpture collection was curated from the private collection of developer Christian Ringnes, and includes stunning pieces by artists such as Renoir, Rodin, Maillol, Vigeland and Dali. Contemporary artists are also well represented, with works by Louise Bourgeois, Marina Abramović, Jenny Holzer, Tony Oursler, Sarah Lucas and Tony Cragg displayed.

→

A visitor admiring paintings exhibited in Oslo's Munch-museet

Ringnes' company also restored the 1920s Ekeberg-parken restaurant into a New Nordic temple of cuisine, with breathtaking views over the fjord. There's another stunning viewpoint at the Ekeberg Stairs, which offers a vista of Oslofjord islands Langøyene, Hovedøya and Gressholmen.

## Munch-museet

⌂ Tøyengata 53 🅃 Tøyen/Munch-museet 🚌 20, 60 🕐 Mid-May-mid-Sep: 10am-5pm daily; mid-Sep-mid-May: 10am-4pm Tue-Sun (check the website for possible closures as the collection moves) 🚫 1 Jan, 1 & 17 May, 24 & 25 Dec 🌐 munchmuseet.no

The largest collection of work by Edvard Munch (1863–1944) is housed in Oslo's Munch-museet. Prior to his death, Munch bequeathed all the paintings in his possession to the City of Oslo, and the museum opened in 1963, a century after Munch's birth. This original building is too small, however, to display the entire sprawling collection of 28,000 paintings, sketches and prints. It has also struggled to handle the foot traffic from visitors curious about Norway's most well-known and much-loved artist. Consequently, the Munch Museum is on the move. Architect Juan Herreros has designed a marvellous 15-storey museum called Lambda in Bjørvika on the East Oslo waterfront (*p99*), beside Oslo Opera House. The project is part of Oslo's push to be a modern Fjord City with its key cultural institutions lining the fjord, and will open in June 2020.

In the meantime, sections of the original Munch-museet in Tøyen will remain open to the public. During the transition period, Munch-museet will display pop-up exhibits to promote contemporary Norwegian artists in various neighbourhoods between Tøyen and Bjørvika. A dedicated gallery space in Dronning Eufemias Gate 34 in Bjørvika also has an exhibit that draws parallels between the new Norwegian artists and the masters of the 19th and 20th century, such as Edvard Munch.

# EAT

### Kontrast
The most highly acclaimed of Oslo's recent wave of New Nordic restaurants. Expect beautifully orchestrated seasonal plates from chef and owner Mikael Svensson, served in a stylish space.

⌂ Maridalsveien 15a 🚫 Lunch, Mon 🌐 restaurant-kontrast.no

ⓀⓀⓀ

### Bass Oslo
This New Nordic bistro specializes in grazing plates and wine pairings. Head here for a relaxed vibe and friendly staff.

⌂ Thorvald Meyers Gate 26C 🚫 Lunch, Mon 🌐 bassoslo.no

ⓀⓀⓀ

# EXPERIENCE
# NORWAY

Stunning Northern Lights over Senja

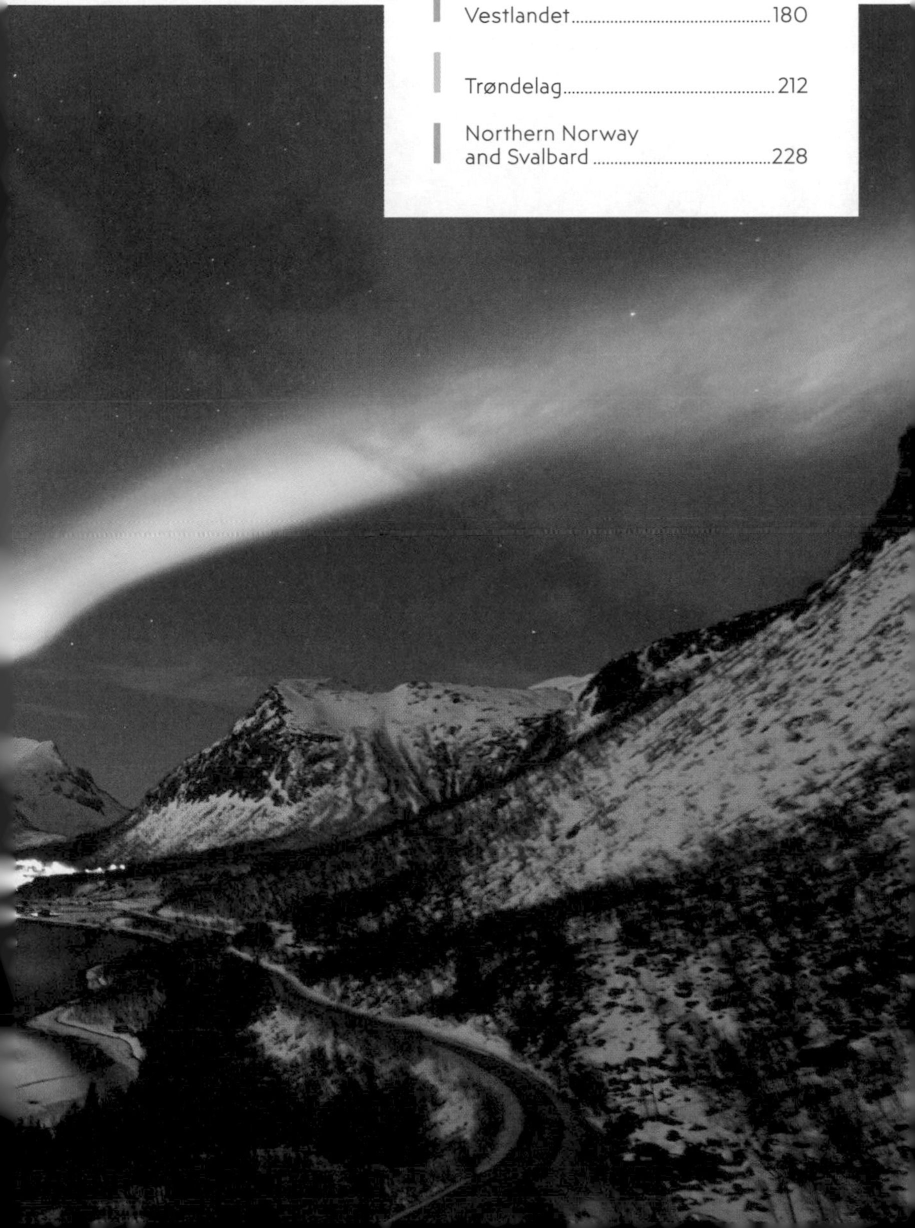

Wooden boats docked at Fredrikstad's pier

# AROUND OSLOFJORDEN

The oldest settlements in the Oslofjorden area date from the Stone Age and Bronze Age, and it was here that the world's best-preserved Viking ships were unearthed. Today, more than one million people – a fifth of Norway's total population – live along the region's 100 km (60 miles) of fjord shoreline, in some of the oldest towns and villages in the country. Many of these settlements have a long history of trading and seafaring, as reflected in the castles, burial mounds and wooden, waterside villages that remain. This ancient cultural heritage merges with modern industry and commerce, and the entire region bears evidence of its proximity to the capital, with many Norwegians commuting into Oslo from their homes around the fjords. Although the land around Oslo is built-up, further south it is a haven of serene villages with quaint clapboard houses, quiet islands and boats galore. Summers are usually warm around Oslofjorden, and the winters seldom severe.

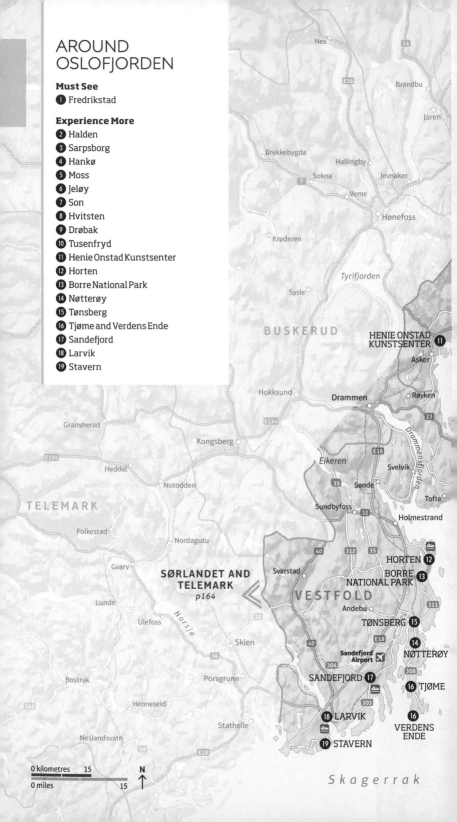

# AROUND OSLOFJORDEN

**Must See**

**1** Fredrikstad

**Experience More**

**2** Halden
**3** Sarpsborg
**4** Hankø
**5** Moss
**6** Jeløy
**7** Son
**8** Hvitsten
**9** Drøbak
**10** Tusenfryd
**11** Henie Onstad Kunstsenter
**12** Horten
**13** Borre National Park
**14** Nøtterøy
**15** Tønsberg
**16** Tjøme and Verdens Ende
**17** Sandefjord
**18** Larvik
**19** Stavern

❶ 🍴 🍵 🛍️

# FREDRIKSTAD

🅰️ D6  🅰️ County of Østfold  🅰️ St Olavsgate 2  🚌 Torvbyen
🚢 Tollbodbrygga Frederikstad  ℹ️ Tøihusgate 41, Gamlebyen; 69 30 46 00

Once a strategic stronghold, now a creative centre, Fredrikstad is enchanting. Cobblestone streets are lined with historic weapons stores and timbered houses, which have been converted into modern art galleries, bars and restaurants. These buzzy streets are bordered by the town's distinct star-shaped moat.

When Sarpsborg was burned down in 1567 during the Nordic Seven Years' War, Frederik II gave permission for the inhabitants to move to a spot closer to the mouth of the Glomma river, which would be better placed for trading, shipping and fishing, as well as defending the country from foreign invasion. And so Fredrikstad was established, based on Dutch architectural models. It became a fortress town in 1663, and Gamlebyen (the Old Town) developed within the bastion walls. Gamlebyen is a particularly attractive and lively place to explore. The modern waterfront district is just across the bridge.

## EAT

### Restaurant Slippen

Slippen has an atmospheric riverside location, plus a pretty terrace. An upscale clientele visit regularly for oysters and the catch of the day.

🅰️ Verkstedveien 12
🕒 Mon  🌐 restaurant slippen.no

Ⓚ Ⓚ Ⓚ

---

### Havnelageret Gastropub

Regional craft beer selections and hearty pub grub are served in wood and leather surroundings. There's also an excellent bottle shop on the premises.

🅰️ Storgata 17
🌐 havnelageret.no

Ⓚ Ⓚ Ⓚ

1. Restaurant Slippen, with its waterside terrace, is particularly popular in summer. Fredrikstad has a number of excellent places to eat, not to mention a fantastic craft beer scene.

2. The historic drawbridge. If the mounted postman arrived after the drawbridge was raised, his sack was winched across on the moat on a line.

3. Traditional wooden boats moored on the River Glomma, Fredrikstad.

← Market stalls in Kongens Tarv, or King's Square, Fredrikstad

Fredrikstad's first aldermen had their seat in the Old Town Hall, built in 1784. In 1797, a lay preacher was imprisoned here.

↓ Bird's-eye view of Fredrikstad's moat

The King's Square has a statue of Frederik II, who founded the town in 1567. Criminals were put in the stocks here.

Mellomporten, the Middle Gate, 1727, is adorned with Frederik IV's monogram.

The Provisions House, dating from 1674 to 1696, is the oldest building in the city.

The drawbridge was raised between last post and reveille.

The Rampart Gate was built in 1695. Above the gateway is Christian V's monogram and motto, 'Piety and Justice'.

The Old Penitentiary was built in 1731 as a detention centre. It's now a city museum.

The Laboratory was constructed in 1802 as a gunpowder factory.

# EXPERIENCE MORE

## ② Halden

**Ⓐ D6** **Ⓐ County of Østfold**
**Ⓐ ⬛** **ⓘ Torget 2; www.
visithalden.com**

The town of Halden is the gateway to Norway for those arriving to the southern regions from Sweden. It is set back on Iddefjorden between a beautiful archipelago and lake-dotted forests. The town developed in the 16th and 17th centuries as an outpost on the border with Sweden, and has many well-preserved old buildings and Neo-Classical houses.

Halden's crowning glory is **Fredriksten Festning**, an imposing fortress on the ridge above the town, complete with ramparts and a warren of passageways. The first fortifications were built around

### Did You Know?

Fredriksten Festning is Norway's largest and most historically significant fortress.

1643–5, and the Swedish king, Karl XII, was shot here in 1718 during his second attempt to attack the fortress. Its museums contain extensive collections of war history and civil memorabilia.

**Fredriksten Festning**
Ⓐ Ⓐ Ⓣ Ⓐ Ⓐ **Ⓐ 1 km (half a mile) S of the centre Ⓒ 6919 0980 Ⓐ Fortress: all year; Museum: mid-May–late Aug: daily; Sep: Sun

## ③ 🏛 Sarpsborg

**Ⓐ D6** **Ⓐ County of Østfold**
**Ⓐ ⬛** **ⓘ Torget 5; 69 13 00 70**

King Olav Haraldsson (later St Olav, Norway's patron saint) founded his capital, Sarpsborg, here in 1016. The area is rich in accessible ancient history. Burial mounds indicate that people lived here 7,000 years ago, and you can walk among over 150 burial sites at Opstad from 1500 BC through to the Viking Age. Sarpsborg also

→
A jetty and boathouse on pretty Hankø bay

boasts a greater concentration of ancient rock carvings than anywhere else in Norway.

The thundering Sarpfossen waterfall is also worth a visit. While not the tallest in Europe, it pounds out the most water per minute, the force of which is captured by three local power stations.

**Borgarsyssel Museum**, which takes its name from the Old Norse name for the region, draws visitors with more recent history. Built on the ruins of Olav's castle, the open-air museum features 30 period buildings from various parts of the country.

**Borgarsyssel Museum**
Ⓐ Ⓐ Ⓐ **Ⓐ Gamlebygaten 8 Ⓐ Jun–Aug: daily; Sep–Jun: Thu–Sun Ⓠ Public hols Ⓦ ostfoldmuseene.no

## ④ Hankø

**Ⓐ D6** **Ⓐ County of Østfold**
**⬛ 302 to Vikane**
**ⓘ Fredrikstad; 69 30 46 00**

The picturesque island of Hankø lies towards the outer part of Oslofjorden. It became especially popular as a holiday resort in the 1950s and 1960s when King Olav had a summer residence, Bloksberg, here. Hankø's sheltered eastern

↑ The ramparts and powder houses of Fredriksten Festning, standing above Halden

side is forested, providing a much favoured harbour and anchorage. The Norwegian Association of Yachting was founded here in 1882, and since then the island has been a venue for national regattas, sailing races and world championship events. Rowing has also had a long tradition on Hankø. The Fredrikstad Rowing Club was established here around 1870.

---

### ⑤ Moss

**Ⓐ D5  Ⓒ County of Østfold**
**Ⓖ🍴🛏 ⓘ Skogaten 52; www.visitmoss.no**

An important industrial and trading centre for the County of Østfold, Moss is also known for its art galleries and streets lined with sculptures. Its harbour has long been a junction for Oslofjorden boat traffic.

Moss by-og Industrimuseum, the Town and Industry Museum, charts Moss's industrial development. Konventionsgården was built in 1778 and is the main building of Moss Jernverk (Moss Ironworks), which was constructed in the mid-18th century. It was here that the Moss Convention was signed in 1814 to ratify the union between Norway and Sweden rather than Denmark.

### ⑥ 🍴🛏🛍
### Jeløy

**Ⓐ D5  Ⓒ County of Østfold**
**Ⓦ oslo-fjord.com/jeloy-moss-norway**

To the west of Moss is the island of Jeløy, dubbed the pearl of the Oslofjord by locals, thanks to its luminescent beauty. Walking trails wind through forests, home to strings of mistletoe, and emerge along the quiet sand and pebble beaches. Trail information can be found at the local tourist office. There are also numerous hiking and biking excursions to choose from on the 20-sq-km (8-sq-mile) island.

Jeløy's special beauty and light have long captivated artists, and the island's former manor houses have been converted into edgy galleries displaying their works. Alby Gård is now home to the leading **Galleri F15**, which displays Norwegian, Nordic and international contemporary art. Next door Røed Gård, a 300-year-old restored manor house, holds exhibitions and sells regional crafts.

### Galleri F15

♿🚭🅿📷 Ⓒ Alby Gård
4 km (2 miles) W of Moss
Ⓒ 69 27 10 33  Ⓞ Tue–Sun
Ⓧ Some public hols

## EAT

**Kafé F15**
After wandering the exhibitions at this idyllic manor turned modern art gallery, head straight for the café. Renowned for its *Albykringle* (apple cake with whipped cream), it also serves traditional and hearty Norwegian lunches. Head out for a swim or woodland walk afterwards.

Ⓐ D5  Ⓒ Bjørn
Bjørnstads vei 28380,
Jeløy  Ⓦ alby.no

Ⓚ Ⓚ Ⓚ

---

**Bakgården**
This Halden institution offers both a casual bistro and a coffee roastery. Make for the former to savour local flavours of fresh halibut and shrimp or deer steaks. If you're looking for something lighter, stop by the roastery for your caffeine fix and a cake baked to perfection.

Ⓐ D6  Ⓒ Storgata 22B,
1776 Halden
Ⓦ bakgarden-halden.no

Ⓚ Ⓚ Ⓚ

death in 1944. In the early 1900s, Oslo's creative set moved here in droves, and a vibrant art community still thrives in Hvitsten today.

Hvitsten's other claim to fame is the prominent shipping magnate Fred Olsen, who shaped the town at the turn of the century. Olsen funded the lovely white church (1903) and other significant buildings. His son, Petter Olsen, is in the process of restoring Munch's former home to a grand hotel, opening in 2019.

## Drøbak

**🅰D5** **🚗County of Akershus** **🚢Summer only** **🚌** **ℹHavnegaTen 4; www.visitdrobak.no**

Half an hour's drive south of Oslo on the eastern side of Oslofjorden is the attractive wooden village of Drøbak. Originally a pilot station, it served as Oslo's winter port when the fjord closer to the capital was ice bound. Today the village, with its narrow 18th- and 19th-century streets, is a popular place to live and a favourite summer holiday spot. From here, the 7-km (4-mile) Oslofjord Tunnel, opened in 2000, runs deep under the fjord to its western shore.

Drøbak has Norway's largest year-round Christmas exhibition, with Julehus (Christmas House) and Julenissens Postkontor (a post office run by Father Christmas's pixie-like helper). The main square, Torget, and its adjoining streets have shops, art galleries and places to eat.

At the small harbour, the seawater aquarium, Saltvannsakvariet, displays local species of fish and other marine life. Next to it, **Drøbak**

## Son

**🅰D5** **🚗County of Akershus** **🌐oslo-fjord.com/son**

Small, white clapboard houses, twisted narrow streets, sandy beaches and a busy harbour characterize Son, the coastal gem located along the sunnier side of the Oslofjord. Son is known as Norway's "northernmost southern town" because of its milder climate. A booming timber port during the Renaissance period, Son was once populated by the Dutch, who even named Oslofjord 'Zoon' after their base. And even after the Dutch left, their quaint architecture remained; the town is one of the best-preserved on the fjord.

Today Son is known for its bustling recreational harbour and the community of artists living here, including Nils Kjær,

Ludvig Karsten, Ronald Fangen and Karl Dørnberger. Osloites flock here for a tranquil weekend at the waterfront Son Spa, or to dine out at one of the many top-notch seafood restaurants.

## Hvitsten

**🅰D5** **🚗County of Akershus**

This dreamy fjord town has two picture-perfect beaches and colourful clapboard houses stacked along the hillsides. The main beach is in Hvitsten harbour, while Emmerstadbukta lies further off the beaten track and has family-friendly wading areas and nearby forests.

Hvitsten has long attracted bohemians. Edvard Munch bought a summerhouse here in 1910 and owned it until his

> **Small, white clapboard houses, twisted narrow streets, sandy beaches and a busy harbour characterize Son, the coastal gem located along the sunnier side of Oslofjord.**

**Båtforenings Maritime Samlinger** (the Maritime Collection) focuses on the area's coastal heritage.

Close to the town centre is the open-air **Follo Museum,** which has a collection of 200 to 300-year-old buildings. On an island just west of Drøbak lies **Oscarsborg Festning,** a fortress best known for its role in the sinking of the German warship *Blücher*, on 9 April 1940. Torpedoes fired from here hit the vessel as it approached Oslo with the first occupational forces on board. This delayed the occupation and gave the king time to flee. In summer, plays are staged at the fortress.

### Drøbak Båtforenings Maritime Samlinger
⊛ 🏠Kroketønna 4 📞64 93 50 87 🕒May–Sep: daily

### Follo Museum
⊛⊗🕑🍴🛍 🏠Belsjøveien 17 📞66 93 66 36 🚌504 🕒Mid-Jun–Oct: 11am–3pm Tue–Sun; Oct–mid-Jun: 11am–3pm Tue–Fri 🚫Some public hols

### Oscarsborg Festning
⊛⊗ 🏠Kaholmene 📞64 90 41 61 🚢From Sjøtorget to Drøbak 🕒Daily

---

**⑩** ⊗ 🍴 🍵 🛍
## Tusenfryd

🅰D5 🏠County of Akershus 🚌10am–1pm: every 30 min from Oslo Bussterminal 🕒Times vary; check website 🌐tusenfryd.no

Norway's largest amusement park, Tusenfryd, is situated 20 km (12 miles) south of Oslo.

The park's main attraction is Thundercoaster, the biggest wooden roller-coaster in Northern Europe. It thrills visitors with drops of 32 m

→
Post office for Christmas letters to Santa Claus, Drøbak

(105 ft). There are numerous rides, places to eat, shops and entertainments, as well as an area for water activities. Nearly half a million guests visit Tusenfryd every year.

---

**⑪** ⊗ Ⓜ 🍴 🍵 🛍
## Henie Onstad Kunstsenter

🅰C5 🏠County of Akershus 🚌160 from Oslo 🕒11am–7pm Tue–Fri, 11am–5pm Sat & Sun 🌐hok.no

The remarkable centre for modern art was a gift to the nation from the three-time Olympic gold medal-winning skater, Sonja Henie (1928, 1932, 1936), and her husband, Niels Onstad. It houses their art collection, including works by Matisse, Picasso and Miró, as well as Expressionist and abstract painters from the post-war period.

The trophy collection from Henie's exceptional sporting career is also on show. There are also medals and cups for outstanding performances at the Olympic Games and in ten world championships.

On site is a library, children's workshop, shop, café and a reliable restaurant.

# STAY

### Son Spa
A two-storey sauna and therapy centre, indoor pool and outdoor jacuzzi with stunning sea views are just some of the draws at Son Spa. When guests have had their fill of pampering, the cute beach town awaits exploration.

🅰D5 🏠Hollandveien 30 🌐sonspa.no.

Ⓚ Ⓚ Ⓚ

---

### Hotel Refsnes
Set on the idyllic Jeløy island, this boutique hotel was built in 1776 and has a vast garden sloping down to the Oslo Fjord. Its rooms are elegantly furnished and original Munch artworks hang in the restaurant.

🅰D5 🏠Godset 5, 1518 Moss 🌐refsnesgods.no

Ⓚ Ⓚ Ⓚ

**12** 🍴 🖥 🛍

## Horten

🗺 C6 🏠 County of Vestfold
✈🚆🚌 To Skoppum, 10 km
(6 miles) W of town
ℹ Tollbugata 1A; www.
visithorten.com

A bronze statue known as Hortenspiken (the Girl from Horten) welcomes visitors approaching the town from the north. The boat she is holding hints that this is a harbour town popular with pleasure-boat owners.

Horten developed around the 19th-century naval base of Karljohansvern, with its shipyard and harbour. In the well-preserved garrison buildings is **Marinemuseet**, the world's oldest naval museum, which was established in 1853. The museum contains an extensive collection of model ships, artifacts and exhibits relating to naval history. The world's first torpedo boat, *Rap* (1872), is on display outside. A recent acquisition is the submarine KNM *Utstein* (1965), which is open to the public.

Next door is **Preus Museum**, Norway's national museum for photography, which was founded in 1976. The museum is located in a blocky brick building that was previously used as a grain store for the

Royal Norwegian Navy. Cameras, images and other items are used to illustrate the development of the art.

Horten town centre, with its timber houses, retains much of its 19th-century character. In summer, the streets are decorated with flowers, and speed restrictions force cars to drive slowly. Outdoor cafés add to the charming atmosphere, but perhaps the town's main claim to fame is Storgaten, lit with quaint lamps and said to be Norway's longest shopping street.

**Marinemuseet**
🎥 🛍 🏠 Karljohansvern,
1 km (half a mile) E of the
centre 📞 33 03 33 91
🕐 May–Sep: daily; Oct–Apr:
Sun 🚫 Public hols

**Preus Museum**
🎥 🎥 🖥 🛍
🏠 Karljohansvern, 1 km
(half a mile) E of the centre
📞 33 03 16 30 🕐 Noon–4pm
Tue–Fri (to 5pm Sat & Sun);
Jul: noon–5pm daily

---

**13** 🎥 🎥 🖥 🛍

## Borre National Park

🗺 C6 🏠 County of Vestfold
📞 33 07 18 50 🚌 01 from
Horten 🕐 Park: all year;
Midgard Historical Centre:
11am–6pm daily 🚫 Public
hols; Sep–May: Mon

The site of the most extensive collection of kings' graves in Scandinavia, Borre has seven large and 21 smaller burial mounds. Excavations at the end of the 1980s revealed that

←

The rooms at the Marinemuseet in Horten, with fascinating exhibits

←

Remarkable Viking burial mounds within Borre National Park

area at the water's edge. Each season outdoor events with a historic theme, such as Viking Age Markets, are hosted here. The Historical Centre has displays of finds from the area.

**Did You Know?**

The Oseberg Viking ship, discovered in Tønsberg, took 21 years to piece together after excavation.

the oldest of the mounds dates from AD 600, before the Viking age, and it is likely that some of the mounds contain kings of the Ynglinge dynasty who had settled in Vestfold after fleeing from Sweden. The burial ground remained in use for a further 300 years. A remarkable selection of craftwork – which was given the name Borrestilen – has been unearthed. The pieces feature intricate animal and knot ornaments, which were often used to decorate harnesses. The finds also confirm that the mounds might have contained ships similar to the Gokstad and Oseberg ships discovered around Oslofjorden *(p112)*.

Borre was Norway's first national park. The grassy mounds are set among woodlands in a well-tended

**⑭**

## Nøtterøy

🅐C6 🅖County of Vestfold 🅦visittjome.no/notteroy

From above, the intricate Nøtterøy archipelago looks like scattered seeds, comprising 175 islets. The population triples here every summer, with visitors seeking sun-dappled beaches and excellent fishing areas. The coastal hiking trails are popular for their sea views, not to mention the animal and plant life that can be found here. Nøtterøy church is an imposing but beautiful stone building from the end of the 12th century.

**⑮**

## Tønsberg

🅐C6 🅖County of Vestfold 🅦visitvestfold.com/en/tonsberg

Founded in 871 AD, Tønsberg was once a prosperous Viking town and medieval trading centre. The town is situated on a narrow archipelago, which juts out into the Skagerrak strait. It was here that a local farmer discovered the Viking Oseberg burial mound quite by chance. Here, a 9th-century, 22-m (72-ft) ship was excavated, and the original Oseberg ship is now displayed at the Vikingskipshuset in Oslo *(p112)*. A replica remains

afloat in Tønsberg harbour. The town is also home to Slottsfjellet Tower, or "Castle Rock". This was Norway's largest medieval fortress in the 1300s, and it functioned as a royal residence and a key power centre. The tower stairs are worth climbing for the mind-boggling views.

The region is also visited for the surrounding Gullkronene, Ilene and Presterødkilen nature reserves, which offer sea-to-forest hikes and abundant wetland bird life.

Vippefyret, the quirky lighthouse that stands at Verdens Ende ↑

**PICTURE PERFECT**
**To the Lighthouse**

If you're visiting Verdens Ende you need a shot of the Vippefyret lighthouse - its pale grey stones standing out starkly against the unending blue. Get there early in the day, before crowds descend.

16 

## Tjøme and Verdens Ende

🏔 C6 🧭 County of Vestfold
🌐 visittjome.no

To the south of Tønsberg is the lovely, sun-drenched archipelago of Tjøme, which comprises some 478 islands in total. This is a destination historically popular with Norwegians during the summer months; the royal family holidays regularly here. Tjøme has all the *sommerbyer*, or holiday town paraphernalia, from painted wooden houses perched at the edge of the sea to clear, sparkling harbours. Bridges connect the larger islands on the journey south, and coastal nature reserves dot the region.

Renowned children's author Roald Dahl, the son of Norwegian parents, was also a regular visitor to the idyllic archipelago of Tjøme. He directly referenced summers in this region as inspiration for a number of his books, including *The Twits* (1980) and *The Witches* (1983).

Verdens Ende – or World's End – sits at the very southern tip of Tjøme, in Færder National Park. Here you can walk to the water's edge and gaze out at the seemingly endless horizon. Vippefyret, a lighthouse built in 1932 and constructed entirely of stones from local beaches, also stands here. A fire basket leans over its roof and once acted as a beacon.

17 

## Sandefjord

🏔 C6 🧭 County of Vestfold
🚆🏠🚌🚢 ℹ Thor Dahls Gate 1; 33 46 05 90

The present town of Sandefjord is relatively new, but archaeological finds from the Bronze and Viking Ages, such as the Viking ship unearthed at Gokstadhaugen in 1880, point to a long history of trading and seafaring. The harbour on the fjord around 1200. In 1800, Sandefjord was burned to the ground and rebuilt. Today, it is a popular holiday destination with Norwegians; its coastline stretches for almost 150 km (93 miles), so visitors have plenty of choice when it comes to both secluded, attractive beaches and more bustling regions.

Until the early 20th century, the spa, **Kurbadet** (1837), was renowned for its health-giving mud bath. It has been restored and is now a protected building, although the mud bath is no more. It can be visited by previously arranged guided tours only.

Whaling was a dominant industry at Sandefjord for many years until it was halted in 1968. **Hvalfangstmuseet** (the Whaling Museum) shows the development of the industry from the primitive methods of catching whales to the introduction of factory ships. There is a special section on Arctic and Antarctic animal life, but the most eye-catching exhibit is undoubtedly the life-size replica of a blue whale.

The whaling monument on Strandpromenaden is a rotating bronze statue, which was designed by Knut Steen, a prominent Norwegian sculptor (1924–2011).

→

Midnight sky over beautifully peaceful Sandefjord

### Kurbadet

⌖ 🏛 Thor Dahls Gate
☎ 33 46 58 57 🕐 For cultural
events and guided tours only

### Hvalfangstmuseet

⌖⌖⌖⌖ 🏛 Museumsgate
39 ☎ 94 79 33 41 🕐 Daily
🔒 Some public hols

---

### ⓲
## Larvik

🅰 C6 🏛 County of Vestfold
🚉🏛🛳🚌 ℹ Feyersgate 7;
33 17 10 00

Larvik came into its own in
the 17th century, when Ulrik
Frederik Gyldenløve was
appointed count of Larvik
and the county of Laurvigen.
In 1671 the town achieved
market town status.

The count's residence,
**Herregården**, was built in
1677 and is one of Norway's
finest secular Baroque buildings. In 1835 the estate was
acquired by the Treschow
family, who have played a
prominent role in Larvik's
economic life since then,
mostly in the forestry industry
alongside the Fritzøes. The
**Larvik Museum** is housed in a
manor south of the town, and
charts their business dealings
from 1600 onwards. There are
also exhibits on Kaupang,
Norway's first Viking town.
**Larvik Sjøfartsmuseum**

(Maritime Museum) focuses
on Larvik's nautical history and
the age of sailing ships. Models
by the famous boat-builder
Colin Archer are on display
and there is an exhibition on
Thor Heyerdahl (p114). Larvik is
also the location of Norway's
only mineral water spring.

### Herregården

⌖⌖ 🏛 Herregårdssletta 2
☎ 48 10 66 00 🕐 End Jun-
mid-Aug: Tue-Sun; mid-Aug-
Sep & May-end Jun: Sun
🔒 Public hols

### Larvik Museum

⌖⌖⌖⌖ 🏛 Nedre Fritzøe
Gate 2 ☎ 48 10 66 00
🕐 End Jun-mid Aug: Tue-
Sun; mid-Aug-end Jun: Sun
🔒 Public hols

### Larvik Sjøfartsmuseum

⌖⌖ 🏛 Kirkestredet 5
☎ 48 10 66 00 🕐 End Jun-
mid-Aug: Tue-Sun; mid-Aug-
Sep & May-end Jun: Sun
🔒 Public hols

---

### ⓳
## Stavern

🅰 C6 🏛 County of Vestfold
🚉 To Larvik 🚌 ℹ Summer:
Skippergaten 6 (33 19 73 00);
winter: Larvik (33 13 91 00)

A quaint mixture of old
and new, Stavern is a
charming place beloved by

holidaymakers. In summer
the population more than
doubles, due partly to the
town's record of more than
200 days of sunshine a year,
with temperatures well above
Norway's average.

From the mid-1750s
until 1864, Stavern was
Norway's main naval base
with a shipyard, Fredriksvern.
A gunpowder tower and
commandant's house remain
on Citadelløya (Citadel Island),
which today is a refuge for
artists. The town is made
up of wooden buildings,
most of them brightly painted
in a cheery colour known as
"Stavern yellow". Minnehallen,
a pyramid-shaped monument
with a plaque containing the
names of seamen killed
during World Wars I and II,
is a fitting memorial to those
who lost their lives.

Stavern's most famous
residents were husband and
wife Herman (1886–1959)
and Gisken Wildenvey (1895–
1985); he was famed for his
poetry and she for her novels.
Their blue-roofed home of
Hergisheim – an amalga-
mation of their names – is
still owned by the Wildenvey
family today.

### Did You Know?

The use of salmon in
sushi was suggested to
Japan by a Norwegian
delegation in
the 1980s.

Mountains reflected in a lake at Rondane National Park

# EASTERN NORWAY

Although Eastern Norway is by far the country's most populated region, vast areas of nature are the domain of ancient animal herds and remain virtually untouched by humans. Sandwiched between Norway's coastline and neighbouring Sweden, the three counties of Hedmark, Oppland and Buskerud together make up one-fifth of Norway's total land area. Here, mountains, valleys and lakes dominate the rugged landscape and have inspired literary giants, such as Hendrik Ibsen. The opportunity for outdoor activities in the area is legion. Rondane, Jotunheimen and Dovrefjell are among Norway's most exceptional national parks and are perfect spots for canoeing and hiking, with a network of mountain huts providing comfortable accomodation. Stretching through the heart of Eastern Norway, the valleys of Gudbrandsdalen, Numedal and Østerdalen are lush and green in temperate weather, transforming into winter sports playgrounds when the snow arrives.

❶ Ⓜ️ ▭

# JOTUNHEIMEN

🄰 C3 🏠 County of Oppland (RV15 from Strynefjellet or FV55 from Sognefjellet) 🚌 To Lom, then change to a local bus (summer only) 🈺 Jotunheimen Reiseli; 61 21 29 90 🌐 visitjotunheimen.no

**The 'Home of the Giants' is Norway's most famous wilderness destination, and rewards hikers with stunning views of turquoise lakes and plunging waterfalls.**

Although it's Norway's top hiking destination, the Jotunheimen mountain range was known only to local fishermen and herdsmen until the late 19th century. Tourists then began to discover this wild and craggy mountain region in the heart of the county of Oppland and the National Park was established in 1980. Norway's highest peaks – which exceed 2,400 m (7,546 ft) – are found here at Jotunheimen, interspersed between colossal glaciers, waterfalls, lakes and valleys. A well-developed network of footpaths crosses the mountains, linking 30 mountain huts, and attracting some 60,000 hikers every year. Jotunheimen also offers opportunities for skiing, mountain biking and rafting.

💬 INSIDER TIP
**Besseggen hike**

A low-stress way to accomplish the iconic Besseggen hike is to catch the morning boat to Memurubu and trek back on the ridge to Gjendesheim. This allows more time to enjoy the views. The trail is also more manageable uphill.

**2,469 (m)**
Height of Galdhøpiggen mountain - Norway's highest (8,100 ft).

↑ Beautiful Lake Gjende surrounded by mountains, Jotunheimen National Park

**Vettisfossen**
4–6 hours; 12.6 km (7.8 miles); easy. A wide gravel trail leads to a rocky path and a spectacular waterfall.

**Knutshø**
4–5 hours; 12 km (7.4 miles); fairly challenging. Stunning views of Lake Gjende.

**Spiterstulen to Galdhøpiggen**
7 hours; 13 km (8 miles); challenging. Forest paths and rocky trails pass three peaks.

**Besseggen Ridge**
6–8 hours; 14 km (8.7 miles); very challenging. Knife-edge hike on a narrow ridge overlooking two glacial lakes.

↑ Hikers climbing Galdhøpiggen, the tallest mountain in Scandinavia

→ A stone sculpture by Knut Wold on the icy Sognefjellet Tourist Road, Jotunheimen

↑ Sunrise over snow-covered cabins, Lake Lillehammer

② 🍴 🖥 🏛

# LILLEHAMMER

🅰C4 🏛County of Oppland 🚉🚌 𝑖Jernbanetorget 2; 61 28 98 00 🌐lillehammer.com

As the skier in the city's coat of arms signifies, Lillehammer has long been a hub for winter sports. Its skiing tradition dates back to 1206, when royal infant Håkon Håkonsson was carried from Lillehammer and across the mountains by skiers, saving the future king from threat. The annual Birkebeiner Race is run on skis from Rena in Østerdalen to Lillehammer in memory of the rescue. In 1994 the city hosted the Olympic Winter Games, solidifying this as a popular winter destination, though there is plenty to entertain during the summer months too. Travellers and artists alike flock to Lillehammer for charming museums and beautiful scenery surrounding the city, where locals hike, cycle and forage for fruits.

① 🎿 🎿 🍴 🖥 🏛

## Maihaugen

🏛Maihaugvegen 1 🕐Mid-Jun-mid-Aug: 10am-5pm daily; mid-Aug-mid-Jun: 11am-4pm Tue-Sun 🔒Public hols 🌐maihaugen.no

In 1887, Anders Sandvig established one of the biggest museums of farming culture in Norway, De Sandvigske Samlinger in Maihaugen.

Sandvig was a dentist who, during his travels in Gudbrandsdalen, collected objects and houses His collection grew to include 200 historical buildings reflecting the everyday lives of locals. The open-air museum includes a farming estate and mountain farm and aims to show a living environment with animals and people . One of Norway's oldest stave churches, Garmokirken, can be seen here. Maihaugen also houses the Post Museum.

② 🎿 🎿 🖥 🏛

## Lillehammer Kunstmuseum

🏛Stortorget 2 📞61 05 44 60 🕐11am-4pm Tue-Sun (late Jun-mid-Aug: to 5pm daily) 🔒Some public hols

It was the 19th-century artist, Fredrik Collett, who first became fascinated by the light and motifs at Lillehammer. Erik Werenskiold, Frits Thaulow and Henrik Sørensen were among the many artists to follow in his footsteps. Their work forms the basis of the collection of painting, sculpture and graphic design on show at this museum. The building itself is strikingly modern and also features a stone and water garden of stark beauty.

③ 🎿 🎿 🖥 🏛

## Bjerkebæk

🏛Sigrid Undsets Veg 16 🕐Jun-Sep: daily 🔒Public hols 🌐maihaugen.no

Lillehammer's most notable resident was Nobel Prize-winning author Sigrid Undset (p34), who settled here in 1921. She lived in splendid isolation in this house, with its magnificent garden. Undset's great work about the medieval heroine Kristin Lavransdatter was published at the time she moved to Lillehammer.

---

④

## Norges Olympiske Museum

🏠 Maihaugvegen 1
🕐 Jun-Aug: daily; Sep-May: Tue-Sun 🚫 Some public hols 🌐 ol.museum.no

The Olympic Museum offers a chance to experience the atmosphere of the 1994 Winter

↑ A cosy room in Bjerkebæk, home of Sigrid Undset

Olympic Games, when 1,737 participants from 67 countries descended on Lillehammer. Displays convey the history of the Olympics, travelling back to the Greek summer and winter games of 776 BC. A re-creation of the games in Athens in 1886 is shown, as are the first Winter Olympics, held in Chamonix in 1924.

---

⑤

## Lillehammer Olympiapark

🏠 1 km (half a mile) E of city centre 🕐 Daily
🌐 olympiaparken.no

The investment for the 1994 Winter Olympics provided Lillehammer with magnificent amenities, including Lysgårdsbakkene Ski Jumping Arena. In winter it is possible to take the chairlift to the top for a fantastic view. Håkons Hall, the ice-hockey arena, has facilities for other sports, such as handball and golf. It also has a 20-m (66-ft) climbing wall. Birkebeineren Skistadion is the starting point for a floodlit skiing track and cross-country trails.

# EAT

### Bryggerikjelleren

Rub shoulders with the locals in this former brewery, dating back to 1955, and dine on delectable steak and fish dishes. Booking is advised.

🏠 Elvegata 19
🕐 Lunch
🌐 bblillehammer.no

Ⓚ Ⓚ Ⓚ

---

⑥

## Lilleputthammer

🏠 Hundervegen, 14 km (9 miles) N of city centre
📞 61 28 55 00
🕐 Jun-Aug: daily

The pedestrian part of Storgata is known as "Gå-gata", and is the model for the miniature town of Lilleputthammer. Here there's an adventure park with lots of rides, a great spot for children.

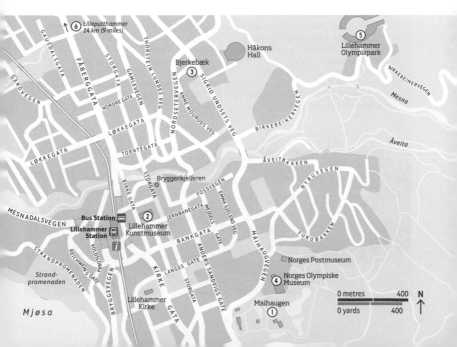

# EXPERIENCE MORE

## ❸ Kongsvinger

**🅐D5 🅐County of Hedmark 🅐🅐 🅘Glommengata 33; 90 06 64 86**

Situated on the Glåma River, the fortress town of Kongsvinger was established during the Hannibal Feud in 1644, when a fortification was built here and grew to become a solid fortress. Øvrebyen (the Upper Town) was situated near the castle ramparts.

With the arrival of the railway in the 1860s, Kongsvinger became a market town. New building was concentrated around the train station, and the quarter between the station and Øvrebyen developed into the town centre. In 1965 the town was designated as a "Development Centre", which led to industrial growth.

**Kongsvinger Festning** is an irregular star-shaped fortress with 16 batteries, fine old buildings and a museum that is dedicated to the armed forces. There are splendid views over the town and river towards Sweden from the castle ramparts.

The forests between Glåma and the Swedish border were settled by Finnish immigrants in the 17th century. **Finnetunet**, a museum of Finnish culture in Grue Finnskog, is made up of 13 buildings, the oldest of which dates from the end of the 18th century. It gives a picture of farming culture and the daily life of the people of Finnskogene (Finn Forest).

### Kongsvinger Festning

**🅐1 km (half a mile) N of town centre 🅒81 57 04 00 🅐Castle: daily; Museum: Jun–Aug: daily; Sep–May: Tue–Fri**

### Did You Know?

Defensive stronghold Kongsvinger Festning has never been conquered by foreign enemies.

### Finnetunet

**🅐🅐🅐 🅐40 km (25 miles) NE of Kongsvinger 🅒62 94 56 90 🅐Jun–Aug: daily**

## ❹ Elverum

**🅐D4 🅐County of Hedmark 🅐🅐 🅘Solørvegen 151; 62 40 90 45 🅦visiter.no**

On 9 April 1940, the day on which the Germans invaded,

---

### ØSTERDALEN AND RENDALEN

The valleys of Østerdalen and Rendalen run parallel in a south-north direction. The RV3 road through Østerdalen follows the Glåma, Norway's longest river, past several small towns of interest. Rena, just north of Elverum, has had a ferry crossing since the Middle Ages, and today is a skiing centre. A further 55 km (34 miles) upriver, Koppang has an intriguing folk museum that features traditional buildings from the region. Further north is the tiny town of Alvdal, the starting point for family mountain walks, and of Norway's second-highest tourist

road, which runs up to Tronfjellet mountain. At Tynset, the RV30 leads north to the old mining centre of Tolga and Os village.

Rendalen valley can be reached by taking the RV30 south from Tynset through Tylldalen, or a road from Hanestad, south of Alvdal, across the mountain passes. From here, there is a mountain road to the pretty fishing village of Fiskevollen *(below)* on Sølensjøen lake. The RV30 runs towards Otnes by Lomnessjøen lake, a beautiful part of Rendalen, and the RV217 leads to two fishing spots: Galten and Isterfossen.

←

Cross-country skiers in the shadow of the vast Trysilfjellet mountain

the Norwegian Parliament approved the Elverum Mandate, giving the fleeing Norwegian government considerable powers for the remainder of World War II. The following day, King Haakon rejected Germany's demand for a new Norwegian government. On 11 April, Elverum was bombed, and 54 people died. A monument at the high school commemorates the king's stand.

After the war, the city quickly rose from the ashes to become an administrative, commercial, educational and military centre.

The quarter on the eastern side of the Glåma River is known as Leiret, and evolved from the buildings below the old fortification, Christiansfjell. Grundsetmart'n, once the most important winter market in Scandinavia, is still held here.

**Glomdalsmuseet**, Norway's third-largest open-air museum, is a collection of 91 buildings from the mountain villages and rural lowland communities and contains some 30,000 exhibits.

Connected by a bridge across the Glåma is **Norsk Skogmuseum** (the Norwegian Forestry Museum), founded in 1954. This is the only museum in the country specializing in forestry, hunting and fishing, with different types of buildings, from lumberjack cottages to boathouses in the open-air section.

### Glomdalsmuseet

Museumsveien 15 62 41 91 00 Jun-Aug: daily; Sep-May: Sun only

### Norsk Skogmuseum

Solørveien 151 Daily Some public hols skogmus.no

---

### 5

## Trysil

D4 County of Hedmark Storvegen 3; www. trysil.com

In the past, the slow road through dense forest from Elverum to Trysil was known as "the seven-mile forest". Trysil is a typical woodland valley with spruce and pine forests and marshland topped by mountainous terrain.

The valley follows the Trysil River from the lake of Femunden, Norway's third-largest lake, to the Swedish border. Ferries operate in summer, and the administrative centre is at Innbygda.

The mountain of Trysilfjellet (1,137 m/3,730 ft) is the site of Norway's biggest alpine skiing centre. Fishing is good in the Trysilelva and "little" Ljøra.

In the eastern wilderness is Femundsmarka National Park and Gutulia National Park, with its 300–400-year-old primeval forests.

# STAY

### Scandic Central Elverum

Strategically located midway between Oslo and Lillehammer, this hotel has airy, modern rooms. The in-house restaurants feature regional specialities and an impressive list of Norwegian aquavit.

D4 Storgata 22, 2406 Elverum scandichotels.com

Ⓚ Ⓚ Ⓚ

---

### Rondvassbu

This red timber lodge sits at the edge of a dazzling turquoise lake in Norway's first national park. Built in 1903, it offers stunning views and hike-in-hikeout access.

C3 Rondvassbu, 2675 Otta rondvassbu.dnt.no

Ⓚ Ⓚ Ⓚ

---

### Trysil Hotell

In a sea of ski-resort chains, Trysil stands out. Rustic 17th century lodges are divided into airy, contemporary rooms - furnished with wood, leather and sheepskin - while an in-house bakery and gastro brewpub have breakfast and dinner sorted.

D4 Storvegen 24, 2420 Trysil trysilhotell.net

Ⓚ Ⓚ Ⓚ

## 6

# Mjøsa

**⚑D4** 🏛 **Counties of Hedmark & Oppland** 🛈 **Grønnegata 52, Hamar, 40 03 636; Lillehammer, 61 28 98 00**

Norway's largest lake, Mjøsa, is 117 km (72 miles) long and lies at the heart of an agricultural area. Many of the farms in Hedemarken, Helgøya and Totenlandet have been settlements since Viking times. They are bordered by forests and mountains, including Skreiafjellene (700 m/2,296 ft). Three towns – Lillehammer (p154), Hamar and Gjøvik – are spread around the lakeshore.

Before the arrival of cars and trains, Mjøsa was an important communications centre, even in winter when horses and sledges would cross the frozen lake. The completion of the railway to Eidsvoll in 1854 led to the arrival of a paddle steamer, *Skibladner*, known as "the White Swan of Mjøsa". It is the world's oldest paddle steamer still in regular service.

Helgøya, "the holy island", is situated in the widest part of the lake and was the site of medieval mansions built for bishops and the aristocracy, and a seat for the king. Among the farming estates are Hovinsholm and Baldishol, where the Baldishol Tapestry

> 💬 **INSIDER TIP**
> **Say cheese!**
>
> Be sure to sample the local salted-caramel-style *brunost*, or "brown cheese" in Eastern Norway. Invented by milkmaid Anne Hov in Gudbrandsdalen in 1863, this sweet cheese is made by boiling whey from cow or goat milk until it caramelizes. *Brunost* is available in local supermarkets.

↑ The striking exterior of indoor sports venue Hamar Olympic Hall

(1200) was found. Further north, between Brumunddal and Moelv, lies Rudshøgda, the childhood home of renowned writer and singer Alf Prøysen.

---

## 7

# Aulestad

**⚑C4** 🏛 **County of Oppland** 🚌 🛈 **Lillehammer; 61 28 98 00**

The writer Bjørnstjerne Bjørnson (1832–1910) bought the farm of Aulestad, in Østre Gausdal, slightly northwest of Lillehammer, in 1874. He moved here the following year with his wife, Karoline.

As well as writing Norway's national anthem, stories, poems and plays, Bjørnson was an outstanding orator and played a key role in the country's 19th-century politics. He was awarded the Nobel Prize for Literature in 1903 (his contemporary Ibsen was also nominated that same year).

The author's home, known as Dikterhjemmet på Aulestad, remains as it was when he lived here. It contains a varied selection of Bjørnson memorabilia and the couple's fine collections of photographs, art and manuscripts. The property was bought by the state in 1922.

## 8

# Hamar

**⚑D4** 🏛 **County of Hedmark** 🚊🚌 🛈 **Grønnegata 52 (summer only); 40 03 636**

Hamar is the largest town on Lake Mjøsa. It was a Norse market borough from 1049 until 1567, when a fire destroyed the cathedral. In 1849 Hamar achieved town status.

The remains of the cathedral, **Domkirkeruinene**, are protected by a glass dome. Built in 1100, the church was noted for its triple nave, but today only crumbling columns and arches give an idea of its original appearance.

**Hedmarksmuseet** is a folk museum comprising more than 50 traditional buildings. The **Norsk Utvandrermuseum** (Norwegian Emigrant Museum) is nearby, with a section devoted to North American emigrants. The railway museum, **Jernbanemuseet**, features an unusual narrow-gauge railway (the *Tertitbanen*). Hamar Olympic Hall looks like an upturned boat, and was built as a skating rink for the 1994 Winter Olympics.

### Domkirkeruinene

♿🚻♿🅿🏠 **Strandvegen 100** ☎ **62 54 27 00** 🕐 **Mid-May-Aug: daily; Sep-mid-May: by arrangement**

### Hedmarksmuseet

⊗⊗☺🏛 **⌂**Strandvegen 100 **☎**62 54 27 00 **○**Mid-May–Aug: daily; Sep–mid-May: by appointment

### Norsk Utvandrermuseum

⊗⊗☺🏛 **⌂**Åkershagan **☎**62 57 48 50 **○**Jun–Aug: daily; Sep–May: Tue–Thu **✕**Some pub hols

### Jernbanemuseet

⊗☺🏛 **⌂**Strandvegen 163 **☎**40 44 88 80 **○**Daily **✕**Public hols; Sep–May: Mon

---

**9**

## Ringebu Stavkirke

**🅰C3 ⌂**County of Oppland, 1 km (0.5 miles) S of town centre **🌐**stavechurch.no

Like other stave churches across the country, Ringebu Stavkirke was built using the

**Did You Know?**

Some 892 medieval coins from Scandinavia and Germany were found at Ringebu Stavkirke.

same woodwork skills that the Vikings applied to their long-houses and longboats. Set in the Gudbrandsdalen valley, Ringebu Stave Church was built around 1220 and the striking red tower was attached during restoration in the 17th century – a response to a growing population and increase in religious practices following the Reformation. The dragon-adorned doorway is from the original stave church, while the altarpiece and pulpit are Baroque.

---

**10**

## Vinstra

**🅰C3 ⌂**County of Oppland **🚉🚌 ℹ**Vinstra Skysstasjon; 61 29 53 76

At Vinstra, the **Peer Gynt-samlingen** contains considerable material on both the historical and the literary figure of Peer Gynt. The town also celebrates its most famous son with a festival in his honour every August.

The 65 km (40 mile) long Peer Gyntveien (Peer Gynt Road) is a mountain toll road running west of the Gudbrandsdalen valley from Tretten to Vinstra.

---

### PEER GYNT

Henrik Ibsen's dramatic poem *Peer Gynt* (1867) is regarded as one of Norway's most important literary works. It is much more than a fairy tale, questioning selfhood and reflecting on Norwegian culture, nature and legend. Ibsen was inspired to pen it after hiking through the Gudbrandsdalen and over the Sognefjell mountains, from where the beloved legend originates.

---

Offering splendid views, it passes a number of hotels and mountain lodges, among them Skeikampen, Gausdal, Gålå, Wadahl and Fefor. The highest point on the road is at 1,053 m (3,455 ft). At Gålå there is the open-air theatre, Gålåvatnet Friluftsteater, which stages a musical interpretation of Ibsen's *Peer Gynt* every year in early August as part of the region's festival.

**Peer Gynt-samlingen**
⊗🏛 **⌂**S of town centre **☎**61 29 20 04 **○**End Jun–mid-Aug: daily

→ Historic Ringebu Stavkirke, with its distinctive red spire

Sunset over the imposing Rondeslottet, in Rondane National Park ↑

## ⑪ Otta

🄰C3 🄰County of Oppland
🄰🚌 🄻Ola Dahl's Gate 1;
61 23 66 70

Since the arrival of the railway in 1896, Otta has been a tourist hub thanks to its proximity to the national parks of Rondane, Dovre and Jotunheimen. The town is the regional centre for North Gudbrandsdalen and a main terminus for buses to and from the adjoining valleys and mountain areas. Historically, Otta is known for the Battle of Kringen in 1612, when an army of local farmers destroyed a Scottish army of mercenaries who were on their way to fight for Sweden in the Kalmar War.

## ⑫ Rondane National Park

🄰C3 🄰County of Oppland
🄻Otta Tourist Information;
61 24 14 44 🅆visitrondane. com

Renowned for its lovely alpine hiking, Rondane was founded in 1962. Many Norwegian artists and writers have been inspired by the glaciated, lichen-covered landscape of Rondane – Norway's first national park; Ibsen based *Peer Gynt* on a fictional reindeer hunt here, while Solberg's *A Winter's Night in Rondane* (1914) has been voted the country's national painting.

Most of the terrain lies above 1,400 m (4,590 ft). There are 10 peaks in excess of 2,000 m (6,562 ft); the tallest, Rondeslottet ("Ronde Castle") climbs 2,178 m (7,145 ft). Rondane has both gentle, rounded mountains and wild, near-inaccessible parts with deep glacial cirques. Among the geological oddities from the last Ice Age are strange hollows of dead ice (a glacial deposit left behind after the glacier melted). Rondane is also one of the last refuges of wild reindeer.

Beyond its sheer beauty, visitors are attracted to the park for its well-developed trail network with several picturesque tourist lodges, including Rondvassbu and Bjørnhollia. Rondane also offers stunning lake views.

> Many Norwegian artists and writers have been inspired by the glaciated, lichen-covered landscape of Rondane - Norway's first national park.

### Did You Know?

The wild reindeer herds in Rondane and Dovrefjell have roamed here since the Ice Age.

## ⑬ Dovrefjell

🄰C3 🄰County of Oppland
🄻Dombås; 61 24 14 44

The mountain plateau of Dovrefjell marks the conceptual divide between Norway "north of the mountains" and Norway "south of the mountains". In 1814, Dovrefjell was used to signify the unity of the nation when the men at Eidsvoll *(p51)* sang *Enige og tro til Dovre faller* ("In harmony and faith till Dovre falls").

Kongeveien, the old King's Road from the south, crosses the plateau. Mountain huts built nearly 900 years ago have saved the lives of many travellers in these parts. The Dovrebane railway was completed in 1921. Hjerkinn is the highest point on both the road and the railway. Here, Eysteins Kirke was consecrated in 1969 in memory of King Eystein (c 1100) who built the mountain huts.

**Fossheim Steinsenter**
🏛🍴🏨 🏠Lom 📞61 21 14 60
🕐Daily 🚫Some public hols

## ⑮ Elveseter

🗺B3 🏠Bøverdalen,
25 km (16 miles) SW of Lom
🕐Mid-May–mid-Sep
🌐elveseter.no

Lying in Bøverdalen valley, in the shadow of Galdhøpiggen (2,469 m/8,100 ft), Norway's highest mountain, is the farming estate of Elveseter. In use since 1880, and with its oldest building dating from 1640, it has been repurposed as a hotel. Nearby stands Sagasøylen, a monument decorated with historic Norwegian motifs and crowned by Harald Fair-Hair (p49) on horseback.

From here, the scenic RV55 continues to Skjolden in Sogn. Maintained by farmers from Lom and Sogn since around 1400, a traffic survey from 1878 states that 16,525 people and 2,658 horses used the mountain road in that year. The current road was built in 1938 and its highest point is 1,440 m (4,724 ft) above sea level. Along its route is the Sognefjell tourist hut, and Turtagrø hotel, a centre for climbers since 1888.

---

Wild reindeer and musk oxen inhabit the region and rare species of birds live on the moorlands of Fokstumyrene.

Dovrefjell National Park was established in 1974. It surrounds Norway's fourth-tallest mountain, Snøhetta ("Snow Cap").

---

## ⑭ Lom

🗺C3 🏠County of Oppland
🚉To Otta 🚌 ℹNorsk Fjellmuseum; 61 21 16 00

The rural centre of Lom, on the banks of the Otta river, is a good gateway to the valley of Bøverdalen, the Jotunheimen mountain range and Sognefjellet mountain. Its stave church, **Lom Stavkirke**, was built in 1000 and retains its original deep foundations. It acquired its cruciform shape around 1600.

**Norsk Fjellmuseum** (the Norwegian Mountain Museum) opened in 1994 and is a good source of practical information on the mountain wilderness as well as on local natural history. Just across the Bøvra river, the Fossheim Hotel houses

**Fossheim Steinsenter** (the Fossheim Stone Centre), comprising a museum and a silversmith workshop.

East from Lom, at a crossing on the Otta river, is Vågå, which is also known for having a stave church (1130). Vågå is the burial site of the reindeer hunter Jo Gjende. Its main claim to fame is Jutulporten, a giant "door" in the mountainside that appears in Norwegian legend.

**Lom Stavkirke**
🚶🏠 🏠Lom 📞97 07 53 97
🕐Mid-May–mid-Sep: daily

**Norsk Fjellmuseum**
🏛🍴🏨🏠Lom
📞61 21 16 00 🕐May–Sep: daily; Oct–Apr: Mon–Fri

→
The wooden interior of Lom Stavkirke, the town's stave church

## TOP 5 SKI RESORTS

**Geilo**
A winter wonderland popular with families (www.skigeilo.no).

**Hafjell**
Perfect powder for cross-country skiing in a former Olympic park (www.hafjell.no).

**Hemsedal**
The 'Alps of Norway', this resort offers a huge range of terrain (www.hemsedal.com).

**Trysilfjellet**
Well-groomed slopes at Norway's largest alpine resort (www.trysil.com).

**Galdhøpiggen**
Glacier skiing in summertime (www.jotunheimen.com).

---

**16**

# Valdres and Fagernes

🅰C4 🄰County of Oppland
🚆🚌 𝒊Jernbaneveien 7, Fagernes; visitvaldres.no

North Aurdal is the biggest community in Valdres, and attracts a large number of visitors year-round. Around 150 years ago it was little more than a farming community, but that changed with the arrival of the railway in 1906. Long-distance buses then arrived, and in 1987 Leirin airport was built, Norway's highest at 820 m (2,690 ft). Despite the closure of the railway in 1988, the area remains easily accessible.

The main valley through Valdres follows the river Begna to Aurdal and Fagernes, where the valley divides into Vestre and Østre Slidre. The Slidre valleys are home to several stave churches. **Valdres Folkemuseum** is situated on Fagernes, a peninsula in Strandafjorden. It has 100 buildings and houses some 20,000 artifacts.

**Valdres Folkemuseum**
♿🄰♟🕐📷 🄰Tyinvegen 27
📞61 35 99 00 🄰Jun–Sep: daily; Oct–May: Mon–Fri

---

**17**

# Geilo

🅰B4 🄰County of Buskerud
🚆🚌📷 𝒊Vesleslåttveien 13; 32 09 59 00

Thanks to its proximity to Hardangervidda (*p168*) and the mountain of Hallingskarvet, Geilo has become one of Norway's most popular tourist destinations. There are opportunities for hiking, fishing and cycling, a great selection of accommodation, and many places to eat.

Geilo has also gained a reputation as a winter sports centre, with 33 alpine pistes and good snow conditions from November until May.

---

**18**

# Hallingdal

🅰C4 🄰County of Buskerud
𝒊Stasjonsgata 7, Nesbyen; 32 07 01 70

The long, narrow valley of Hallingdal, sided by steep mountains, widens out beyond Gol to form an agricultural landscape. Nesbyen, one of the populated areas along the way, is known for its extreme temperatures: the lowest recorded was –38° C, and the highest +35.6° C (a Norwegian record). Nesbyen's open-air **Hallingdal Folkemuseum** comprises 20 old houses, including one that dates from around 1300.

---

←

Dogs resting in the snow in Geilo, a hub for winter activities

←
The humble exterior of
Uvdal Stavkirke

Those looking for adventure outdoors should head for Hallingdal's magnificent mountain regions. There's a ski centre in the valley of Hemsedal – one of Scandinavia's finest.

### Hallingdal Folkemuseum
⊛⊕☺⊜ 🅰Møllevegen 18, Nesbyen 📞32 07 14 85 🅲Apr-May & Sep-Oct: Sun; Jun-Aug: Tue-Fri 🅺Public hols

---

## ⑲
## Numedal

🅰C5 🅰County of Buskerud
🚌 𝒊Stormogen in Uvdal;
www.visitnumedal.com

The landscape of Numedal is dominated by Norefjorden, 18 km (11 miles) long. Near the lake is an animal park, **Langedrag Naturpark**, which is home to species adapted to mountain life, such as polar foxes, wolves and Norwegian Fjord Horses.

The valley wends further into Uvdal, where the richly decorated Uvdal Stavkirke (stave church) dates from 1175. Another stave church (1600) stands on the eastern side of Norefjorden, alongside some weather-worn houses.

### Langedrag Naturpark
⊛⊕☺⊜ 🅰30 km (19 miles) NW of Nesbyen 📞32 74 25 50 🅲Daily 🅺Some public hols

## ⑳
## Kongsberg

🅰C5 🅰County of Buskerud
🚆🚌 𝒊Schwabes Gate 2, N3611; 32 29 90 50

For 335 years silver mining was the main focus of activity at Kongsberg, until the Sølvverket (Silverworks) were closed in 1957. It was also the site of Norway's royal mint.

The town was laid out by Christian IV in 1624, and developed rapidly. The large Baroque church, Kongsberg Kirke, was opened in 1761. Its organ (1760–65), by Gottfried Heinrich Gloger, is considered a masterpiece.

Kongsberg is also the location of the Norwegian Mining Museum, **Norsk Bergverksmuseum**, home to the Royal Mint Museum and the Sølvverket collections.

### Norsk Bergverksmuseum
⊛⊕☺⊜ 🅰Hyttegata 3 🅲Mid-May-Aug: daily; Sep-mid-May: Tue-Sun 🅺Public hols 🆆norsk-bergverksmuseum.no

---

## ㉑
## Drammen

🅰C5 🅰County of Buskerud
🚆🚌 𝒊Engene 1, 03008
🆆drammen.kommune.no

The location of the river port of Drammen on the navigable Drammenselva has long been the source of its prosperity. It was mentioned as early as the 13th century as a loading place and remains Norway's largest harbour for importing cars.

**Drammens Museum**, at the manor house of Marienlyst Herregård, has collections of city and farming culture. The art gallery, **Drammens Kunstforening**, has Norwegian 19th- and 20th-century paintings and a large collection of Italian art.

The Drammenselva river is one of the best in the country for salmon fishing.

### Drammens Museum
⊛⊕☺⊜ 🅰Konnerudgatan 7 📞32 20 09 30 🅲11am-3pm Mon-Fri (to 8pm Wed), 11am-5pm Sat & Sun

### Drammens Kunstforening
⊛☺ 🅰Konnerudgatan 7 📞32 20 09 30 🅲11am-3pm Mon-Fri (to 8pm Thu), 11am-5pm Sat & Sun 🅺Public hols

---

# SØRLANDET AND TELEMARK

Telemark and Sørlandet (the "southern lands") create a gentle transition between the east and west. The county of Telemark is dominated by the mountain plateau of Hardangervidda, topped by the 1,883-m (6,178-ft) high peak of Gaustatoppen to the northeast. Valleys criss-cross the landscape and a multitude of lakes shine like jewels. Here the Skienvassdraget underwent a major makeover in the 19th century to create the Telemark Canal, an important waterway in its time. There are few places in the country with such a rich and diverse folklore – many fairy tales and folk songs were composed in the region. Buildings preserve history, and you can smell the sunburnt, tarred timber of centuries-old cabins and log barns. Meanwhile Sørlandet – made up of the counties of Vest-Agder and Aust-Agder – has a coastline 250 km (155 miles) long, more if you include the fjords and skerries here. This is an area much loved by visitors, with its white-painted villages and towns, bobbing boats and busy quays. The archipelago is a haven for fishing and swimming, and the pleasant, though sometimes old-fashioned, towns make Sørlandet a paradise for holidaymakers.

# SØRLANDET AND TELEMARK

**Must Sees**
1. Hardangervidda
2. Kristiansand
3. Heddal Stavkirke

**Experience More**
4. Heddal
5. Kragerø
6. Risør
7. Arendal
8. Grimstad
9. Mandal
10. Lindesnes
11. Flekkefjord
12. Setesdal
13. Rauland
14. Rjukan
15. Lyngør
16. Bø Sommarland

HORDALAND

Odda

Hardangervidda
National Park

HARDANGERVIDDA

1

Røldal

E134

Botnen

Vassdalsegga
1658m

Haukeligrend

362

13

Suldal

Hovden

9

Byklehelene

Bykle

45

12

SETESDAL

Valle

VESTLANDET
*p180*

13

Rysstad

Otra

Jørpeland

Lysefjorden

Suleskard

45

Austad

Stavanger

9

ROGALAND

Sinnes

Sandnes

468

Byrkjedal

Sira

Bryne

Åseral

E39

Vikeså

Tonstad

VEST-
AGDER

Varhaug

42

42

44

Helleland

Mygland

Eiken

Sveindal

Egersund

Byremo

455

Eide

Sira

Gyland

Kvina

41

Byremo

FLEKKEFJORD

11

E39

Snartemo

Konsmo

461

Kvinesdal

Hidra

465

Lyngdal

Lyngna

Mandalselven

Øyslebø

455

Vanse

Farsund

E39

Søgne

9 MANDAL

LINDESNES 10

0 kilometres    25
0 miles    25

N
↑

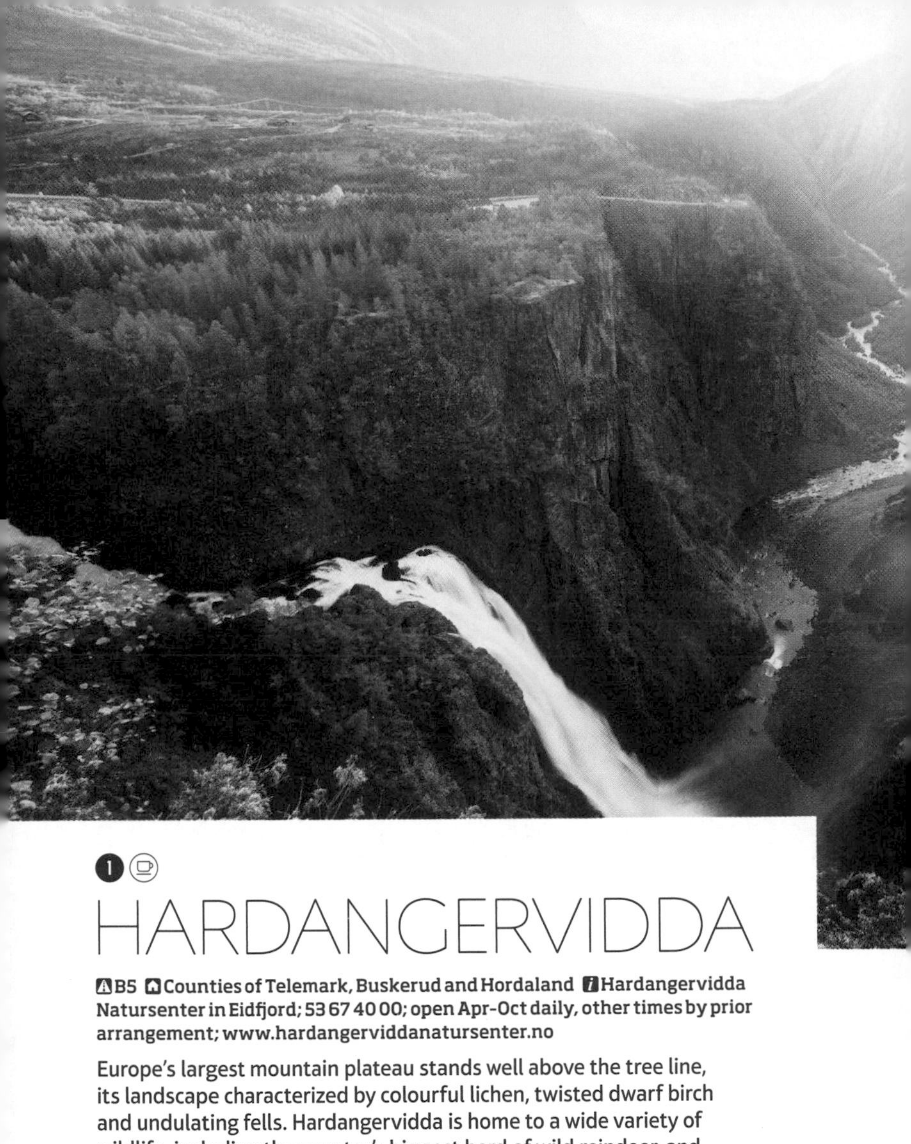

# ❶ 🖵

# HARDANGERVIDDA

**🅰 B5** 🏔 Counties of Telemark, Buskerud and Hordaland 🚹 Hardangervidda Natursenter in Eidfjord; 53 67 40 00; open Apr-Oct daily, other times by prior arrangement; www.hardangerviddanatursenter.no

Europe's largest mountain plateau stands well above the tree line, its landscape characterized by colourful lichen, twisted dwarf birch and undulating fells. Hardangervidda is home to a wide variety of wildlife, including the country's biggest herd of wild reindeer, and attracts visitors drawn to its bleakly beautiful landscape.

---

🗻 **GREAT VIEW**
**Gaustatoppen, Rjukan**

For sensational views of Hardangervidda, scale the peak of Gaustatoppen, Norway's most dazzling summit. Gaustatoppen is an 8.6 km (5.3 mile) hike, or a more relaxing cable-car ride from Svineroi.

---

Hardangervidda stands at an impressive 1,100–1,400 m (3,608–4,593 ft) and is punctuated with prominent peaks, including Hårteigen, Big Nup summit on Haukeli Mountain, Hardangerjøkulen glacier and – perhaps most grand and famous of them all – Gaustatoppen. Many rivers have their sources in the mountain lakes here, the best known being Numedalslågen and Telemarksvassdraget (commonly known as Skiensvassdraget) in the east, and Bjoreia with the Vøringsfossen waterfall in the west. Ancient tracks and well-trodden paths bear witness to the passage of walkers across the mountains in times past, along with an ancient reindeer herd that still roams and grazes along the plateau. Today, *hytte*-to-*hytte* (hut-to-hut) hikers trek around Hardangervidda's primitive landscape.

### GREAT HIKES

**Falkeriset, Rauland**
1 hour; 3 km (2 miles); easy. This child-friendly hike entails a gently inclining pathway passing grazing animals. It ends with great views of the moor.

**Solstien**
1.5 hours; 3.5 km (2 miles); fairly challenging. The stone-paved 'sun trail' leads from Rjukan to Hardangervidda, with fantastic vistas.

**Dyranut-Kjeldebu-Finse**
2 days; 26.5 km (16.5 miles); challenging. Takes in Dyranut ('the roof of Norway') and Hardangerjøkulen glacier. Advance planning required.

←

Vøringsfossen waterfall, plunging from the Hardangervidda plateau

① Gaustatoppen stands at 1,883 m (6,178 ft), its views attracting some 30,000 people every year. On a clear day you can see one sixth of Norway from its summit.

② Hardangervidda is home to a wide variety of wildlife. Male bluethroats are particularly busy in spring when they forage for insects and berries.

③ Well-marked trails allow walkers to easily explore Hardangervidda National Park.

1

3

2

**2** 🍴 🍽 🛍

# KRISTIANSAND

**🅐 B7** 🏛 **County of Vest-Agder** ✈🏠🚌⛴
**ℹ Rådhusgaten 6; 38 12 13 14**

The capital of Sørlandet, Kristiansand was founded by Christian IV in 1641 and immediately obtained trading privileges. The town expanded in 1922 and again in 1965. It's now the fifth-largest town in Norway, and a delightful mix of old and new. In addition to the town itself, the municipality incorporates the surrounding hills, forests, tranquil lakes, farmland and coastline.

## ① Posebyen

**🏛 NE part of town centre**

In Kristiansand's early days as a fortress and garrison town, the soldiers lived in private houses in what has become the best-preserved part of the old town. The small, pretty houses in this area of town are complete with courtyards, stables and wagon sheds, wash-houses and outbuildings. They've survived several fires and the threat of demolition, and are now very desirable to Norwegians. The historic houses are maintained in good order by the inhabitants.

## ②  Domkirken

**🏛 Gyldenløves Gate 9**
**🕐 Mon-Fri 🌐 kristiansand domkirke.no**

Kristiansand became a diocese in 1682 when the bishopric was moved here from Stavanger. The Neo-Gothic cathedral, Domkirken, is the fourth to be built on the site. It was completed in 1885, after a fire five years earlier, and can hold a congregation of 2,000. The organ in the east gallery dates from 1967 and has 50 pipes. A painting on the altarpiece by Eilif Peterssen shows Jesus in Emmaus.

## ③ 🎭 Christiansholm Festning

**🏛 Østre Strandgate 📞 38 07 51 50 🕐 Jun-Jul: daily; Sep-May: call ahead**

Christian IV wanted a town on the south coast to strengthen the Danish-Norwegian union. A permanent fortification was established in around 1640, and the Christiansholm Festning was eventually erected. The town became a garrison and the fortress was regarded as the country's most important after Akershus.

↑ The undulating interior of Kilden Performing Arts Centre

← Motorboats navigate a canal in colourful Kristiansand

Nordic species that can be seen at the park. From further afield, there are giraffes, apes, alligators and boa constrictors.

⑥ 🛈 🍴 🖾 🏛

## Kilden Performing Arts Centre

🏠 Vigeveien 22 🕒 For performances 🌐 kilden.com

This striking oak and glass concert hall on the town's waterfront is a unique venue and cultural powerhouse. With several halls of varying sizes, and wonderful acoustics, touring ballet and opera companies perform here. The oak building references Kristiansand's history as an oak export hub.

### Did You Know?

After a fire broke out in 1892, Posebyen was Kristiansand's only neighbourhood to survive.

④ 🛈 🎟 🖾 🏛

## Vest-Agder Museum Kristiansand

🏠 Vigeveien 22 🕻 38 10 26 90 🕒 20 Jun–20 Aug: daily; 21 Aug–19 Jun: Sun 🚫 Some public hols

Established in 1903, this open-air museum features wooden buildings from around the county, arranged according to origin. This includes farmyards, store and bath houses, and 19th-century town houses. In the museum itself there is a display of folk costumes and examples of the typical rustic decorations known as *rosemalt*.

⑤ 🛈 🍴 🖾 🏛

## Kristiansand Dyrepark

🏠 10 km (6 miles) E of town centre 🕻 38 04 97 00 🕒 Daily 🚫 Some public hols

Wolves, lynx, elk, capercaillies and eagle owls are among the

# EAT

**Fiskebrygga**
A cluster of clapboard buildings on the pier house fishmongers and seafood restaurants with fresh and affordable options (including takeaway).

🏠 Gravane 6
🕻 91 14 72 47

Ⓚ Ⓚ Ⓚ

**Bonder i Byen**
Hearty breakfast, lunch and dinner plates made exclusively with inputs from nearby producers.

🏠 Rådhusgata 16
🕻 91 14 72 47 🕒 Sun

Ⓚ Ⓚ Ⓚ

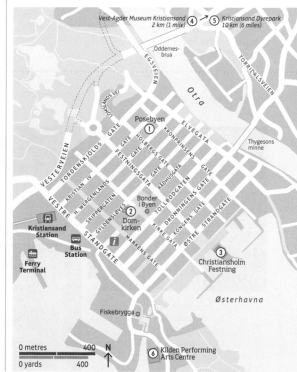

Vest-Agder Museum Kristiansand ④ ⑤ Kristiansand Dyrepark
2 km (1 mile)    10 km (6 miles)

Oddernes-brua

Otra

Posebyen ①

Thygesons minne

Bonder i Byen ②

Kristiansand Station

Bus Station

Dom-kirken

Ferry Terminal

③ Christiansholm Festning

Østerhavna

Fiskebrygga

0 metres   400   N
0 yards    400

⑥ Kilden Performing Arts Centre

3 🏛️ 🎞️ 🍴

# HEDDAL STAVKIRKE

**🅰C5** **🏠Heddalsvegen 412, Notodden** **🚇To Notodden**
**🚌4 to Heddal Barneskule** **🕙10am–5pm Mon–Sat, 12:15–5pm Sun**
**🌐heddalstavkirke.no**

As if plucked straight from a fairy tale, Heddal Stavkirke's intricate, shingled roof surfaces and turreted spire soar 25 m (82 ft) into the sky. Built in the 12th century, and still in use today, this is the largest of Norway's famous wooden cathedrals.

## Step Back in Time

The oldest part of Heddal Stavkirke is the chancel, built in 1147. About a century later, in 1242, the church was enlarged to the shape it keeps today. Twelve large pillars and six smaller ones create structural support for the three naves, portico and apse. The roof gables are adorned with fearsome dragons that reference Viking Sigurd, a legendary dragon-slayer. Notable features inside the church itself include the richly carved bishop's chair, the altarpiece and the late-17th-century wall paintings.

## Visiting the Church

Group tours are offered in both Norwegian and English, or visitors can explore the church under their own steam. The vicarage barn houses various exhibitions and a restaurant, where you can enjoy a bite to eat with lovely church views. The church is a popular wedding venue and is closed to visitors on such occasions.

### BISHOP'S CHAIR

The wooden bishop's chair (c 1250) is a star attraction within the church, and grabs visitor attention. Its elaborate carvings depict the epic Norse legend of Sigurd the Dragon-slayer. Christians are said to have repurposed the pagan myth, recasting Sigurd as Jesus and, perhaps not surprisingly, the dragon as the devil. The chair also portrays two knights on horse-back approaching a warrior maiden.

① A wooden corridor, with intricate decoration around doorways.

② Dragon carvings, intended to ward off evil, on a church portal.

③ The altar features various depictions of Christ, including a carved figure at the top.

↑ Norway's largest stave church, Heddal Stavkirke

# EXPERIENCE MORE

## ❹
## Heddal

🅐C5 🏛County of Telemark
🚉🚌 ℹTeatergaten 3; 35 01
50 00

The main attraction in the village of Heddal is Heddal Stavkirke (p172), but there is more to see here. A stone's throw from the church is the open-air museum **Heddal Bygdetun,** which displays traditional local buildings from medieval times to the early 20th century. This includes a house decorated in 1784 in the rustic style known as "rose painting", by the well-known painter Olav Hansson. There are also animals to give a tangible sense of farm life.

The Norsk Hydro company was established in the neighbouring city of Notodden in 1905. The company museum, **Bedriftshistorisk Samling**, is a small collection that shows its first years of operation, and looks at the history and lives of the local railway navvies.

### Heddal Bygdetun
Ⓐ Ⓦ Ⓟ 🏛6 km (4 miles) W of Notodden ℂ35 02 08 40
🌐Mid-Jun–mid-Aug: daily

### Bedriftshistorisk Samling
Ⓐ Ⓦ Ⓟ Ⓔ 🏛Notodden city centre ℂ35 09 39 99
🌐15 Jun–18 Aug: daily; other times by arrangement

---

## ❺
## Kragerø

🅐C6 🏛County of Telemark
🚂To Neslandsvatn 🚌
ℹTorvgata 1; 35 98 23 88
🌐visitkragero.no

A popular holiday resort since the 1920s, Kragerø is surrounded by a magnificent archipelago of small islands that are divided by narrow, twisting waterways. The picturesque little town was the home of the artist Theodor Kittelsen (1857–1914), best known for his fine illustrations of Asbjørnsen & Moe's collection of Norwegian folk tales. Some of these

illustrations can be seen in his house-turned-museum, which is situated in the centre of the town.

The morainic island of Jomfruland, the outermost in the Kragerø archipelago, has a distinctive flora and bird life. There is also an old, charming brick lighthouse from 1839 plus a newer one from 1939. The island can be reached by local ferry from Kragerø.

→
Narrow and atmospheric streets of Arendal at dusk

---

### TELEMARK CANAL

In 1861, during the heyday of waterways transport, Telemark's greatest river, Skiensvassdraget, was transformed into the Skien-Nordsjø Canal. Thirty years later, the Nordsjø-Bandak Canal to Dalen was completed, creating the Telemark Canal, 105 km (65 miles) long. At the time it was hailed as the "eighth wonder of the world". Today, it has become one of the biggest attractions in the county. Highlights include fairy tale architecture in Dalen, the towering Ulefoss waterfall and lush forest landscapes, all of which contrast with the remarkable canal engineering. The best way to experience this old-fashioned glory is to glide along the brick-lined waterways in a boat. The MS *Henrik Ibsen* or MS *Victoria* (www. visittelemark.no) offer day trips and extended cruises. Canoeing and cycling are also popular ways to explore.

**6**

## Risør

🅰 C6  📍 County of Aust-Agder  🚌 To Gjerstad, then bus  ℹ️ Torvet 1; 37 15 22 70

Protected from the sea by just a few islets, Risør is known as the "White Town of Skagerrak". It is the row of dazzling white merchants' and ship owners' houses on Solsiden ("the sunny side") by the harbour, as well as the pristine cottages nestling on Innsiden ("the inside") that have given the town its nickname. Despite several fires, the town has preserved much of its 19th-century layout.

Risør had its heyday towards the end of the sailing ship era, from around 1870. Many traditions from this period live on, as proved by the Wooden Boat Festival held here every August. Magnificent vessels fill the harbour and boat builders can be seen at their craft.

The wooden church at Risør, **Den Hellige Ånds Kirke**, was built in 1647 with Baroque details and a 17th- to 18th-century interior. The 1885 deactivated Stangholmen Fyr lighthouse features a summer restaurant and bar offering glorious views, as well as temporary exhibitions in its lamp room.

### Den Hellige Ånds Kirke

🕐 📍 Prestegata 6  📞 37 15 03 12  🕐 Jul: daily; other times by arrangement

---

**7**

## Arendal

🅰 C7  📍 County of Aust-Agder  ➡️ Kristiansand  🚤🚌 ℹ️ Sam Eydes Plass; 37 00 55 44

Sørlandet's oldest town, Arendal first began to develop in the 1500s, although it was only granted town status in 1723. Arendal is often referred to as the "Norwegian Riviera", and this most southerly part of Norway has been a popular holiday destination for years; it has remained relatively untouched by international tourism but is a firm favourite with domestic travellers. Arendal's historic buildings have been carefully preserved, and the town was awarded the Europa Nostra conservation medal in 1992. The town hall, **Rådhuset**, is similarly an architectural gem, and was built in Neo-Classical style in the early 19th century. At that time, Arendal was the biggest shipping town in the country, with a merchant fleet larger than that of Denmark. The area still has a small boat-manufacturing industry.

**Aust-Agder Museet** has archaeological and seafaring exhibits. In the harbour of Merdøy (half an hour by boat from Langbrygga) the former captain's home of Merdøgård is open to the public.

From Tvedestrand, there are boat trips on the M/S Søgne to the islands beyond.

### Rådhuset

🕐🕐 📍 Rådhusgaten 10  📞 37 01 30 00  🕐 For pre-booked tours only

### Aust-Agder Museet

🕐🕐🕐 📍 Park Veien 16  📞 37 07 35 00  🕐 Tue–Fri & Sun  🕐 Public hols

> **Arendal is often referred to as the "Norwegian Riviera", and this most southerly part of Norway has been a popular holiday destination for years.**

## 8

# Grimstad

**△C7** **△County of Aust-Agder** **☒Kristiansand** **🚌**
**ℹ Storgata 1a; 37 25 01 68**

The old centre of Grimstad dates from the days of sailing ships, and has narrow streets winding between the hills. **Grimstad Bymuseum**, which features arts and crafts and a maritime section, is situated in the town centre together with the pharmacy that dates from 1837, where Henrik Ibsen was an apprentice and where he wrote his first plays.

Northeast of the town is Fjære Kirke, a church with a memorial stone to Terje Vigen, about whom Ibsen wrote. This brave seaman came rowing from Denmark to Grimstad with two tons of barley in the year of starvation, 1809.

Craft beer aficionados should venture further north to take a tour of the award-winning Nøgne Ø brewery.

Nørholm, on the south-western outskirts of Grimstad, was the home of Nobel prize-

↑ Boats moored in the harbour of Lillesand, outside Grimstad

winning novelist Knut Hamsun. The coast towards Kristiansand is renowned for its charming holiday resorts.

Further south, Lillesand is a charming skerries town, with an elegant town hall and white-washed wooden houses. Sightseeing boats depart from here for Blindleia, a 12-km-(7-mile-) long series of inlets.

The beauty spots of Justøy island and Gamle Hellesund in Høvåg are close by. There is a Bronze-Age settlement at Høvåg. A ferry calls at one idyllic place after another, including Brekkstø, an artists' community on Justøy.

**Grimstad Bymuseum**
⊛ ⊛ ⊛ **△Henrik Ibsens Gate 14** **⊙Mid-Jun–mid-Aug: daily; mid-Aug–mid-Jun: by arrangement** **🆆gbm.no**

---

## 9

# Mandal

**△B7** **△County of Vest-Agder** **☒Kristiansand** **🚌To Marnardal or Kristiansand** **🚌** **ℹ Bryggegata 10; 38 27 83 00**

Mandal owes its fortunes to the timber trade in the 18th century. But its boom years were shortlived and with the transition from sail to steam,

around 1900, one in four inhabitants departed for America. But despite mass emigration, floods and fires, the town has retained more of its former characteristics than many others in Sørlandet. **Vest-Agder Museet**, located in an old merchant's house, has a large art collection, a ship gallery and a fishing museum. Nearby, the sizeable town church dates from 1821.

The coastal road to Mandal passes near the harbour of Ny-Hellesund, where the writer Vilhelm Krag (1871–1933) lived. This was also where Amaldus Nielsen painted his famous picture *Morning at Ny-Hellesund* (1885, Nasjonal-galleriet, Oslo). Norway's finest beach is close by, the 800-m (2,625-ft), eggshell-white Sjøsanden.

---

> **BEST BEACHES**
>
> Towns such as Risør, Grimstad and Mandal are strung along the southern coast like pearls. Narrow streets lined with clapboard houses slope towards the sea, where secluded beaches are dotted with smooth rock formations, ideal for sunbathing. Tiny Stangholmen island, off Risør's coast, is bordered with peaceful swimming coves. Grimstad's archipelago has many idyllic spots accessible by the Østerøy ferry. Near Mandal, Furulunden Park has a famously long, white sand beach – Sjøsanden – and tiny coves including Lille Banken and Lordens.

**Vest-Agder Museet**
Store Elvegata 5 · 38 25 60 23 · End Jun–mid-Aug: daily; mid-Aug–end Jun: Sun · vestagdermuseet.no

## 10 Lindesnes

B7 · County of Vest-Agder · Lindesnes Informasjonssenter; 38 27 83 00

The southernmost point on Norway's mainland is the Lindesnes peninsula, 2,518 km (1,565 miles) from the North Cape in the Far North. Here stands Lindesnes lighthouse, built in 1915 on the site of Norway's first lighthouse, which was lit in 1655.

The peninsula marks a distinctive change in the landscape between the small fjords and gently rounded islands to the east and the longer fjords to the west. Here there are more barren islets and wilder-looking mountains.

The Skagerrak and North Sea meet at this point, some days with great force. This can be the roughest place on the south coast, but at other times the water can look quite inviting. Two small harbours, Lillehavn and Vågehavn, enable sailors to shelter the worst of the storms.

## 11 Flekkefjord

B7 · County of Vest-Agder · To Sira · Elvegata 9, 38 32 80 00

This port is the biggest fishing and fish-farming town on the Skagerrak coast. The Dutch were early trading partners, hence Hollenderbyen (Dutch Town), dating from 1700. The town museum, **Flekkefjord Museum**, is housed in a 1720s patrician building and recreates old shipping scenes.

At the mouth of the fjord is the island of Hidra (reached by car ferry from the mainland). It is known for its scenic harbours and vibrant island community.

To the west of Flekkefjord is the fishing village of Åna-Sira, at the border between Sørlandet and Vestlandet. Nearby, the **Sira-Kvina Kraftselskap**, a renewable power station (one of seven on the Sira-Kvina waterway), can be toured.

**Flekkefjord Museum**
Dr Krafts Gate 15 · Jun–Aug: daily; other times by prior arrangement · vestagdermuseet.no

**Sira-Kvina Kraftselskap**
Stronda 12, 440 Tonstad · End Jun–mid-Aug: daily (guided tours only) · sirakvina.no

## EAT & DRINK

**Smag & Behag**
This charming restaurant and gourmet shop is a local favourite, offering innovative seasonal delicacies and more casual lunches.
C7 · Storgaten 14, 4876 Grimstad · smag-behag.no
Kr Kr Kr

**Apotekergaarden**
Authentic Neapolitan-style pizzas and back-garden concerts draw crowds to this lively restaurant and bar.
C7 · Skolegaten 3, 4876 Grimstad · apotekergaarden.no
Kr Kr Kr

**Nøgne Ø**
Head to this friendly brewery for full-bodied session ales and an evolving list of experimental brews.
C7 · Lunde 8, 4885 Grimstad · Dinner, Sat, Sun · nogne-o.com

**Jacob & Gabriel**
This intimate, upscale spot bases its seasonal menu on the local catch of the day or a phone call with a nearby farmer.
C6 · Bruene 1, 3724 Skien · Lunch, Mon, Sun · jacoboggabriel.no
Kr Kr Kr

← Lindesnes lighthouse, perched at Norway's most southerly point

↑ Charming turf-roof farmhouses at Setesdalsmuwseet

## ⑫ Setesdal

🅰B6 🏠County of Aust-Agder 🚌 🛈Valle Sentrum; 37 93 75 00

The biggest of the Agder valleys is Setesdal, with the steep Setesdalsheiene mountains forming towering walls on each side of the River Otra. **Setesdalsmuseet** has a medieval open-hearth house and a small barn dating from c 1590. The fine Hylestad stave church once stood nearby; it was demolished in 1668. Its portal, with motifs from the *Volsunga* saga, is now in Oslo's Historisk Museum.

At **Setesdal Mineralpark** in Hornnes, rare minerals glitter within exhibition halls hollowed out inside the mountain.

### Setesdalsmuseet

🏵🏵😑🏛 🏠Rysstad on RV9 ☎37 93 63 03 🕒Mid-Jun-Aug: daily; Sep-mid-Jun: Mon-Fri ✖Public hols

### Setesdal Mineralpark

🏵🏵😑🏛 🏠10 km (6 miles) S of Evje ☎37 93 13 10 🕒May-Sep: daily

## ⑬ Rauland

🅰B5 🏠County of Telemark 🚌 🛈Raulandshuset; 35 06 26 30 🖥rauland.org

The mountainous area around the beautiful Totakvatnet lake is known for its well-preserved buildings and its culture. Many artists had strong ties with the lake-side village of Rauland, and their works are on display at **Rauland Kunstmuseum**. Just east of here is an abundance of historic buildings, such as the old farmhouses near Austbøgrenda, one of which has wood-carvings from the 1820s. Other wooden buildings can be seen at Lognvik farm by lake Lognvikvatnet.

### Rauland Kunstmuseum

☺ 🏠1 km (half a mile) W of Rauland centre ☎35 06 90 90 🕒20 Jun-Sep: Tue-Sun; other times by arrangement

## ⑭ Rjukan

🅰C5 🏠County of Telemark 🚌🛈Torget 2; visitrjukan.com

Rjukan's international claim to fame was as the site of the hydrogen factory that was blown up in 1943 by Norwegian Resistance fighters. Before that, however, the small rural community played a key role in Norway's industrial development when a power station was built here in 1911. Fuelled by the Rjukanfossen waterfall, the power station helped the village expand into a self-sufficient industrial community. When a new power station was built in 1971, the old structure became a museum, **Norsk Industriarbeidermuseum**, which tells the story of the thrilling wartime sabotage and of Norway's industrial past. The waterfall itself was a

## GAUSTATOPPEN

The loftiest mountain in southern Norway stands at 1,883 m (6,178 ft) and is widely considered Norway's most noble peak. Some 30,000 people ascend the summit every year to enjoy the sublime views of almost one sixth of Norway, down the southern coast and east to Sweden. It's a moderate 2-hour hike from Stavsro (near Rjukan) to reach the summit. Alternatively, you can take it easy and jump on the cable car (www.gaustabanen.no).

key tourist attraction, but the power station means it can only be seen occasionally.

On the opposite side of the valley is the **Krossobanen** cable car, erected in 1928 to enable the residents of the shaded valley to glimpse the sun in winter. It rises to 886 m (2,907 ft) and is an excellent starting point for walking trips on Hardangervidda.

Gaustatoppen is another popular peak on the plateau. It can be reached via a well-marked path from the Stavsro car park in about 2 hours.

### Norsk Industriarbeidermuseum

⊛⊛⊛⊜⊜ ⬛ 7 km (4 miles) W of town centre ☎ 35 09 90 00 ⬛ Apr & Oct: Tue–Sat; May–Sep: daily; Nov–Mar: Tue–Fri

### Krossobanen

⊛ ⬛ 1 km (half a mile) W of town centre ☎ 35 09 00 27 (bookings) ⬛ Daily

---

### ⑮ Lyngør

⬛ C6 ⬛ County of Aust-Agder ⬛ To Vegårshei, then bus ⬛ To Gjeving, then boat taxi ⬛ Summer only ⬛ Wrold Wroldsens Gt 2 (Tvedestrand); 37 16 40 30

A former winner of the "best-preserved village in Europe" award, Lyngør is one of the idyllic islands

in Skjaergårdsparken (Archipelago Park), which covers most of the coast of Aust-Agder county. Accessible only by boat taxi from Gjerving on the mainland, the island has no roads for motor vehicles and is a peaceful haven.

Lyngør has fine historic buildings near the old pilot and customs station. Narrow footpaths wind past painted houses with white picket fences and fragrant gardens. The forests that once covered the islands are long gone, but there is an abundance of flowers, initially brought here as seeds in the ballast of sailing ships.

In 1812, Lyngør was the scene of a bloody sea battle when the Danish-Norwegian frigate, *Najaden*, was sunk by

the English vessel, *Dictator*. The population sought refuge in Krigerhola, a pothole near the sea. A cultural history museum is connected to the restaurant, *Den Blå Grotte*.

The islands share an early 13th-century church at Dybvåg on the mainland.

---

### ⑯ Bø Sommarland

⬛ C6 ⬛ County of Telemark ⬛ Jun–Aug: daily ⬛ sommarland.no

Norway's biggest waterpark, Bø Sommarland, offers more than 100 activities, appealing to different ages. There are paddling pools and water activities for young, while older kids will enjoy the water carousel, slides, rafting and a wave pool.

Thrill-seekers should head for the diving towers, water rollercoaster, surf waves or the heart-stopping free-fall slide, Magasuget. Dry land attractions include a fair-ground and several places to eat. The park lies just north of the small town of Bø.

→ A lighthouse in Lyngør, affording spectacular sea views

# VESTLANDET

The long, thin westerly region bordering the North Sea is the land of fjords, where fingers of deep blue water cut spectacularly through the mountains. Here, picturesque villages edge the shoreline, linked by ferries, tunnels and precipitous winding roads. Vestlandet comprises four counties, each with their own unique landscape, which together cover about 15 per cent of Norway's total land mass: Rogaland, Hordaland, Sogn and Fjordane, and Møre and Romsdal. Beautiful Bergen – Norway's second city – can be found in Hordaland. Its stunningly preserved wooden warehouses are mementos of Bergen's centuries-old trading role. Today this historic hub makes a good starting point for excursions out to the enchanting fjords and impressive stave churches – both prolific in this part of Norway and once more remind travellers of the country's ancient history. Vestlandet offers excellent opportunities for mountain hiking in both easy and more challenging terrains. For the angler, there is superb sea fishing and salmon and trout fishing in the lakes and rivers.

# VESTLANDET

**Must Sees**

*North Sea*

*North Sea*

VESTLANDET

0 kilometres 50

0 miles 50

N

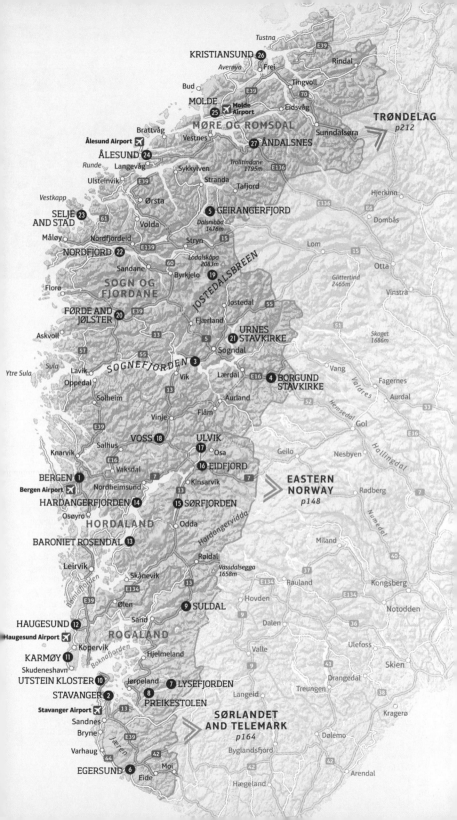

# BERGEN

🅐A5 🚗County of Hordaland 🚃20 km (12 miles) S of town 🚌🚉Strømgaten 8 ⛴Frieleneskaien (Hurtigruten), Strandkaiterminalen (regional) 🛈Strandkaien 3; 55 55 20 00; www.visitbergen.com

This charming, World Heritage City has as much appeal as Oslo and with a less frenetic vibe. The waterfront is the city's atmospheric heart and there are world-class museums, photogenic buildings and chic restaurants aplenty.

Granted town status by King Olav Kyrre in 1070, Bergen was at the time the largest town in the country and the capital of Norgesveldet, a region that included Iceland, Greenland and parts of Scotland. Even after Oslo became capital of Norway in 1299, Bergen continued to grow as a trading centre, especially for the export of dried fish and other fish products during the era of the Hanseatic League trading company, which eventually ended in the mid-18th century. Following a period of decline in the 15th century, the town entered a new era of prosperity as a centre for shipping and trading, and benefited from Norway's neutrality during World War I.

## Bryggen

🅐North side of Vågen harbour 🌐whc.unesco.org

The old timber warehouses on the harbour's northern side were first known as Tyske-bryggen (the German Quay). Until 1754 they were at the hub of Hanseatic trade in Norway, though, long before, this part of the town had been a trading centre for fish. Over the centuries the gabled medieval houses facing the harbour have been ravaged by fires; the last, in 1955, left only 10 gables standing. Today, Bryggen is an artistic centre and restaurant area, and is included in UNESCO's World Heritage List.

## Håkonshallen and Rosenkrantztårnet

🅐Bergenhus Festning
📞55 31 60 67
🕐Håkonshallen: daily; Rosenkrantztårnet: mid-May-Aug: daily; Sep-Dec: Tue-Sun; Jan-mid-May: Sun
🚫Public hols

Håkonshallen is a Gothic ceremonial hall built by King Håkon Håkonsson for the coronation and wedding of his son, Magnus Lagabøter, in 1261. It is thought to be the largest secular medieval building remaining in Norway. Originally, the ceremonial hall was situated on the top floor. The middle storey comprised living areas and the cellar was used for provisions. The building was later restored and decorated with paintings by

---

🔍 HIDDEN GEM
**Theta Museum**

This tiny, one-room museum, at Bredsgården 2B, was the secret headquarters of the Theta Group – a resistance cell during Nazi occupation from 1941-2 (p52).

---

←

Stunning sunset over Bergen, seen from Mount Fløyen

Gerhard Munthe, but it suffered extensive damage in World War II. Restoration work followed and it became a grand function venue.

The Rosenkrantz Tower is, along with Håkonshallen, part of the old fortifications of Bergenhus (Bergen Castle). The main building dates from the same period as Håkonshallen. The present tower was built in 1560 by the governor of Bergen Castle, Erik Rosenkrantz, as a defence post and residence.

> Mariakirken's splendid Baroque pulpit is decorated with representations of Christian values, such as Faith, Hope, Love, Chastity, Truth and Temperance.

③ ♿

## Mariakirken

🏠 Dreggsallmenningen 15
📞 55 59 32 70 🕐 Jul-Aug: 9am-4pm Mon-Fri (group visits at weekends & after 1 Sep by arrangement)

Part of the chancel in Mariakirken (St Mary's Church) dates from the 11th century, around the time when Bergen was granted town status by King Olav Kyrre. As such Mariakirken is the city's oldest surviving church.

In Hanseatic times the German merchants used the building as their own special church and richly embellished it. Dating from 1677, Mariakirken's splendid Baroque pulpit is decorated with representations of Christian virtues such as Faith, Hope, Love, Chastity, Truth and Temperance.

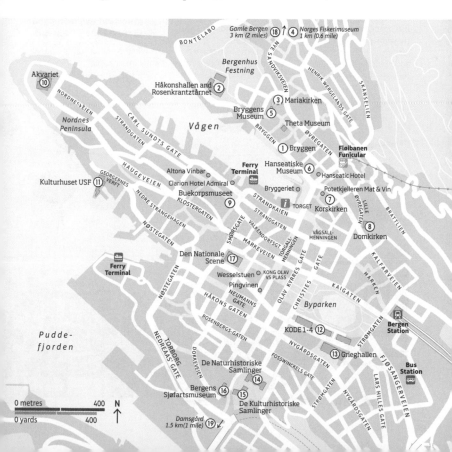

### GREAT VIEW
## Fløyen Funicular

Ride Fløibanen funicular 320 m (1,050 ft) to the top of Mount Fløyen for a spectacular vista of Bergen. Once up, linger over pancakes at Fløistuen Café or, if you're feeling energetic, take a forest hike.

④
## Norges Fiskerimuseum

⌂ Sandviksboder 23
🕐 Jun-Aug: daily; Sep-May: Sun-Fri ⓦ fiskerimuseum. museumvest.no

Situated on the city's pretty waterfront, Norges Fiskeri-museum (the Norwegian Fishing Museum) provides a comprehensive insight into Norway's long-established fishing industry, including the management of its resources. Fishing boats and equipment through the ages are on show, while other displays cover various types of fishing, such as herring and cod fishing, fish farming, whaling and sealing. Historical films are also screened, along with a slideshow.

⑤
## Bryggens Museum

⌂ Dreggsalmenning 3
🕐 For restoration until May 2019 ⓦ bymuseet.no

After a catastrophic fire at Bryggen in 1955, the city began a series of excavations, which were then to be the largest of their kind in northern Europe. Bryggens Museum is based on the archaeological finds unearthed during these excavations, and provides a picture of everyday life in a medieval town such as this. It features a wealth of well-presented material, both graphic and written, including runic inscriptions dating from the 14th century, clothing, accessories, pottery, tools and even human skulls.

⑥
## Hanseatiske Museum

⌂ Finnegårdsgaten 1A
🕐 For restoration
ⓦ hanseatiskemuseum. museumvest.no

Established in 1872, this museum is located in one of Bryggen's expansive German merchant's houses, dating from the end of the Hanseatic era. A number of traders were housed here, next to rooms for drying fish, offices and storerooms. The early 18th-century interiors give a good impression of how they lived and worked. The museum also features four assembly rooms used for eating, entertainment and keeping warm in winter.

⑦
## Korskirken

⌂ Korskirkealmenningen
📞 46 98 12 25 🕐 Mon-Sat

To the east of Torget and the innermost part of Vågen is Korskirken (the Church of the

↑ A sense of medieval life at Bergen's Hanseatiske Museum

Cross). It was erected around 1100, originally as a three-aisled Romanesque church. A south wing was added in 1615 and a north wing in 1623. A beautiful Renaissance portal with Christian IV's monogram graces the northern end.

---

### ⑧
## Domkirken

🏠 Domkirkeplassen 1
📞 55 59 71 75 🕐 Daily

Bergen's cathedral was originally a parish church, Olavskirken, dating from the

← Enjoying a drink on the terrace outside the Norges Fiskerimuseum

latter half of the 12th century. When a Franciscan monastery was established in Bergen around 1250, the church was taken over by the monks. As with so many other buildings in Bergen, Olavs-kirken was ravaged by fire. On one occasion it was restored by Geble Pederssøn, who became Norway's first Lutheran bishop in 1537. He built a new tower and installed the clock above the western entrance. The multi-sided Gothic choir, with its high windows, has remained untouched, and the church's large Rieger organ has an impressive 61 stops.

The poet Ludvig Holberg, considered to be the founder of modern Norwegian literature, was a pupil at the nearby Latin School from 1698 to 1702.

---

### ⑨
## Buekorpsmuseet

🏠 Strandsiden 📞 55 23 15 20 🕐 Sat & Sun 🕐 Mid-Jul-mid-Aug

The 400-year-old Muren (Wall Gate) was originally the private home of a high-ranking official, Erik Rosenkrantz, and today houses the Buekorpsmuseet. The Buekorps (literally "Bow Corps") are boys' brigades, with its members ranging from 7 to 20 years in age. They originated in 1850s Bergen, and have become a very special part of the town's cultural traditions.

At one time the various Buekorp groups were rivals, but today their drills and marches are more light-hearted. Their longbows, banners and historic photographs are on display in this small museum.

---

# EAT

### Potetkjelleren Mat & Vin

A long-time favourite with locals, this Nordic kitchen is housed in a 600-year-old cellar. The speciality under the vaulted ceilings is regional cuisine, with a strong focus on seafood and local, seasonal vegetables. Unsurprisingly, there is a good wine menu.

🏠 Kong Oscars Gate 1A
🕐 Lunch, Sun
🌐 potetkjelleren.no

Ⓚ Ⓚ Ⓚ

---

### Wesselstuen

The oldest restaurant in Bergen is renowned for dishing up filling, traditional fare, including Norway's national favourite *klippfisk* (salted cod). Meat-eaters might also like to try *reinsdyrstek* (reindeer steak).

🏠 Øvre Ole Bulls Plass 6
🌐 wesselstuen.no

Ⓚ Ⓚ Ⓚ

---

### Pingvinen

Rub shoulders with the locals at Plingvinen, whether for a hearty evening meal or a preprandial drink. Expect fishcakes, dumplings and other dishes based on local seafood, plus a number of lamb dishes and a wealth of potato-based side dishes.

🏠 Vaskerelven 14
🌐 pingvinen.no

Ⓚ Ⓚ Ⓚ

⑩ 🚴 🏔 🍴 🛍

## Akvariet

🏠 Nordnesbakken 4
🕐 Daily 🚫 17 May, 24 & 25 Dec 🌐 akvariet.no

The aquarium is one of Bergen's most popular attractions, home to Europe's largest collection of sea and freshwater fish and invertebrates. Inside, there are nine large and 50 smaller tanks plus two pools with sea birds, seals and penguins. One section is dedicated to the development of marine life. The tropical section has crocodiles, snakes, lizards and common marmosets.

Every day 3 million litres (666,000 gallons) of seawater are pumped up from the depths of Byfjorden, through 8,000 m (26,246 ft) of plastic pipes, and into the tanks.

⑪ 🍴 🛍

## Kulturhuset USF

🏠 Georgernes Verft 12
📞 55 30 74 10 🕐 Daily

The former United Sardines Factories (USF) have been renovated to house the USF Cultural Centre, a large contemporary arts complex featuring music, films, theatre, dance, visual arts and handicrafts. It also has a lovely terrace café, which is a particularly fine spot for a coffee or drink during the summer months.

⑫ 🚴 🏔 🍴 🛍 🛍

## KODE 1-4

🏠 Around Lars Hilles gate
🕐 15 Sep-14 May: 11am-4pm Tue-Fri, 11am-5pm Sat & Sun; 15 May-14 Sep: 11am-5pm daily 🚫 1 & 17 May, 24 Dec-4 Jan
🌐 kodebergen.no

The KODE museum is an umbrella for Bergen's quartet of world-class art museums. At the heart of the city, the collection fills four impressive buildings on the edge of Lille Lungegård. Each building has its own focus: KODE 1, refurbished in 2017, houses the national silver collection and the Singer painting collection, with works by old European and Asian masters. KODE 2 is the organisation's venue for temporary, rotating exhibitions, while KODE 3 has a stunning collection of works by Edvard Munch. Finally, KODE 4 focuses on much-loved Norwegian artist Nikolai Astrup, and international greats including Pablo Picasso, Paul Klee and Asger Jorn. It also houses KunstLab, an art museum for children.

↑ Artworks by Edvard Munch, in Bergen's KODE 3

⑬ 🛍 🛍

## Grieghallen

🏠 Edvard Griegs Plass 1
🕐 Box office: Mon-Sat and before events
🌐 grieghallen.no

Bergen's modern concert hall, Grieghallen, opened in 1978. Designed by the Danish architect Knud Munk, it is the country's largest auditorium, with 1,500 seats. A smaller hall accommodates 600 people. Grieghallen is also used for opera, ballet, theatrical productions and congresses. It is the central venue for events during the Bergen International Festival (Festspillene), held annually in May and June since 1953.

Bergen Filharmoniske Orkester (the Bergen Philharmonic Orchestra), also known

### Did You Know?

Bergen is famous for *skillingsboller*, an enormous cinnamon and cardamom spiced bun.

> **Bergen Museum's botanical gardens, known as Muséhagen, are a mass of blooms in summer. Tropical plants can also be seen every season.**

as Harmonien, holds concerts every Thursday at Grieghallen from September to May. The orchestra was founded in 1765.

---

⑭ 🏃 🏃

### Bergen Museum: De Naturhistoriske Samlinger

📍 Muséplass 3  🕐 Jun–Aug: 10am–4pm Tue–Fri, 11am–4pm Sat & Sun; Sep–May: 10am–3pm Tue–Fri, 11am–4pm Sat & Sun  🌐 uib.no

Comprehensive botanical, geological and zoological collections, as well as a botanical garden and plant house, make up Bergen Museum's De Naturhistoriske Samlinger (the Natural History Collection). Both the natural history and the cultural history collections were founded by the president of the Norwegian Parliament, W F K Christie, in 1825. The natural history collection is housed in an imposing hillside building on Nygårdshøyden dating from 1866 and 1898. It was designed by J H Nebelong and H J Sparre.

The zoological section shows stuffed animals, birds and fish from all over the world, including an exhibition titled "Wild Life in Africa".

The geological section features an eye-catching mineral collection with fine samples from Bergen and further afield. The life of our early ancestors is exposed in "The Evolution of Man". Other exhibits focus on "Oil Geology" and "The Green Evolution – the Development of the Planet".

Bergen Museum's botanical gardens, known as Muséhagen, are a mass of blooms in the summer. Tropical plants can also be seen every season in the greenhouse. Muséhagen was established in 1897 and over the years it has amassed 3,000 different species. The selection of plants is particularly large and varied. When the gardens outgrew their original site, new gardens and an arboretum were created at Milde, about 20 km (12 miles) south of the town centre. The extensive research carried out by Bergen Museum's natural and cultural history departments paved the way for the establishment of Bergen University, which today has more than 17,000 students, seven faculties and 90 institutes.

→

The Whale Gallery, De Naturhistoriske Samlinger

# DRINK

**Altona Vinbar**
Founded 1614, this is Bergen's oldest tavern; you'll be spoiled for choice when it comes to wine and *aquavit* – a Scandinavian spirit.

📍 Strandgaten 81
🕐 Sun  🌐 augustin.no/vinbar

---

**Bryggeriet**
Microbrewery with 15 seasonally rotating beers on tap and a gastro-pub menu. Live music and craft beer tours are also available.

📍 Torget 2  🕐 Sun
🌐 bryggeriet.biz

## Did You Know?

Bergen is statistically one of the wettest cities in Europe. An umbrella is essential.

(15)

## Bergen Museum: De Kulturhistoriske Samlinger

🏠 Håkon Shetelings Plass 10
🕐 Tue–Sun 🕐 Public hols
🌐 visitbergen.com

Situated opposite the Natural History Museum, on the other side of Muséhagen, is the Cultural History Collection of Bergen Museum, De Kultur-historiske Samlinger. The collection occupies a large building designed by Egill Reimers in 1927.

Innovative displays focus on Norwegian culture and folk art, as well as some exhibits from foreign cultures. The unusual archaeological collection is based on finds from the counties of Hordaland, Sogn and Fjordane, and Sunnmøre in Western Norway. Exhibits are shown in themed displays such as "The Stone Age" and "The Viking Age". "Legacy from Europe" depicts the cultural exchange between Norway and the rest of Europe.

The colourful motifs of Norwegian folk art are explored in the "Roses and Heroes" exhibition, while folk costumes are part of the "Rural Textiles" collection.

"Ibsen in Bergen" describes Henrik Ibsen's inspirational work at Det Norske Scene (the National Theatre) in Bergen from 1851–7.

Anthropological exhibitions include "Between Coral Reef and Rainforest", "Indians, Inuit and Aleut: The Original Americans" and "Eternal Life: Egyptian Mummies".

(16)

## Bergens Sjøfartsmuseum

🏠 Håkon Shetelings Plass 15
🕐 Daily (times vary, check website) 🌐 bsj.uib.no

The story of Norwegian shipping can be explored in Bergens Sjøfartsmuseum (Maritime Museum), with special emphasis on Vestlandet. The ground floor covers up to 1900; the first floor focuses on the 20th century to the present day.

There is an extensive model collection of Viking ships and various working boats, including the deckhouse of the training ship *Statsraad Lemkuhl*. "Coastal and Fjord Boats" describes life aboard for the crew and passengers of the vessels working up and down the coast.

The Maritime Museum was founded in 1921. It is housed in a striking stone building, with an atrium in the centre, designed by Per Grieg and completed in 1962.

In summer children of all ages congregate in the atrium to play with remote-controlled model boats. The "promenade deck" is perfect for relaxing in deckchairs and looking out over one of Bergen's busy harbours.

(17)

## Den Nationale Scene

🏠 Engen 1 🕐 For performances 🌐 dns.no

The first Norwegian National Theatre has its roots in Det Norske Theater in Bergen, founded in 1850 by the violinist Ole Bull. Henrik Ibsen was a director here for six years, starting his tenure in 1851, followed by Bjørnstjerne Bjørnson from

### EDVARD GRIEG

Edvard Grieg (1843-1907) was Norway's foremost composer, pianist and conductor. He was born in Bergen in 1843. At the age of 15, on the advice of the violinist Ole Bull, he enrolled at the Leipzig Conservatory to study music. Later, in Copenhagen, he came into contact with influential composers of the time, such as Niels Gade. Grieg's aim was to create a Norwegian style of music for which he sought inspiration in folk music. Among his most well-known works is the music for Ibsen's *Peer Gynt*. In 1867 he married his cousin, the soprano singer Nina Hagerup.

1857 to 1859. Since 1909 the theatre has been housed in a splendid Art Nouveau building. Sadly, the original theatre building, "the Theatre in Engen", was destroyed by bombs in 1944. Den Nationale Scene has played a significant role in Norwegian theatre history, thanks to its rich repertoire.

---

18 ⬡ ⬡ ⬡ ⬡ ⬡

## Gamle Bergen

⌂ Elsesro, 5 km (3 miles) N of town centre ☎ 55 30 80 30 ⊙ 12 May–1 Sep: daily

An open-air museum, Gamle Bergen was founded in 1949 on the old patrician site of Elsesro in Sandviken. The buildings, furniture, domestic utensils, clothes and everyday items on show provide a graphic illustration of life in Bergen in the 18th and 19th centuries. Workshop interiors and shops give an idea of the living conditions of the different social classes, such as sailors and high-ranking officials, artisans and labourers. Around the

↑ Pretty, pastel-coloured, clapboard houses at Gamle Bergen

houses are streets and paths, squares and alleys designed to imitate the style of the times.

---

19 ⬡ ⬡ ⬡ ⬡

## Damsgård

⌂ Alleen 29 ⊙ Jun–Aug: daily ⬡ bymuseet.no

Europe's best-preserved wooden Rococo building, was built by a nobleman in 1770 when Bergen was a large, bustling and wealthy port town. Of the 80 wooden mansions built during this period, Damsgård is the most impressive. The house was used for entertaining, while the surrounding land was used for nominal farming. The pleasure palace still features the original luxurious interior. The sculpture garden is a lovely place for a picnic and a stroll. There are daily tours of both the interior and exterior in spring and summer.

# STAY

### Clarion Hotel Admiral

Situated in historic warehouse buildings dating from 1904, the Clarion has gorgeous views of the sea, mountains and Bryggen. Rooms are modern and spacious. There's also an excellent terrace bar.

⌂ C Sundts Gate 9 ⬡ nordicchoice hotels.com

---

### Hanseatic Hotel

The height of luxury in Bergen, this opulent boutique hotel is set in a 16th-century building, right in the heart of UNESCO Bergen. It's located right next door to the Hanseatic Museum – perfect for culture vultures.

⌂ Finnegården 2A ⬡ dethanseatiske hotel.no

Ⓚ Ⓚ Ⓚ

↑ Gorgeous houses and cobbled streets in Gamle Stavanger

② Ⓜ Ⓨ ▭ 🛍

# STAVANGER

🅰 A6  🏠 County of Rogaland  ✈ 12 km (7 miles) SW of town centre  🚉🚌 Jernbaneveien 3  ⛴ Østre Havn
ℹ Strandkaien 61; www.regionstavanger.com

Before the cathedral was built around 1125, Stavanger was little more than a fishing village – a reputation it held for centuries. The town prospered in the 1960s when oil was discovered off the coast. Today, it's Norway's fourth-largest city, and a foodie destination.

## ①
### Gamle Stavanger

🏠 Stavanger town centre

To the west and southwest of Vågen harbour is Gamle ("Old") Stavanger, a residential and commercial quarter known for its attractive wooden houses and winding cobbled streets. Between Øvre Strandgate and Nedre Strandgate, there are complete terraces of well-preserved, 19th-century whitewashed timber houses, with small, manicured front gardens and picket fences. Once the homes of seafarers and local workers, the 156 protected houses are lovingly cared for by their modern-day owners.

## ②

### Norsk Hermetikkmuseum

🏠 Øvre Strandgate 88A
📞 51 84 27 00  🕑 Mid-May-mid-Sep: 10am-4pm daily; mid-Sep-mid-May: 11am-3pm Tue-Fri, 11am-4pm Sat & Sun  🔒 Public hols, Dec

Stavanger's canning museum is housed in an old cannery in pretty Gamle Stavanger. It provides an overview of an industry that was of great importance to the town; in the 1920s there were a staggering 70 canneries in Stavanger. Learn about 19th-century markets, developments in technology and the international launch of tinned sardines in the 20th century.

---

### GREAT VIEW
### Valbergtårnet

This 19th-century look-out tower on the hill of Valberget has seen many fires rage through Stavanger. Today, however, the tower offers great views of the town, the harbour and Boknafjorden.

---

③ Ⓢ Ⓜ ▭ 🛍

### Stavanger Maritime Museum

🏠 Nedre Strandgate 17-19
🕑 Daily  🔒 Public hols
🌐 stavanger.museum.no

The sailing vessel *Anna of Sand* was launched in 1848 and is Norway's oldest sailing ship. Between voyages, it can be seen here at the Maritime Museum. The museum is in two converted warehouses.

---

④ Ⓢ Ⓜ Ⓨ 🛍

### Norsk Oljemuseum

🏠 Kjerringholmen  🕑 Daily
🔒 Some public hols
🌐 norskolje.museum.no

Oil and gas production in the North Sea created an economic

boom in Stavanger, making this one of the most cosmopolitan towns in the country. The ultra-modern Norsk Oljemuseum (Petroleum Museum) offers a graphic account of life at work on a drilling platform, with a top-to-bottom presentation of an oil rig. Models of the equipment used are on display, including drilling bits, diving bells and a survival capsule.

---

## ⑤
# Domkirken

🏠 Haakon VII's Gate 7 📞 51 84 04 00 ⏰ 11am-4pm Mon-Sat, Sun for services

Reinald, the first bishop of Stavanger, was an Englishman from Winchester, where St Swithun had been a bishop in the 9th century. During the reign of King Sigurd Jorsalfar, Reinald was given the means to construct a cathedral. The imposing Romanesque nave was completed around 1100, and dedicated to St Swithun, who thus became the patron saint of Stavanger.

After a fire in 1272, the cathedral was rebuilt with a Gothic choir. About the same time, the Gothic eastern façade and the Bishop's Chapel were added. The two towers on the eastern façade date from 1746. The Baroque pulpit was added in 1658, and the stained-glass paintings behind the altar are were installed in 1957.

↑ Exhibit on the water at Stavanger's Norsk Oljemuseum

---

⑥ 🐾 Ⓜ 🖥 🛍
# Stavanger Museum

🏠 Muségaten 16 ⏰ Jun-Aug: 10am-4pm Tue-Sun; Sep-May: 11am-3pm Tue-Fri (to 7pm Thu), 11am-4pm Sat & Sun ⏰ Public hols
🌐 stavangermuseum.no

Completed in 1893, Stavanger Museum houses exhibitions on local, natural and cultural history. It also comprises the Norwegian Children's Museum, which has a play park with historical games – perfect for modern-day kids.

---

⑦ 🐾 Ⓜ 🖥 🛍
# Sverd i fjell

🏠 6 km (4 miles) south of Stavanger

These three Viking swords pay tribute to the historic Viking Battle of Hafrsfjord (p49). The striking sculpture by Fritz Røed was unveiled by King Olav V of Norway in 1983.

---

# EAT

**Re-naa**
The menu here is based on the very best foods from the sea, fjords, forests and mountains, served with a curation of wines chosen by expert sommeliers.

🏠 Steinkargata 10
⏰ Lunch, Mon, Sun
🌐 restaurantrenaa.no

Ⓚ Ⓚ Ⓚ

**Sabi Omakase**
Watch the sushi master chef prepare and serve your dinner at this exclusive restaurant.

🏠 Pedersgata 38
⏰ Lunch, Sun-Wed
🌐 omakase.no

Ⓚ Ⓚ Ⓚ

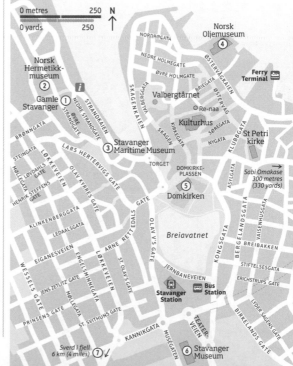

# SOGNEFJORDEN

🅰A4 🏠County of Sogn and Fjordane 🚌🚆🚢 𝒊Kulturhuset, Sognda; 99 23 15 00; www.sognefjord.no

Nicknamed "King of the Fjords", Sognefjorden is Norway's longest, deepest fjord and cuts straight through the heart of the country. A number of smaller fjords splinter off from the main, majestic waterway and idyllic fjord villages punctuate the surrounding scene.

Extending for 206 km (128 miles) and reaching a maximum depth of 1,308 m (4,291 ft), Sognefjorden is magnificent. Five large arms subdivide into long fjord fingers and it is these innermost sections that arguably have the most to offer. Each is well known for its beauty: Fjærlandsfjorden, Sogndalsfjorden and Lustrafjorden to the north, Årdalsfjorden to the east, and Lærdalsfjorden, Aurlandsfjorden and Nærøyfjorden to the south – the last of which is a UNESCO World Heritage Site. They encompass some of the world's finest natural scenery. Dotted throughout this landscape are small and charming villages that hold their own appeal, from irresistible local delicacies and well-preserved Viking mounds, to attractive waterfronts bounded by bucolic countryside.

> **INSIDER TIP**
> ## Getting there
>
> Public transport around Sognefjorden is superb. Check out Nettbuss (www.netbuss.no) for bus links and Norled (www.norled.no) for passenger express boat services. There are also ferries and car ferries.

① This is a popular place for glacier hiking tours. Here, intrepid walkers scale Nigardsbreen, an arm of the larger Jostedalsbreen glacier.

② The Stegastein viewpoint is famed for its brilliant Aurlandsfjorden views as well as its stunning design. Standing at 650 m (2,133 ft) and protruding 30 m (98 ft) from the mountainside, it's an amazing work of art.

③ A journey on the Flåmsbana railway guarantees stunning views of mountains, waterfalls, picturesque hamlets and curious-looking rock formations. The train passes on a short, steep route between the villages of Flåm and Myrdal.

## TOP 5 BEAUTIFUL VILLAGES

**Flåm**
Catch the famous train here and head for a meal on the harbour-front on arrival.

**Undredal**
Home to just 80 people and Norway's smallest stave church.

**Aurland**
Cute village not far from the unmissable Stegastein viewpoint.

**Vik**
Don't miss the 1130 stave church here.

**Balestrand**
Viking burial mounds, the historic Kviknes Hotel and stunning fjord views.

←

Beautiful Nærøyfjord, an arm of the mighty Sognefjorden

↑ Borgund Stavkirke, bounded by rolling green hills

④ 🖉 🕅 🖵 🗁

# BORGUND STAVKIRKE

🅰 B4  🅰 County of Sogn and Fjordane  🚌 From Lærdal  📞 57 66 81 09  ⏰ Mid-Jun–mid-Aug: 8am–8pm daily; mid-Apr–mid-Jun & mid-Aug–Sep: 10am–5pm daily

Norway's best-preserved medieval church is a staggering sight, with its shingled roof soaring skyward. Travel back in time and step inside this intricately decorated wooden cathedral.

Borgund Stavkirke at Lærdal is the only stave church to have remained unchanged since the Middle Ages. Dedicated to the apostle St Andrew, it was completed around 1150. Built entirely of wood, the interior is very simple: there are no pews or decorations, and the lighting is limited to a few small openings high up on the walls. The exterior is richly decorated with carvings and runic inscriptions. The visitors' centre, where you can purchase entry tickets, also houses exhibits on the role of the stavkirke in the Middle Ages, and early Viking finds from a nearby archaeological dig.

↑ Wooden posts supporting the roof of the nave

> 💬 INSIDER TIP
> **Follow ancient footsteps**
>
> Don't miss the 2-hour circular "Vindhellavegen to Sverrestigen" hike, which follows an ancient footpath. This picturesque loop starts and ends at the church.

The church's roof is composed of an intricate framework using numerous rafters and joists.

The tower has a three-tiered roof. The first tier is decorated with pagan dragon heads on the gables, similar to those on the main roof.

Crosses decorate the gables above the apse tower and the doorways.

The windows were originally simply circular openings in the outer walls.

→
The wooden exterior of Borgund Stavkirke

The altar has an altar-piece dating from 1654.

The exterior of the church is richly adorned. The Romanesque west door shows dragon battles and vines.

Twelve posts – or staves – around the centre of the nave disappear into the semi-darkness of the roof, giving an increased sense of height.

**5**

# GEIRANGERFJORD

🅐B3 🚉Åndalsnes ✈Ålesund International Airport 🚌Geiranger
(Panorama, Highlight and CitySightseeing tours all depart from here)
ℹ Geiranger Tourist Information Office, Geirangervegen 2; 70 26 30 99

**The colossus of Norway's fjords, Geiranger astounds whether you approach by boat or on foot. The fjord's 16 km (10 miles) of snaking, emerald waters are bounded by cliffs that soar at 1,700 m (5,577 ft), and waterfalls thunder down the mountainsides in a spectacular showcase of nature.**

The mother of all fjords, Geiranger is a 16 km- (10 mile-) long UNESCO-ranked beauty. The area's unique natural surroundings were created during a succession of ice ages, when glaciers carved out deep ravines and shaped the surrounding mountains. Geiranger is the quintessential fjord-cruise experience; some 600,000 people visit every summer, meaning it can be overrun at peak times. A basic ferry trip from the port of Hellesylt and Geiranger provides a budget-friendly alternative, while tour operators such as Geiranger Fjordservice offer longer jaunts. Perched at the head of the fjord, Geiranger village is among the most well-known resorts in the fjord country, and a good base camp for exploring this verdant landscape. Other popular ways to view the fjord include hiking and kayaking.

### HIKING

Escape the crowds of tourists disembarking from cruise ships and see the fjord on foot. There are numerous hiking trails offering quiet, unique vistas of the stunning fjord and its lush terrain. Hiking also means you can explore nearby farmland. One of the most memorable treks is from Geiranger village to Skageflå Mountain Farm. The trail on a Storsæterfossen waterfall hike goes behind the waterfall, providing a thrilling experience. Further up the valley, the famous Dalsnibba trek takes you to the highest point, giving truly breathtaking views back towards Geiranger. Don't forget to take your camera!

## Go Chasing Waterfalls

Waterfalls are one of Geirangerfjord's distinguishing features. Some of the most famous to crash down the vertical cliff faces and leave clouds of mist in their wake are the spectacular *De syv søstrene* (the Seven Sisters), *Friaren* (the Suitor) and *Brudesløret* (the Bridal Veil).

↑ Bridge crossing Geirangelva River, Geiranger village

→ Seven Sisters, comprising seven separate streams

→ A cruise ship passing the Seven Sisters waterfall on Geirangerfjord

## Did You Know?

After Geirangerfjord was used as a backdrop in Disney's *Frozen* (2013), tourism increased here by 40 per cent.

# EXPERIENCE MORE

**6**

## Egersund

**A7** **County of Rogaland**
**Jernbaneveien 18;**
**www.eigersund.**
**kommune.no**

When the sea is rough,
Egersund is the only natural
harbour along the Jæren coast
to provide good shelter. It is
Norway's largest fishing
harbour, but quaint old white
wooden houses still perch on
the steep rocks around the
wharves. The cruciform church
dates from 1620.

The cultural history museum,
**Dalane Folkemuseum**, is
located at Slettebø, once the
residence of a high-ranking
civil servant. Handicrafts,
old farming tools and
industrial equipment are
on display. At Eide, glazed
earthenware – once a major
local industry – is exhibited in
a former faience factory (part
of the Dalane Folkemuseum).

Northwest of Egersund is a
waterfall, Fotlandsfossen,
with salmon steps to aid the
migrating fish.

The agricultural and
industrial region of Jæren
is one of Norway's flattest
areas. There are some sandy
beaches, but no islands to
protect the shore. The
towering Eigerøy lighthouse
presides over the coast.

### Dalane Folkemuseum

**2 km (1 mile) N of town
centre** **51 46 14 10** **Mid-
Jun–mid-Aug: daily; other
times by prior arrangement**

---

**7**

## Lysefjorden

**B6** **County of Rogaland**
**Stavanger–Lysebotn**
**Turistinformasjonen,
Stavanger; 51 85 92 00**

The breathtaking Lysefjorden
cuts through the mountains

like the blow of an axe.
Formed by enormous
glaciers during the Ice Age,
it stretches through the
landscape for over 40 km
(25 miles). Only in very few
places is the starkness of the
mountainside interrupted by
some sparse greenery and a
solitary farm.

At the inner end of the
fjord, the Lyseveien road is
famous for featuring 27
hairpin bends, and affords
views of Kjerag peak, which
stretches to 1,000 m (3,281 ft)
above the water. South of
Lysefjorden is Frafjorden,
where the waterfall of
Månafossen tumbles into
the water below from a
height of 92 m (302 ft).

### Did You Know?

Tom Cruise dangled
from the cliffside at
Preikestolen for
*Mission: Impossible -
Fallout* (2018).

## ⑧ Preikestolen

🅰B6 🏛County of Rogaland
🚌🚢Stavanger-Lysebotn
🌐preikestolen.no

Pulpit Rock is a world-famous, spine-tingling fjord and cliff viewpoint that tops travellers' bucket lists. Norway's most emblematic photo opp is not for the faint of heart. The narrow mountain plateau in Rogaland juts out over a sheer 604-m (1,980-ft) plummet to Lysefjord. The views from the top of the rock, reached only by hike, are dizzyingly breathtaking, with the emerald fjord unfurled glassily below. Hiking season runs from April to September. The 8-km (5-mile) round-trip from Preikestolen Mountain Lodge takes about 5 hours, with a 350 m (1,150 ft) ascent.

It's essential to check the weather conditions before departure and to avoid starting out too late in the day, to ensure there are enough daylight hours for the return journey.

## ⑨ Suldal

🅰B5 🏛County of Rogaland
🚌 ℹTuristinformasjonen, Sand; www.suldal-turist kontor.no

The famous salmon river, Suldalslågen, flows into Sandsfjorden through the town of Sand. Here, beside a waterfall, is **Laksestudioet** (the Salmon Studio), where a glass wall enables visitors to watch the salmon and trout as they negotiate the cascade on their journey up-river. The studio dates from 1988, one year after a fish ladder was put in place. The best time to visit for salmon-spotting is between mid-July and the end of September. There is also an exhibition on the history of salmon fishing on the site. The heritage of the English "salmon lords" can be seen throughout Suldal valley in the grand manor houses that they had constructed along the river towards the end of the 19th century.

At the **Kolbeinstveit Museum**, further up the river, is a collection of old wooden cottages, smoke houses, mills, storage houses on stilts and the Guggendal loft and store-house, dating from 1250. From here, a road inland leads to **Kvilldal Kraftstasjon**, Norway's largest power station.

At the eastern end of the river, steep mountains on each side of the water form the mighty Suldalsporten (Suldal gateway), creating a narrow sound before leading into the lake, Suldalsvattnet, from where the river springs.

### Laksestudioet
⊛🐾 🏛Sand town centre
📞52790560 🕐15 Jun-Aug: daily; other times by prior arrangement

←
Emerald waters of the dramatic Lysefjorden in Vestlandet

💬 INSIDER TIP
### Off-peak fjords

Fjord country can get overcrowded in high summer. If it's possible, plan your trip for May or September – it should be quieter, the weather will be mild and you'll find hotels offer better rates.

### Kolbeinstveit Museum
⊛🐾 🏛17 km (11 miles) E of Sand 📞52792950 🕐End Jun-mid-Aug: Tue-Sun

### Kvilldal Kraftstasjon
⊛🐾 🏛Soldalsosen
🕐By prior arrangement; call Suldal Tourist Office (52790560)

---

⑩ ⊛ 🐾 💬
## Utstein Kloster

🅰A6 🏛County of Rogaland 🚌 🕐Mid-May-Aug: daily 🕐Some public hols 🌐utsteinkloster.no

On the island of Mosterøy, northwest of Stavanger, is the 12th-century monastery Utstein Kloster. It stands on what was originally a royal estate from the time of King Harald Hårfagre, with records of the site dating back to the 9th century. Construction of the monastery began in about 1260, and around 1265 it was presented to the Augustinian order. The monastery remained in their ownership until the Reformation, when it became the property of Norwegian and Danish aristocrats.

The monastery, surrounded by a large estate of 139 farms, is considered by many to be the country's best-preserved medieval monastery despite fires and attacks. In 1935 the buildings were taken over by the state and restored as a national monument. Today it houses a museum, and also acts as a concert venue and conference centre.

→

Kjeragbolten, a boulder wedged dramatically in a mountain crevasse

# STAY

### Juvet Landskapshotell

Modern Norwegian architecture at its finest, this hotel is gracefully designed around a picturesque mountain waterfall. Expansive windows take advantage of the stunning views and bring the outside in. Rooms are simple yet luxurious and no two are the same, promising a truly unique experience.

🅰B3 🅰Alstad, 6210 Valldal 🔤juvet.com/no

Ⓚ Ⓚ Ⓚ

### Skåpet Tourist Lodges

Book well in advance for these striking, avant-garde cabins in the hiking area near Lysefjord. The Norwegian Trekking Association (DNT) hired an award-winning team of architects to design seven private zinc boxes, with floor-to-ceiling views of the surrounding mountains and a stream-side sauna.

The minimalist, shipping container-style cabins include cooking equipment for self-catering.

🅰A6 🅰Soddatjørn, Forsand, Rogaland 🔤english.dnt.no

Ⓚ Ⓚ Ⓚ

---

**⑪**

## Karmøy

🅰A6 🅰County of Rogaland 🔲🚌🛳
🅘Turistinformasjonen, Stratsråd Vinjes Gate 25; www.visitkarmoy.no

The 30-km- (19-mile-) long island of Karmøy lies like a shield against the sea (the Old Norse word *karmr* means protection). On the inside is the Karmsundet, a shipping channel that was part of the ancient *Nordvegen* (Northern passage), from which the word *Norge* (Norway) is derived. By the bridge to the island, stone megaliths known as the Five Wayward Virgins guard the sound. It is said that they were raised in honour of the five sons of a monarch who fought the king of Avaldsnes, where there was a royal estate

(870–1450). The area's many burial mounds are proof that Avaldsnes was an important prehistoric centre.

Olavskirken (St Olav's Church) was built at Avaldsnes by King Håkon in around 1250. Next to the church leans the Virgin Mary's Sewing Needle, a 7.5-m (25-ft) stone pillar. The nearby island of Bukkøya hosts a reconstructed Viking estate. Iron Age stone pillars can be seen at Åkrahavn on the western side of Karmøy.

On Karmøy's southern tip lies the whitewashed town of Skudeneshavn, which has a museum at **Mælandsgården**. Karmøy's main town is the lively Kopervik.

### Mælandsgården

⊗Ⓚ 🅰Skudeneshavn 📞52 84 54 60 🕒Jun–mid-Aug: Mon–Fri & Sun; other times by prior arrangement

## ⑫ Haugesund

🅰A6 🄲County of Rogaland 🄳Karmøy, 13 km (8 miles) S of town centre 🚌 🚢Hurtigbåtterminalen 🄸Strandgt 171; www.visithaugesund.no

The three seagulls in the town's coat of arms signify Haugesund's seaside location, and its fishing and shipping industries. This is a young town, but the area has important historical connections; it is known as the birthplace of Norway and the homeland of Viking kings. To the north is the burial mound of **Haraldshaugen**, where King Harald Hårfagre was buried around 940. Norges Riksmonument, Norway's national monument, was erected on this site in 1872 to mark 1,000 years of a united Norway. Haugesund has museums, a gallery and a splendid town hall. The town hosts a number of popular festivals.

Out to sea in the west is the island of **Utsira**, renowned for its rich bird life and accessible by boat.

### Haraldshaugen

🄲3 km (2 miles) N of Haugesund town centre 🚌

### Utsira

🕘 🄲1 hr 20 min W of Haugesund (by boat) 🚢For timetable call Turistinformasjonen, Haugesund (47 88 01 44).

---

⑬ 🄰🄼🄳🄳🄼

## Baroniet Rosendal

🅰A5 🄲County of Hordaland 🚍From Bergen, Haugesund and Odda 🕘Mid-May–mid-Sep: tours daily; mid-Sep–mid-May: by prior arrangement 🌐baroniet.no

In 1658 a magnificent wedding was celebrated at Kvinherad, between Karen Mowatt and the Danish aristocrat Ludvig Rosenkrantz. The groom was the highest-ranking administrator in the then-fiefdom of Stavanger and war commissioner for Norway, while the bride was one of Norway's richest heiresses. Among the wedding gifts was the estate of Hatteberg, and the couple built a small Renaissance palace, Rosendal, here in 1665.

The estate became a barony in 1678. In 1745 it was sold to Edvard Londeman of Rosencrone and remained in the family until it was given to Oslo University in 1927.

The magnificent garden, dating from the 1660s, was extended in the 19th century to include a landscaped park with Gothic towers and fairy-tale houses. The palace interior was also modernized. It contains a number of artworks, among them Meissen porcelain and Norwegian paintings in the National Romantic style.

Note that visitors are welcome to visit by tour only.

---

## ⑭ Hardangerfjorden

🅰A5 🄲County of Hordaland 🚍 🄸Ulvik Tourist Information; 56 55 38 70 🌐hardangerfjord.com

Hardangerfjord stretches 180 km (112 miles) from the island of Bømlo in the North Sea to Odda. The main fjord extends to Utne, at the tip of the Folgefonn peninsula, where it forks into a number of tributaries. The largest of

these are Sørfjorden, Eidfjorden and Ulvikfjorden.

The glacier, Folgefonna, lies 1,600 m (5,249 ft) above the fjord with arms extending down to 500 m (1,640 ft). One of these, Bondhusbreen, resembles a near-vertical frozen waterfall tumbling towards Mauranger. On the western side of the Folgefonn peninsula are Jondal and Utne. Jondal has a ferry quay and museum, **Det Gamle Lensmannshuset** (the Old Sheriff's House). Utne is home to **Hardanger Folkemuseum**, a cultural heritage museum that gives an idea of how life was lived in the region in the 18th and 19th centuries.

Nordheimsund and Øystese are tucked into a bay on the northwestern side of the fjord, near the suspension bridge across Fyksesundet. Both are popular tourist resorts. At Øystese there is a museum featuring the work of the sculptor Ingebrigt Vik.

### Det Gamle Lensmannshuset

🄰🄼🄳 🄲Viketunet, Jondal, RV550 🄲53 66 95 00 🚢 🕘By prior arrangement

### Hardanger Folkemuseum

🄰🄼🄳🄳 🄲Utne 🄲47 47 98 84 🕘Daily

↑ A boat moored in the tiny harbour of Jondal

Moody skies above Skei in Hardangerfjorden

## 15 Sørfjorden

**B5** **County of Hordaland** **Odda Tourist Information; 53 65 40 05**

Sørfjorden is the longest arm of Hardangerfjorden, and runs along the eastern side of the Folgefonn peninsula. On its western side, below the 1,510-m- (4,954-ft-) high peak of Aganuten, is the cultural heritage site of **Agatunet**, which has 32 medieval timber houses, and Lagmannsstova, a court house dating from 1300.

In the region of Ullensvang, where the fjord villages of Lofthus and Kinsarvik are found, Sørfjorden is at its most scenic, especially in spring when more than 200,000 fruit trees bloom on the slopes. Nearly a fifth of all the fruit trees in Norway grow here. The district has always been a centre of prosperity, and the monks from the Lysekloster monastery near Bergen grew fruit here in the Middle Ages. They also educated the local farmers, as did the clergyman Niels Hertzberg (d 1841).

The Gothic-style Ullensvang church dates from the early Middle Ages. Its stone walls are 1.4 m (5 ft) thick. In the garden of Hotel Ullensvang is Edvard Grieg's composing hut, where he wrote *Spring* and parts of *Peer Gynt*.

Around the industrial town of Odda are a number of beautiful waterfalls, including Låtefoss, which has a fall of 165 m (541 ft), and the 612-m- (2,008-ft-) high Langfoss.

### Agatunet

⊛ ✿ 🖼 🏛 **25 km (16 miles) N of Odda** **47 47 98 02** **Mid-May–Aug: daily; other times by prior arrangement**

## 16 Eidfjord

**B5** **County of Hordaland** **Ostangvegen 1; 53 67 34 00**

Even by Norway's standards, the scenery around Eidfjord is dramatic. Almost vertical valleys have been scoured out by glaciers and rivers. The Bjoreia river flows through the valley of Måbødalen to Vøringsfossen, a dramatic waterfall that plunges 145 m (476 ft) into a formidable gorge extending down towards upper Eidfjord.

The valley's main road passes through a series of unremarkable tunnels, while cyclists and pedestrians can opt to travel on the old road cut into the gorge instead. A footpath up Måbøgaldane comprises 1,500 steps and 125 bends. A bridleway leads to Vøringsfossen.

A nature centre at Sæbø, **Hardangervidda Natursenter**, offers information about the Hardanger mountain plateau.

Also in the region is the largest Iron Age site in western Norway. Some 350 Viking burial mounds can be found in Eidfjord, dating from between AD 400 and 1000.

### Hardangervidda Natursenter

⊛ ✿ 🖼 🏛 **7 km (4 miles) E of Eidfjord** **53 67 40 00** **Apr–Oct: daily; other times by prior arrangement**

→

The thundering Vøringsfossen waterfall in Eidfjord

↑ Kayaks lined up beside the Austdalsbreen glacier, in Jostedalsbreen

## ⑰
## Ulvik

**🅐B4** **🄲County of Hordaland** **🚌🚢Summer only** **🛈Tyssevikvegan 9-11; www.visitulvik.com**

The village of Ulvik sits at a softly curving bow at the inner end of a small fjord. Terraced farms rise from the fjord with their lush green fields and abundant orchards – it's almost as if the glacier made a special effort to leave a particularly rich type of soil here. A 19th-century church, the altarpiece of which dates from the Middle Ages, stands on the site of a 13th-century stave church.

The area is ideal for hiking and winter sports. About 10 km (6 miles) from Ulvik, the impressive Røykjafossen waterfall is at Osa.

## ⑱
## Voss

**🅐A4** **🄲County of Hordaland** **🚂🚌** **🛈Skulegata 14; www.visitvoss.no**

Isolated until the arrival of the railway in 1883, Voss is today the largest winter sports resort in Western Norway. It has chairlifts, ski lifts and a cable car, Hangursbanen, which rises

660 m (2,165 ft) into the mountains. The beautiful landscape attracts visitors all year round.

The resort's cultural heritage museum, **Voss Folkemuseum**, focuses on items of historical interest found in Finnesloftet, a building thought to date from around 1250. The museum incorporates the farmstead of Mølstertunet, complete with 16 well-preserved, 400-year-old buildings.

Voss Kirke (1270) is a Gothic-style church with fine interiors.

### Voss Folkemuseum

🖻🖻🖻🖻🖻 **🄲Mølsterveien 143** **🕒Jun–Aug: daily; Sep–May: Mon–Fri & Sun** **🛇Public hols** **🖳vossfolkemuseum.no**

## ⑲
## Jostedalsbreen

**🅐B3** **🄲County of Sogn and Fjordane** **🚌🛈Breheimsenteret; www.jostedal.com**

The largest glacial area in Continental Europe, Jostedalsbreen is a whopping 100 km (62 miles) long and 15 km

(9 miles) wide. Together with Jostefonn, which used to be joined to it, Jostedalsbreen covers 486 sq km (188 sq miles). Its highest point is Lodalskåpa (2,083 m/6,834 ft).

The ice cap sends fingers into the valleys below. In the 18th century a number of these glacial spurs extended so low that they destroyed cultivated fields, but they have since receded.

The starting points for glacier tours include Jostedalen (Nigardsbreen and Bergsethbreen glaciers), Stryn (Brīksdalsbreen glacier) and Fjærland (Bøyabreen and Supphellebreen glaciers).

On the innermost reaches of the Fjærlandsfjorden is **Norsk Bremuseum** (the Norwegian Glacier Museum), an award-winning "activity museum" devoted to snow, ice, glaciers, glacier hiking and climbing. A panoramic film presentation takes the viewer on a virtual glacier experience.

### Norsk Bremuseum

🖻🖻🖻🖻 **🄲Fjærland** **🕒Apr–Oct: daily; other times by prior arrangement** **🖳english.bre.museum.no**

> **The village of Ulvik sits at a softly curving bow at the inner end of a small fjord. Terraced farms rise from the fjord with their lush green fields and abundant orchards.**

## 20
# Førde and Jølster

🅐 A4 🏛 County of Sogn and Fjordane 🚆🚌
ℹ️ Langebruveien 20; 57 72 19 51 🌐 sunnfjord.no

The town of Førde lies within the district of Sunnfjord, at the heart of the county of Sogn and Fjordane. It has a cultural centre, Førdehuset, which is home to an art gallery, library, cinema and theatre. **Sunnfjord Museum**, which comprises 25 buildings from around 1850, is just outside of Førde.

East of the town, in Vassenden, there is another cultural heritage museum, **Jølstramuseet**, with houses from the 17th century. Not far away is the tranquil rural museum **Astruptunet**, where the painter Nikolai Astrup (1880–1928) once lived.

This area is renowned for its excellent fishing. The Jølstra river has a salmon ladder dating from 1871. The river flows from Jølstravatnet lake, which teems with large trout. There is also good fishing in nearby Gaularvassdraget.

### Sunnfjord Museum
🏛🎨😊🕐 📍 9 km (6 miles) E of Førde 📞 57 72 12 20 🕐 Jun–Aug: daily; Sep–May: Mon–Fri 🚫 Public hols

### Jølstramuseet
🏛🎨😊 📍 20 km (12 miles) E of Førde 📞 97 14 09 75 🕐 15 Jun–Aug: Thu–Sun; other times by arrangement

### Astruptunet
🏛🎨😊😊 📍 26 km (16 miles) E of Førde 📞 99 20 26 76 🕐 Late May–mid-Aug: daily; mid-Aug–Sep: Wed, Sat & Sun

---

## 21 🚶🎿
# Urnes Stavkirke

🅑 B4 🏛 County of Sogn and Fjordane, 17 km (11 miles) NE of Sogndal 📞 57 67 88 40 🚌🚢 🕐 May–Sep: daily

Urnes is the queen of Norway's stave churches and is also the oldest. It appears on UNESCO's list of World Heritage sites along with Røros, the Alta rock carvings and Bryggen in Bergen. Built around 1130–50, it contains beams from an 11th-century church that stood on the same site.

The most notable feature of the church is the north portal. This, too, dates from an earlier building and its carvings depict the conflict between

Urnes Stavkirke, Norway's oldest stave church

---

### Refviksanden Beach

A silvery crescent of sand arches around the water at Western Norway's loveliest beach. Head about 10 km (6 miles) outside the city of Måløy to find it, on the coast between Bergen and Ålesund.

---

good and evil in the form of animals engaged in battle with snakes. Such animal ornamentation is hence known as the "Urnes Style".

Two candlesticks on the altar in metal and enamel date from the 12th century and were made in Limoges, France.

Also situated in the district of Luster is Sogn's most beautiful stone church, Dale Kirke, built in 1250.

---

## 22
# Nordfjord

🅐 A3 🏛 County of Sogn and Fjordane 🚆 Sandane 🚌🚢 ℹ️ Stryn Tourist Information; 57 87 40 40 🌐 nordfjord.no

Nordfjord is the northernmost fjord in Sogn and Fjordane county. Measuring 110 km (68 miles) in length, it extends from Måløy in the west inland to Stryn, near the border with Eastern Norway.

The area around Stryn has been a sought-after destination since 1850, when the first English outdoor enthusiasts arrived. Opportunities abound for mountaineering, glacier hiking, skiing and fishing.

There are several glacier spurs from Jostedalsbreen, which itself is the largest glacier in mainland Europe, stretching over 486 sq km (188 sq miles). One off-shoot, Briksdalsbreen, can be reached by horse and carriage from Briksdal (tickets are available

↑ Unbroken views and a meteorological station in Vestkapp

from Stryn tourist office), while the one on Strynfjell is accessible by chairlift from Stryn Summer Ski Centre.

Loen, on Lovatnet lake, was devastated in 1905 when part of the Ramnefjellet mountain fell into the lake, causing a huge wave. It killed 63 people and destroyed many houses.

From Stryn there are two roads around Nordfjorden. The northernmost (RV15) runs along Hornindalsvatnet – Europe's deepest lake – to Nordfjordeid, a centre for the breeding and rearing of Norwegian Fjord Horses. The southernmost (RV60, E39) passes through Innvik, Utvik and Byrkjelo to Sandane. The **Nordfjord Folkemuseum** in Sandane comprises 44 historic houses, mainly from the 18th and 19th centuries. Many of the houses are furnished, with the interiors detailing lifestyles from different periods of time.

**Nordfjord Folkemuseum**
🈂️🈺️⬜️⬜️⬜️ 🏠Sandane
🕐1–4pm daily 🗓Sep–Jun: Sat; public hols 🌐nordfjord. museum.no

## 23
## Selje and Stad

🅰️A3 🏛County of Sogn and Fjordane 🚍🚌 ℹ️Selje Tourist Information; 57 85 85 00

From Måløy on the outer reaches of Nordfjorden it is not far to the Stad peninsula and Vestkapp, one of Norway's westernmost points. Here stands "Kjerringa", a 460-m-(1,509-ft-) high rock that plunges steeply into the water. Below, in Ervik, a chapel commemorates the loss of the coastal passenger ferry *St Svithun*, in World War II.

On the island of Selje are the ruins of a 12th-century Benedictine monastery. It is dedicated to St Sunniva, daughter of an Irish king, who fled east to escape betrothal to a heathen chieftain. Her party came ashore on Selje and sought refuge in a cave.

**㉔**

# Ålesund

**🅰A2 🏛Møre and Romsdal
✈🚌🛥 ℹSkateflukaia;
www.visitalesund.com**

The original centre of Ålesund was destroyed in a catastrophic fire in 1904. Fellow Europeans quickly came to the rescue with help and donations, and in just three years the town was rebuilt, almost entirely in the Art Nouveau style. For this reason, Ålesund occupies a very special place in the architectural history of Europe. It spans several islands linked by bridges. It did not receive town status until 1848, but today is an important fishing port.

The area of Borgund, now part of Ålesund, was a market town and centre of the Sunnmøre region from around 1200. From the mountain lodge, Fjellstua, there is a panoramic view over the town.

**Ålesund Museum** has one section devoted to the town and another to the Arctic. **Sunnmøre Museum** consists of 40 historic houses and boathouses, and 30 different types of fishing boats.

Southwest of Ålesund is the island of **Runde**. It is renowned for its nesting cliffs, which provide a habitat for around one million seabirds, including puffins, kittiwake pairs and the rare northern gannet. The Dutch East India vessel

↑ Colourful, Art Nouveau buildings overlooking Ålesund's waterfront

*Akerendam* went down just off the island in 1725 with a valuable cargo. Divers have since recovered a large haul of gold and silver coins from the wreck.

## Ålesund Museum

◈ 🏠Rønnebergs Gate 16 📞70 16 48 42 🕐May–Sep: daily; Oct–Dec: Tue–Fri & Sun 🚫Some public hols

## Sunnmøre Museum

◈◈◷◷ 🏠5 km (3 miles) E of town centre 📞70 16 48 70 🕐Mid-May–23 Jun: Mon–Fri & Sun; 24 Jun–Aug: daily; Sep–mid-May: Mon, Tue, Fri & Sun

## Runde

🏠30 km (19 miles) SW of town centre 🚌🛥To Fosnavåg ℹ70 01 37 90

---

**㉕**

# Molde

**🅰B2 🏛County of Møre and Romsdal ✈🚊To Åndalsnes 🚌🛥 ℹTorget 4; www.visitmolde.com**

Known as the "Town of Roses" for its rose gardens and lush vegetation, Molde is an attractive, fjord-side spot. The term "Molde Panorama" is used to describe the scenery here; from Varden it is possible to see 87 snow-covered peaks on a clear day. In July, Molde is the site of a lively jazz festival, attracting top musicians from all over the world.

**Romsdalsmuseet**, the outdoor museum of timber houses, also contains a fascinating collection of national costumes. **Fiskerimuseet** (the Fisheries Museum), on the nearby island of Hjertøya, focuses on the cultural history of the coastal population.

While on the Molde peninsula, it is worth visiting both the fishing village of Bud, which faces the infamous stretch of sea known as Hustadvika, and the intriguing marble cave of Trollkyrkja (Troll Church).

**TOP 5**

## BEACHES IN VESTLANDET

**Hoddevik & Ervik, Nordfjord**
Twin aquamarine coves, both much loved by surfers and bathers.

**Retiro, Molde**
A popular family spot, with golden sands and tranquil green water.

**Orrestranden Beach, in Sogn og Fjordane**
Norway's longest sand beach, edged by undulating farmland.

**Flåm Beach, Flåm**
The blue-green waters here demand a dip.

**Hellestø sola,**
Hellestø's sand beach is famed for a summer kite festival and pretty light.

On Eresfjorden, Mardalsfossen waterfall has the highest unbroken vertical drop in northern Europe (297 m/974 ft).

Atlanterhavsvegen, the "Atlantic Road" from Averøy towards Kristiansund, is spectacular. It passes over islets and skerries and across bridges built out in the sea.

## Romsdalsmuseet

◈◈◷◷ 🏠Per Adams Vei 4 📞71 20 24 60 🕐Jun–mid-Aug: daily

## Fiskerimuseet

◈◈ 🏠Hjertøya 🚢 📞71 20 24 60 🕐End Jun–mid-Aug: Tue–Sun

---

**㉖**

# Kristiansund

**🅰B2 🏛County of Møre and Romsdal ✈🚌🛥 ℹKongens Plass 1; www.visit kristiansund.com**

From the cairn on the island of Kirkelandet there is a

Spectacular viewpoint above the hairpin turns of Trollstigveien ↑

magnificent view over this and the two other islands that comprise Kristiansund.

The sheltered harbour gave rise to the coastal settlement of Lille-Fossen, or Fosna. In 1742, when it acquired town status, it was renamed Kristiansund. The country's biggest exporter of *klippfisk* (salted, dried cod) in the 19th century, Kristiansund was almost entirely destroyed by bombs in April 1940. The reconstruction created a new, more modern image for the town.

**Nordmøre Museum** contains a special exhibition of archaeological finds from the Fosna culture, as well as a fisheries exhibition.

North of Kristiansund is the tiny island of **Grip**, inhabited only in summer. All that remains of this former fishing community is a 15th-century stave church, in which the population took refuge from the fearsome storms.

Once accessible only by boat, today Kristiansund has an airport and road connections to the mainland.

**Tingvoll Kirke**, also known as Nordmøre Cathedral, dates from around 1200. Inside there is an exquisite altarpiece and runic inscriptions on the chancel wall.

At Tingvollfjorden the road passes Ålvundeid, where

travellers should divert their journey to visit the magnificent peaks of the Innerdalen valley. At the end of the fjord is Sunndalsøra, where the famous salmon and sea trout river Driva has its mouth.

**Nordmøre Museum**

⊛⊛⊚⊚ 🅰2 km (1 mile) N of town centre 📞71 58 70 00 🕐Mar-Nov: Mon-Fri; Dec-Feb: Tue-Fri

**Grip**

⊚ 🅰14 km (9 miles) N of Kristiansund 🚢From Kristiansund 🛈Turistinformasjonen, Kristiansund; 71 58 54 54

**Tingvoll Kirke**

⊛ 🅰55 km (32 miles) SE of Kristiansund 📞71 53 01 23 🕐May-Sep: daily (concert 5pm Sat)

**㉗**
# Åndalsnes

🅰B2 🅰County of Møre and Romsdal ➡Molde 🚆🚌 🛈Jernbanegt 1; www.visitandalsnes.com

Where the Rauma river enters Romsdalsfjorden lies the resort of Åndalsnes, terminus of the Raumabanen railway. On the eastern side of the valley is Romsdalshorn; opposite are the ragged peaks of Trolltindane, with a sheer vertical cliff to the valley floor. This is a popular mountaineering spot.

Trollstigveien (the Troll's Path) is a thrilling drive between Åndalsnes and Valldalen to the south, with 11 breathtaking hairpin bends and waterfall views en route. Each summer a ski race, Trollstigrennet, is held on the Trollstigheimen pass.

---

**ATLANTERHAVSVEGEN SCENIC ROUTE**

Among the most memorable drives in the world, the Norwegian National Scenic Route, or "Atlantic Road", seems to roll into the Norwegian Sea. This marvel of engineering unfurls along tiny islets from the mainland to the island of Averøy, and across eight bridges. The journey here is incredible in itself; striking architectural installations punctuate the route. There are snaking boardwalks and wide viewing platforms thoughtfully distributed to allow visitors space to stretch their legs and savour the scenery's impact.

# TRØNDELAG

A journey over Dovrefjell to Trøndelag was a challenge in times gone by. The route from southern to northern Norway, undertaken by kings and pilgrims of old, was arduous. Today's roads and railway lines make this an easy trip. Most of those crossing Dovrefjell would have been heading for the city of Trondheim, or Nidaros as it was known originally. Throughout history, Trondheim has been the capital of central Norway; for a time it was the first capital of the kingdom and its cathedral, Nidarosdomen, was a focal point for pilgrimage in Scandinavia. The natural landscape in Trøndelag is coniferous, with deciduous forests tailing off into scraggy mountain woodland in the fells. The mountainous regions of Børgefjell, Sylene, Rørosvidda, Dovrefjell and the spectacular Trollheimen have much of interest in the way of outdoor activities, and many of the rivers offer excellent salmon-fishing. The offshore islands, particularly the archipelago of Vikna, are easily accessible, and bird-watching and sea fishing are among the attractions here.

# TRØNDELAG

**Must Sees**

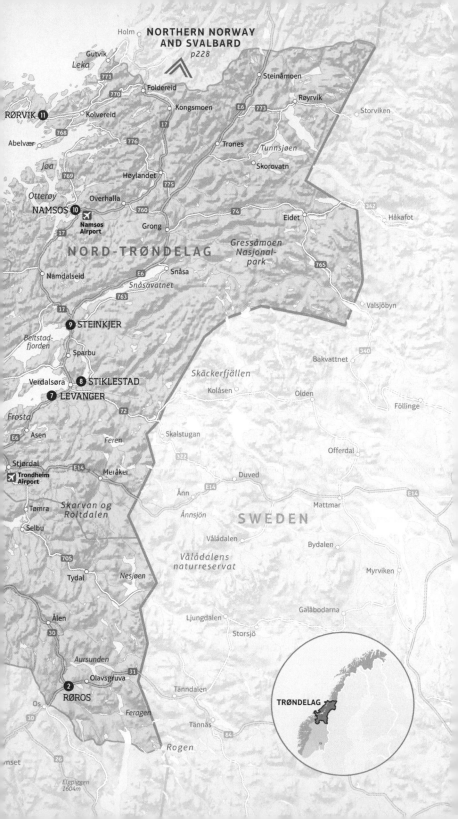

**❶**

# TRONDHEIM

🅰C1 🏛County of Sør-Trøndelag ✈Vaernes, 50 km
(31 miles) E of town centre 🚆Brattøra 🚌Brattøra 🚢Pier 2
ℹ Nordre Gate 11; www.visittrondheim.no

At the mouth of the Nidelva river, Trondheim – or
Nidaros as it was known – was once the capital of
Norway. History is woven into every beam in Trondheim.
This is where King Olav Haraldsson was canonized in
1031, and where fire and war raged in the 17th century.
Today, Trondheim's historic sights can be found along-
side a stylish, urban shopping and dining scene to rival
any of Norway's larger cities.

## ① Bakklandet

🏠1 km (half a mile) E of
city centre

East of the Nidelva river lies
Bakklandet, a charming
quarter with narrow, winding
streets dating back to 1650.
The area originally belonged
to a nunnery. From 1691 it was
owned by Jan Wessel, the
father of the maritime hero
Tordenskiold, who ran a public
house here. The Bakke estate
was burned down by the
Swedes in 1658, and again in
1718 when General Armfeldt
tried to storm the town. It was
quickly rebuilt, with dwellings
for sailors, fishermen and
craftsmen, which have now
been restored.

From the city centre,
Bakklandet can be reached
using the Old Town Bridge,
Gamle Bybro, which acquired
its carved gates in 1861.
High above Bakklandet is
the fortress of Kristiansten,
built by Johan Caspar de
Cicignon in 1682.

## ② Bryggen

🏠Øvre Elvehavn

The warehouses and wharves
at the mouth of the Nidelva
river have been the focus of
Trondheim's business and
trading since early times. As
in many cities, these wooden,
waterside buildings have been
ravaged by fire on various
occasions. Now fully restored,
these colourful buildings
line both sides of the river.
On the city centre side, in
Kjøpmannsgata, they are
based in a terraced area
from where it was possible
to attack the enemy on the
river with cannon fire. On
the Bakklandet side of the
river, the buildings are
situated in the streets of
Fjordgata and Sandgata. The
oldest remaining wharf
dates from around 1700.

## ③ Gammle Bybro

The beautiful Old Town
Bridge dates back to 1861,
though there's been a bridge
at this spot since 1681. The
pedestrianized bridge
connects the city with the
Kristiansten fortress, and is

↑ Attractive Gammle
Bybro, crossing the Nid

←

Beautiful buildings of Bryggen, reflected in the waters of the Nidelva

## Nordenfjeldske Kunstindustri-museum

⊕ Munkegaten 5 ⊕ Jun-Aug: daily; Sep-May: Tue-Sun ⊕ Some public hols ⊕ nkim.no

Next to the cathedral is the red-brick Kunstindustri-museum, or the Museum of Decorative Arts, which houses a collection comprising furniture, silver and textiles. In a section titled Three Women, Three Artists, works by the tapestry artists Hannah Ryggen and Synnøve Anker, and the glass designer Benny Motzfeld, are on show.

### SCANDI STYLE

Scandi fashion and interiors are sought after across the globe, thanks to their sleek designs and quality materials, and shoppers are spoiled for choice in Trondheim. Olav Tryggvasons Gate is a good starting point. At No 19, Livid Jeans sells quality, hand-crafted trousers (www.livid jeans.com). Up the road, at No 10, Ting is a one-stop-shop for Scandi homewares (www. ting.no), and Småting, at No 6, designs toys and clothing for kids (www.smaating.no). This is just scratching the surface; woollen accessories, ceramics, books, souvenirs and much more await here.

the best way to both access and photograph picturesque Bakklandet. Gamle Bybro is also sometimes referred to as the Lykkens portal, which means "Gate of Happiness", and is regarded by locals as a landmark of the city.

---

## Trondheim Kunstmuseum

⊕ Bispegaten ⊕ Jun-Aug: 10am-4pm daily; Sep-May: Wed-Sun ⊕ trondheim kunstmuseum.no

Trondheim Kunstmuseum (Museum of Art) is conveniently located close to Nidaros Cathedral and the Archbishop's Residence. It contains a fine collection of paintings dating back to its precursor, the Trondheim Art Society, founded in 1845.

The most important works in the gallery are Norwegian paintings from the beginning of the 19th century until today, ranging from the Düsseldorf School to the Modernists. There is also a collection of Danish paintings that would be hard to rival outside Denmark, and an international collection of graphic art. The gallery is further known for its excellent programme of temporary exhibitions.

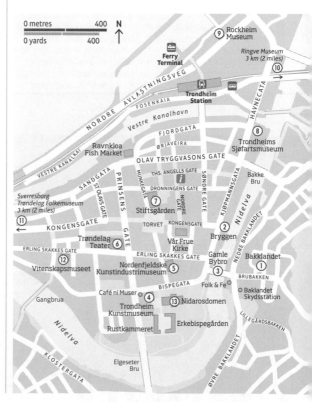

## ⑥ 🍴
### Trøndelag Teater

📍 Prinsens Gate 22
🕐 For performances
🌐 trondelag-teater.no

The splendid Trøndelag Teater complex was completed in 1997. It comprises five separate stages, with seating for between 50 and 500 people in each auditorium, and offers a broad repertoire. Incorporated into the theatre is the main stage from the original theatre, constructed in 1816.

## ⑦ 🎟️ 📷 🛍️
### Stiftsgården

📍 Munkegaten 23
🕐 Jun–Aug: daily (guided tours only)
🔒 For royal visits
🌐 nkim.no

Royal residence Stiftsgården is one of the most imposing old timber mansions in Trondheim and an important example of Norwegian wooden architecture. Designed by General G F von Krogh and completed in 1778, it is Rococo style, with Baroque details.

The original owner was Cecilie Christine de Schøller, widow of the privy councillor.

Connected to the royal court in Copenhagen, she was keen to build a mansion in her attempt to become the "first lady" of Trondheim.

The building is 58 m (190 ft) long with 64 rooms. It was named "Stiftsgården" when it was bought by the government in 1800 as a residence for the chief officer of the diocese, the Stiftsamtmannen. It became a royal residence in 1906. The dining room, with paintings of London and Venice by J C C Michaelsen, is especially worth a look.

## ⑧ 🎟️ 🛍️
### Trondheims Sjøfartsmuseum

📍 Kjøpmannsgata 75
🕐 Jun–Aug: 9am–2pm Mon–Fri, noon–4pm Sat & Sun; Sep–May: 9am–2pm Tue–Fri, noon–4pm Sun
🌐 trondheimsjofart.no

Trondheim Maritime Museum is housed in a prison building dating from 1725. It has a comprehensive collection of sailing ship models, figureheads and artifacts relating to maritime life in Trøndelag from the beginning of the 16th century.

## ⑨ 🎟️ 🍴 🛍️
### Rockheim Museum

📍 Brattørkaia 14
🕐 10am–4pm Tue–Fri (to 8pm Thu), 10am–5pm Sat & Sun
🔒 1, 17 & 15 Nov, 1, 22–26 & 31 Dec
🌐 rockheim.no

Since opening in 2010, the National Museum of Popular Music has become, befittingly, a popular fixture in Trondheim. The state-of-the-art attraction is based in a former grain warehouse and tracks the country's history of pop and rock music from the 1950s to the present day.

Visitors start in the cantilevered 'Top Box', which is decorated with album covers, and work their way down as they progress through the eras. Highlights include the Time Tunnel, where interactive exhibits allow visitors to experience Norwegian music, and the Rockheim Hall of Fame, which honours standout musical stars from Norwegian rock history.

### Did You Know?

Norway's Viking kings were crowned at Oretinget, an assembly hall in Trondheim by the Nidelva River.

⑩ 🖊️ 🎵 🖥️ 🛍️

## Ringve Museum

📍 Lade Allé 60, 4 km
(2 miles) NE of city centre
🕐 18 May-15 Sep: daily;
16 Sep-17 May: Sun
🌐 ringve.no

A brilliant contrast to the Rockheim Museum, Ringve is Norway's national museum for music and musical instruments. It was opened in 1952, after Victoria and Christian Anker Bachke had bequeathed their country estate and collection of musical instruments to become a museum. The instruments had previously been owned by Jan Wessel, father of the maritime hero Peter Wessel Tordenskiold, after whom the museum café, Tordenskiolds Kro, is named. The exhibition takes visitors through musical history, presenting its masters and instruments to the accompaniment of music from each period.

The Botanical Gardens of Ringve, surrounding the mansion, are stocked with 2,000 species of plants and trees.

⑪ 🖊️ 🎵 🖥️ 🛍️

## Sverresborg Trøndelag Folkemuseum

📍 Sverresborg Allé, 4 km
(2 miles) S of city centre
🕐 Daily 🕐 Public hols
🌐 sverresborg.no

Featuring more than 60 buildings from Trondheim and around, Trøndelag Folkemuseum gives a unique insight into the building traditions and daily life of the region. The museum is located next to the medieval fortress of King Sverre, with a splendid view over the city. The 18th- and 19th-century

← 

The exterior of the Rockheim Museum, where old architecture meets new

↑ Cans and bottles on display at Sverresborg Trøndelag Folkemuseum

Gammelbyen (Old Town) has been recreated with a dentist's surgery, a grocery store and a shop selling old-fashioned sweets. Look out for Vikastua, a cottage from Oppdal with an exceptional rose-painted interior. The stave church, originating from Haltdalen, dates from 1170.

⑫ 🖊️

## Vitenskapsmuseet

📍 Erling Skakkes Gate 47
🕐 Daily 🌐 ntnu.no

The rich collections of the Museum of Natural History and Archaeology are housed in three separate buildings, named after the founders of the Royal Society of Norwegian Science (1706). The Gerhard Schøning building traces Norway's ecclesiastical history and exhibits church interiors and religious art. The Peter Frederik Suhms building focuses on the Middle Ages. The Johan Ernst Gunnerus branch contains departments of zoology and mineralogy. Special displays include "From the Stone Age to the Vikings" and "The Culture of the Southern Sami".

Don't miss the ancient Kuli stone, which is carved with a crucifix and runic inscriptions, showing Norway's transition from paganism to Christianity.

# EAT

**Baklandet Skydsstation**
Set in an 18th-century coaching inn, this vintage-inspired restaurant is homely, and serves hearty Norwegian staples.

📍 33 Øvre Bakklandet
🌐 skydsstation.no

Ⓚ Ⓚ Ⓚ

–––––––––

**Folk & Fe**
A modern bistro based in Bakklandet, with a cosy – or *koselig* – interior. Norwegian fare includes foraged ingredients.

📍 66 Øvre Bakklandet
🕐 Mon, Tue L, Wed L
🌐 folkogfe-bistro.no

Ⓚ Ⓚ Ⓚ

–––––––––

**Café ni Muser**
This museum café does affordable and quality light bites, such as antipasti and *smørbrød*.

📍 Trondheim Kunstmuseum, Bispegaten
🌐 nimuser.no

Ⓚ Ⓚ Ⓚ

⑬ Ⓜ Ⓨ Ⓐ

# NIDAROSDOMEN

Ⓐ Pier 2, Bispegata 11 Ⓒ May: 9am-3pm Mon-Fri (to 2pm Sat), 1-4pm Sun; Jun-Aug: 9am-6pm Mon-Fri (to 2pm Sat), 1-5pm Sun; Sep-Apr: 9am-2pm Mon-Sat, 9am-2pm Sun Ⓦ nidarosdomen.no

**Scandinavia's greatest medieval building has attracted pilgrims for centuries. The cathedral is dedicated to St Olav, a Viking king who ended paganism in Norway and officially introduced Christianity to the masses.**

Built on the site of Kristkirken, over the grave of Olav the Holy – the patron saint of Norway – the oldest part of Nidaros Cathedral dates from around 1320 in Norman, Romanesque and Gothic styles. The cathedral is the largest medieval construction in Norway, at 102 m (335 ft) long and 50 m (164 ft) wide. Several fires have ravaged it over time and restoration began in 1869. A Gothic reconstruction has now been completed. One of the chapels houses the Norwegian crown jewels, including the crowns of the king and queen.

### OLAV HARALDSSON

Olav Haraldsson was born in Ringerike in AD 995. Son of Åsta Gudbrandsdatter and Harald Grenske, he was a direct descendant of Harald Fair-Hair, the first king of Norway (p49), a title that Olav would gain in 1016. Olav saw it as his duty to unite his homeland of Norway, much like ancestor Harald Fairhair. Little did he know that he would become the patron saint of Norway (p226).

*Northern transept, from the 12th century in Romanesque style*

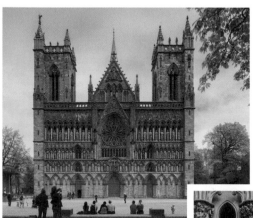

↑ The impressive Gothic façade of Nidaros Cathedral

→ Intricately carved figures line the West Front of the cathedral

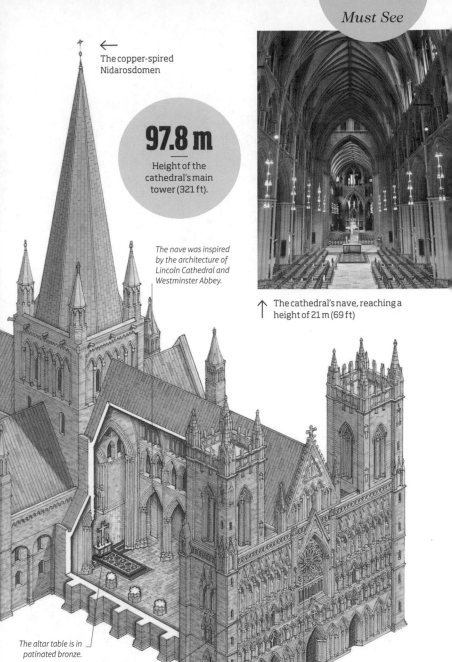

← The copper-spired Nidarosdomen

## 97.8 m

Height of the cathedral's main tower (321 ft).

*The nave was inspired by the architecture of Lincoln Cathedral and Westminster Abbey.*

↑ The cathedral's nave, reaching a height of 21 m (69 ft)

*The altar table is in patinated bronze.*

*West Front. The middle row of sculptures on the ornate west wall shows, from left to right, the Norwegian saints Archbishop Øystein, St Hallvard, St Sunniva and St Olav (Olav the Holy), and the heavenly virtue: Love.*

*Gabriel Kielland created many of the cathedral's beautiful Chartres-inspired stained-glass works, including the magnificent rose window.*

↑ Timber buildings, synonymous with the town of Røros

**2** 🖼🖼🖼🖼

# RØROS

🅰D2 🏛County of Sør-Trøndelag 🚉🚌🚌 🈺Peder Hiorts Gate 2; www.roros.no

Rows of perfectly preserved, colourful houses curve along the snowy hillside in Norway's best-kept secret – Røros. Founded in 1646, the town developed along the Hitterelva river as an agricultural and copper-mining community until mining finally ceased in 1977. Its turf-roofed and wooden cottages survived the fires that ravaged many of Norway's other timber towns, leading to Røros being named a UNESCO World Heritage site. During the cold winter months it's not unusual to see locals zipping through the central snowy streets with kick sleds; you can even rent one for yourself from the tourist office.

**①** 🖼🖼

### Smelthytta

🏛Lorentz Lossius Gata 45 🕐From 10am daily; closing times vary, check website 🌐rorosmuseet.no

Literally "melting hut", this historic building conveys copper mining as a way of life. The museum focuses on the 17th to 19th centuries when mining was prevalent in Røros. Exhibits use detailed, miniature scale models to give insight into the changing methods of extracting ore, modes of transport in the mines and smelting processes. Smelting demonstrations are held in summer.

Those wanting a more authentic experience can join a tour at **Olavsgruva**, a short drive outside of Røros. Journey 50 m (164 ft) below ground and into a mine, used from 1650 to 1972.

### Olavsgruva

🖼🖼 🏛P.b 224 🕐Tours: mid-Sep–May: 3pm Thu & Sat 🌐rorosmuseet.no

**②**

### Flanderborg Gate

The loveliest collection of centuries-old painted houses can be found on the opposite side of the river Hitterelva from Røros Church. These pretty wooden dwellings are famous for their intricately carved and painted doors.

The turf-roof cottages along adjoining 'Sleggveien' provide an insight into the social history of this mining community. The five humble houses at the top of the road were home to local craftsmen and those with little income. Sleggveien is also referred to as 'Pippi's Street' because an episode of *Pippi Long Stocking* (1969) was filmed here.

↑ An attractive wooden door, in typical Røros style

③ ⊛ ⊛ ⊡

### Røros Kirke

⬛ Kjerkgata 39 ⬛ Jun-Aug: 10am-4pm Mon-Sat, 12:30-2:30pm Sun; Sep-May: 11am-1pm Sat
🌐 roroskirke.no

The locals built this Baroque church in 1784 when the copper mining industry was booming. It's one of Norway's largest churches, with room for 1600 worshippers. The 1742 organ is the oldest Norwegian-made organ still functioning.

---

④

### Bergmannsgata and Kjerkgata

Bergmannsgata, known locally as "Storgata" or "Big Street", is the main artery in Røros, along with parallel Kjerkgata. Several stately mansions line the way, such as Rasmusgården and Bekholdgården.

---

⑤

### Slegghaugan

These somewhat unsightly slag heaps are reminders of the huge impact of large-scale mining in Røros, and are listed on the UNESCO World Heritage list as such.

---

⑥

### Harald Sohlbergs Plass 59

⬛ Top of Kjerkgata
🚫 To the public

Norwegian landscape painter Harald Oskar Sohlberg (1869–1935) moved to Røros in 1902 and lived in this quaint, turf-roof and timber house. He used Røros as a regular motif in his paintings of Norway, including *Night* and *Storgaten Røros*, which were shown during the 1906 autumn exhibition in Oslo. His most famous work is the popular *Winter Night in Rondane*, owned by the National Museum in Oslo (*p70*).

---

# EAT

### Vertshuset Inn

This historic inn serves a delightful six-course tasting menu that utilises local produce. Rammkjelleren - their basement brewery - is a further incentive and offers tastings.

⬛ Kjerkgata 34
🌐 vertshusetroros.no

Ⓚ Ⓚ Ⓚ

---

### Skanckebua

Gastro-pub based in Bergstadens Hotel and serving casual fare such as burgers and tacos. On the floor below, sister restaurant Smørkjelleren is known for refined Scandi cuisine. Expect a cosy interior and a friendly atmosphere.

⬛ Kjerkgata 28
🌐 bergstadenshotel.no

Ⓚ Ⓚ Ⓚ

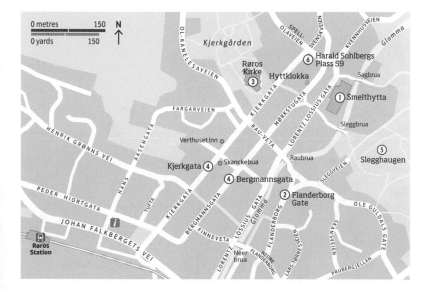

# EXPERIENCE MORE

**3**

## Oppdal

🅐C2 🄰County of
Sør-Trøndelag 🚆🚌
🛈O Skasliens Vei 15;
72 40 04 70

Oppdal is a vibrant tourist centre all year round, but particularly in winter.

Its excellent winter sports facilities include 200 km (124 miles) of ski slopes, a cable car and ski lifts, ski huts, cafés and restaurants. The skiing season starts with the Vintersleppet festival, while the off-piste Free-ride Challenge race attracts daring skiers around Easter.

The town occupies a beautiful mountain setting. It is an important junction on the Dovrebanen railway and has good road connections.

**Oppdalsmuseet**, an open-air museum, has a fine collection of old houses of cultural interest. Outside the town, at Vang, there is a large Iron Age burial ground.

Oppdal is the starting point for the journey northwards to Vårstigen (the Spring Path), the old pilgrims' route, through Drivdalen valley and to Dovrefjell National Park *(p160)*.

From Festa bridge in the west, the toll road heads north to Gjevilvasshytta, a tourist lodge incorporating Tingstua, the old courthouse from Meldal.

### Oppdalsmuseet

🕙🄰🄰Museumsveien 11
🄲41 51 15 09 🄳End Jun–mid-Aug: Thu, Fri & Sun
🅦oppdalsmuseet.no

---

**4**

## Austrått

🅐C1 🄰Opphaug 🄲72 51
40 36 🚌🚌To Berkstad

This beautiful white Viking-era manor house is among the best-preserved medieval attractions in Norway. It is situated in the fertile Ørdlandet region on the Fosen peninsula. While the pastoral farm, coastal scenery and on-site cafe, Borgstua, create an alluring day trip, the history here is also fascinating.

The manor's most famous resident was one of Norway's most powerful women: Ingerd

**INSIDER TIP**
**Dive In**

It might be colder than the south, but the coast north of Trondheim makes for great diving, with shipwrecks and rich biodiversity lying in wait. Visit Deeper Blue for advice *(www. deeperblue.com)*.

Ottesdatter Rømer (1475–1555), who played a key role in the country's Protestant Reformation. At one point Rømer owned a sixth of the land in Norway, and Ibsen based his protagonist in *Lady Inger of Osteråt* (1854) on her.

Also worth a visit is the exquisite manor chapel, which dates from the 12th century and features seven medieval wooden sculptures.

---

**5**

## Munkholmen

🅐C1 🄰Ravnkloa 🚌

Tiny Monk's Island has a storied past. The Vikings used

↑ Turf-roofed houses at the open-air museum in Oppdal

→

Blue waters and a replica Viking boat off the island of Hitra

it for executions, displaying the heads of transgressors on poles. Benedictine monks – after whom the island is named – founded Norway's first monastery here, in around AD 1000. In the 17th century, the island was used as a fort. During World War II it was taken over by the Germans, and an anti-aircraft artillery gun can be viewed as a reminder of their stay.

Today Munkholmen is a picnic spot for Trondheim residents, with a beach and a café. From May to September, ferries for the island leave hourly from Ravnkloa Fish Market. The island lies where the mouth of the Nidelva river meets Tronsheimsfjord. In terms of access via ferry, visitors can choose between a scenic Nidelva tour culminating at Munkholmen, or a direct service to the island.

### Hitra and Frøya

**Ⓐ C1** **Ⓐ Fillan** **📞 72 44 40 10**

The bucolic Hitra and neighbouring Frøya archipelago consist of some 5,400 islands, islets and reefs lying northwest of the entrance to Trondheimsfjorden. Frøya is connected to the mainland by an underwater tunnel. Once out on Frøya, a network of local ferries and bridges connect the islands, where you can visit ancient fishing villages with traditional *rorbu* (red fishermen's cottages) and savour local specialities such as scallops and salmon. The islands are renowned for being a world-class destination for deep-sea fishing. Most visitors on fishing excursions hook cod, coalfish and haddock. Sea kayaking in the midnight sun is another

popular activity here. Also of note is the red-and-white striped Slettringen lighthouse on Frøya's western coast, which is the tallest lighthouse in Norway.

---

### ❼ Levanger

**Ⓐ D1** **Ⓐ County of Nord-Trøndelag** **✈ Værnes, 50 km (31 miles) SW of Levanger** **🚉📨** **ℹ Levanger; www. levanger.kommune.no**

In inner Trondheimsfjorden is Levanger, which is the site of Iron Age rock carvings, burial mounds and graves. South of here, near Ekne, is the **Falstad Fangeleir**, a former World War II concentration camp.

Out in the fjord is the picturesque island of Ytterøy, a popular holiday spot. Beyond this, the Indreøy peninsula almost blocks the fjord before its end at Steinkjer *(p226)*. Strauma on Inderøy is an idyllic timber-housed hamlet.

#### Falstad Fangeleir
🈯🈂 **Ⓐ 20 km (12 miles) S of Levanger** **📞 74 02 80 40** **🕐 Tue–Fri & Sun**

---

# EAT & DRINK

#### Øyna
Among the stops along Inderøy's picturesque peninsula, Øyna shines. With talented chefs working alongside an impressive list of local suppliers, you can truly taste the distinctive fjord landscape.

**Ⓐ D1** **Ⓐ Øynavegen 60, 7670 Inderøy** **🌐 oyna.no**

🈁🈁🈁

#### Inderøy Gårdsbryggeri
This brewery is among the success stories of Norway's recent craft beer boom. There is a bottle shop, beer tastings and an impressive live music line-up.

**Ⓐ D1** **Ⓐ Kvamshaugan 46, Inderøy** **🌐 igb.no**

## 8 Stiklestad

🅐D1 🅠County of Nord-Trøndelag, 4 km (2 miles) E of Verdal town centre
🅡To Verdal 🚌During Olsok feast 🌐stiklestad.no

Stiklestad is one of the most famous places in Norwegian history. It was at a battle here in 1030 that King Olav Haraldsson, later St Olav, was killed. The site is marked by the **Stiklestad Nasjonale Kultursenter** (National Cultural Centre). The St Olav Monument is, according to legend, situated exactly where the body of the king was hidden in a shed the night after the battle. His remains were later buried in Nidaros (now Trondheim) (*p216*).

Every year, around the time of the St Olav celebrations of *Olsok* (29 July), the play *Spelet om Heilag Olav (The Story of St Olav)*, by Olav Gullvåg and Paul Okkenhaug, is performed at the amphitheatre in Stiklestad, which is crowned by a statue depicting Olav the Holy on his horse.

The altarpiece in Stiklestad Kirke – erected on the site of the battle – is said to have been built above the stone against which Olav the Holy died. Tableaux in the church date from the 17th century. The frescoes in the choir are by Alf Rolfsen, and were commissioned for the church's restoration for the St Olav Jubilee in 1928.

**Verdal Museum**, near the church, features a typical 19th-century farm from Verdal among its exhibits.

### Stiklestad Nasjonale Kultursenter

🚳🍷🕐 🅐4 km (2 miles) E of Verdal town centre 🅲74 04 42 00 🕐Daily 🔒Some public hols

### Verdal Museum

🏛️🕐 🅐1 km (2 miles) E of Verdal town centre 🅲74 04 42 00 🕐10 Jun–10 Aug: daily

### ST OLAV AND THE BATTLE OF STIKLESTAD

Olav Haraldsson was declared king of a united Norway in 1016. He went on to convert the entire country to Christianity – and in so doing made many enemies, who feared he would become too powerful. Instead, they gave their support to King Canute of Denmark. In 1028, Canute sent an army to invade Norway, and Olav was forced to flee. He returned in 1030 to re-conquer his realm. Olav was killed in a battle against Canute's forces at Stiklestad, on 29 July 1030. A year later, his undecayed body was exhumed and he was declared a saint. Olav's body was finally laid to rest in Kristkirken, and the site became a place of pilgrimage.

## 9 Steinkjer

🅐D1 🅠County of Nord-Trøndelag 🚉🚌 🅸Sjøfartsgata 2a; 74 40 17 16

Archaeological finds indicate that there has been human settlement in the Steinkjer area for 8,000 years. Burial mounds, stone circles and memorial stones have been discovered at Eggekvammen, Tingvoll and Egge, near the Byafossen waterfall. There are petroglyphs from the Stone Age and Bronze Age near Bardal, and there is also a large area of rock carvings near Hammer, 13 km (8 miles) west of Steinkjer town centre. Other finds indicate that there was an important trade and shipping centre at the head of Beitstadfjorden. Snorre writes in his sagas that Olav Tryggvason established a market town here in 997.

On the hill of Mærehaugen stands Steinkjer church. Before the introduction of Christianity there was a temple to the Norse gods here, and indeed this is the third church to stand on the site. The first, which dated from 1150, burned down; the second was destroyed during a bombing raid in 1940. The present church was designed by Olav Platou in 1965 and is richly decorated by artists including Sivert Donali and Jakob Weidemann.

Steinkjer has good transport and communication links. The Nordlandsbanen train line and the E6 pass through the town, and the RV17 leads to the coastal areas of Flatanger and Osen. On the eastern side of Snåsavatnet lake stands Bølareien, a 6,000-year-old life-size rock carving of a reindeer.

Snåsa is the starting point for trips to Gressåmoen – once a national park in its own right, but now incorporated into the sprawling Blåfjella-Skjækerfjella National Park. The Snåsaheiene hills, noted for their excellent fishing, can also be reached from Snåsa. In the town, **Samien Sitje** is a museum devoted to the southern Sami culture.

### Samien Sitje

🚳🍷🕐 🅐58 km (36 miles) NE of Steinkjer 🅲74 13 80 00 🕐20 Jun–20 Aug: daily; 21 Aug–19 Jun: by prior arrangement

→

Cheerful red-and-white fishing boats moored in the coastal town of Rørvik

**10**

# Namsos

**⚑F7 ⬡County of Nord-Trøndelag** 🚆🚌🚗
**ℹ Dampskipskaia; 73 84 24 40**

Namsos is situated at the innermost tip of the 35-km- (22-mile-) long Namsenfjorden, inside the islands of Otterøy and Jøa, which were featured in the novels of Olav Duun (1876–1939). The town was established in 1845 as a shipping port, particularly for timber. It was twice destroyed by fire, and was razed to the ground by bombs during World War II, but has since been rebuilt.

The Namsen river, the longest in the county of Trøndelag, enters the sea here. It is one of Norway's best salmon rivers, with popular fishing areas including Sellæg, Grong and Overhalla. Fishing is primarily done from boats known as *harling*, but it is also possible to fish from the bank. The Fiskumfossen waterfall, north of Grong, has the longest set of salmon steps in northern Europe, at 291 m (955 ft).

The **Namsskogan Familiepark** in Trones is a nature park where Nordic animals live in their natural environment. Further north, a side road leads to Røyrvik, the starting point for a boat connection to the Børgefjell National Park.

## Namsskogan Familiepark

🎟️🚻🍴☕ ⬡70 km (43 miles) N of Namsos 🚌From Namsos 📞74 33 37 00 🕐Jun–Aug: daily

---

**11**

# Rørvik

**⚑E7 ⬡County of Nord-Trøndelag** 🚌🚗 **ℹ Vikna; 74 36 16 70**

North of Namsos is the archipelago of Vikna, which comprises nearly 6,000 islands. Rørvik, a tiny coastal town that buzzes with life, is Vikna's main administrative centre. Rørvik's coastal museum, the **Nord-Trøndelags Kystmuseum**, is an architecturally stunning building that resembles an enormous sailing ship. Inside, exhibits take visitors through 10,000 years of the region's sailing and fishing history. The in-house seafood restaurant is a fine-dining destination.

A large part of outer Vikna is a conservation area, and an abundance of nesting birds, as well as otters, porpoises and several species of seal, can be found here.

North of Vikna, the mountain of Lekamøya rises from the sea. *Leka-møya* (the Leka Virgin) is the principal character in a Nordland folk tale. The main attractions on Leka are cave paintings in Solsemhulen, Herlagshaugen burial mound and a museum of cultural history, **Leka Bygdemuseum**.

## Nord-Trøndelags Kystmuseum

🎟️🚻🍴☕ ⬡Strandgata 7 📞48 88 00 24 🕐Daily

## Leka Bygdemuseum

🎟️🚻 ⬡1 km (half a mile) N of Leka 📞74 38 70 11 🕐Jul: daily

# NORTHERN NORWAY AND SVALBARD

The author Knut Hamsun described Northern Norway as "the land hidden behind a hundred miles". Other writers have called it "the land of excitement" or "the land of the high flames". These expressions capture the essence of this northern land – the great distances, the rugged scenery, the dancing Northern Lights of winter and the midnight sun that shines day and night in summer. Northern Norway consists of three counties – Nordland, Troms and Finnmark – which cover about a third of the country, and comprise some of the country's harshest environments. Inland, the national parks are the habitat of bears and wolves, while out at sea, birds flock to the steep nesting cliffs. The mountains of Lofoten rise like a wall from a sea of islets to the northwest; here fishing has been the islanders' lifeblood for centuries. Further north is Tromsø, the "Paris of the North", which marks the start of Norway's most severe terrain. Lying 640 km (400 miles) north of the mainland are the Arctic Ocean islands of Svalbard, almost 60 per cent covered in glaciers.

**Arctic
Ocean**

*Arnøya*

*Ringvassøya*

**Tromsø Airport** ✈
**TROMSØ** ❸  Lyngseidet

Fagernes

**SENJA**  **T R O M S**
❿

*Andøya*  Andenes  Finnsnes  Øvergård

*VESTERÅLEN*  Risøyhamn  Andselv
Nykvåg  ❷  Setermoen  ❽⁷
*Langøya*  Sortland  Harstad
Stokmarknes  *Hinnøya*  Bjerkvik  Innset
**Evenes Airport** ✈  E6
**LOFOTEN**  Lødingen  **NARVIK** ❾  E10
Vestvågøya ❶  E10
Leknes  Svolvær  Ballangen  *Abisko*
Stamsund  Bognes  *Storriten*
*Moskenesøya*  *1503m*
Å  Skutvik  *Nikkaluokta*  *Kiruna*
*Værøy*  *Vestfjorden*  Nordfold  E10
*Røst*  Bonåsjøen  *Ritsem*
Kjerringøy  *Vietas*
**BODØ**
**Bodø Airport** ✈ ❽  80  Fauske  *Kvikkjokk*  *Porjus*
Saltstraumen  830  Sulitjelma
17  Rognan
Ørnes  Røkland  *Kvikkjokk*  *Jokkmokk*
*N O R D L A N D*
*Snøtinden*  *Jäkkvik*
*Hestemona*  *1594m* ❻ **SALTFJELLET-SVARTISEN**  **S W E D E N**
*Lovunden*  **NATIONAL PARK**
17  Storforshei
❺  ❼ **MO I RANA**  *Kåbdalis*
Sandnessjøen  E6  95
*Alsten*  Korgen  *Arjeplog*
*Vega*  *Oksskolten*  E45
*1916m*  *Hemavan*
Mosjøen  *Røssvotnet*
Brønnøysund  Trofors  Hattfjelldal  *Arvidsjaur*
*Leka*  17  76  *Ajaureforsen*  *Sorsele*  E12  E45
E6
Kongsmoen  **V**
**TRØNDELAG**
*p212*

0 kilometres 60
0 miles 60  N ↑

---

**Svalbard inset:**

❹ **SVALBARD**

*Kvitøya*

*Nordaust-
Landet*

*Perriertoppen
1717m*  *Kongsøya*

*Spitsbergen*

*Prins Karls
Forland*  *Barentsøya*
✈ Longyearbyen
**Svalbard
Airport**  *Edgeøya*

0 km        100
0 miles     100    N ↑

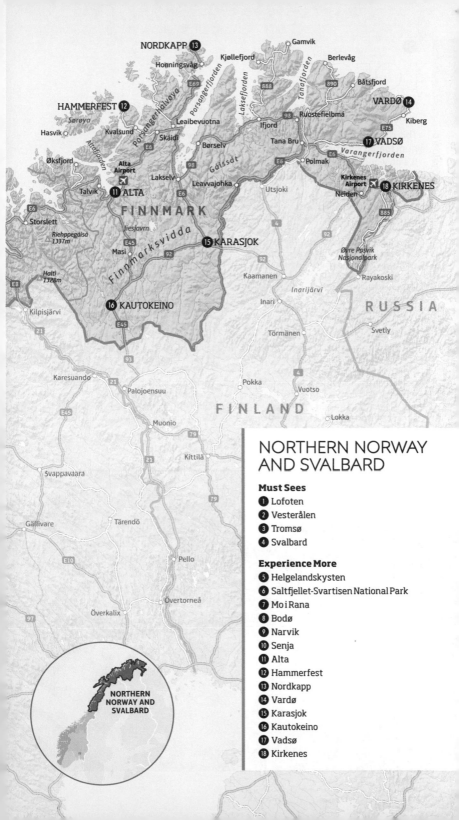

NORDKAPP 13
Honningsvåg
Gamvik
Kjøllefjord
Berlevåg
888
Båtsfjord
890
HAMMERFEST 12
Sørøya
Leaibevuotna
Porsangerfjorden
Lakselfjorden
E69
Tanafjorden
VARDØ 14
98
Ruostefielbmá
Kiberg
E75
Hasvik
Kvalsund
Skáidi
E6
Børselv
Ifjord
Tana Bru
17 VADSØ
Varangerfjorden
Øksfjord
Alta
Airport ✈
Lakselv
Leavvajohka
Polmak
E6
Galssát
Talvik
11 ALTA
E6
FINNMARK
Utsjoki
Kirkenes
Airport ✈
18 KIRKENES
Neiden
885
Storslett
E6
Riehppegáisá
1337m
Jiesjavrn
Finnmarksvidda
Masi
92
15 KARASJOK
Kaamanen
92
Øvre Pasvik
Nasjonalpark
Rayakoski
Halti
1328m
E8
16 KAUTOKEINO
E45
Inari
Inarijärvi
RUSSIA
Kilpisjärvi
21
93
Kaamanen
Törmänen
Svetly
Karesuando
21
Palojoensuu
Pokka
4
Vuotso
FINLAND
Lokka
E45
Muonio
79
Kittilä
21
Svappavaara
79
Gällivare
Tärendö
E10
Pello
Svappavaara
97
Övertorneå
Överkalix

## NORTHERN NORWAY
## AND SVALBARD

### Must Sees
**1** Lofoten
**2** Vesterålen
**3** Tromsø
**4** Svalbard

### Experience More
**5** Helgelandskysten
**6** Saltfjellet-Svartisen National Park
**7** Mo i Rana
**8** Bodø
**9** Narvik
**10** Senja
**11** Alta
**12** Hammerfest
**13** Nordkapp
**14** Vardø
**15** Karasjok
**16** Kautokeino
**17** Vadsø
**18** Kirkenes

NORTHERN
NORWAY AND
SVALBARD

# LOFOTEN

**△E5** **🏠Counties of Nordland** **✈Leknes, Svolvær** 🚌🚢 **ℹTorget 18, 8300 Svolvær; 76 07 05 75** **🌐lofoten.info**

This is the Norway of popular imagination: craggy headlands punctuated with fishing villages, famed for their idyllic red cabins. It's no wonder that Lofoten, comprising six large and many smaller islands, has long attracted artists and travellers alike.

Viewed from Vestfjorden, north of Bodø, the mighty mountains of the Lofoten Islands rise up like a wall in the sea, staggeringly beautiful. Corries, hollows and sharp peaks create an exciting backdrop to the fjords, moorlands and farms, small towns and fishing villages. The island of Moskenesøya is southernmost of the larger islands. Between Moskenesøya and the remote Skomvær Island lie 60 km (37 miles) of steep nesting cliffs, called *nyker*.

## Svolvær

Despite being long regarded as the "capital" of Lofoten, the bustling harbour town of Svolvær only received town status in 1996. Its location on Austvågsøya and good transport links make it an important gateway, and it is generally treated as Lofoton's administrative centre. The town's economy depends on Lofotfisket (the Lofoten Fisheries). In March and April every year the cod arrive in Vestfjorden to spawn and the fishing boats follow. The two-horned, 569-m (1,867-ft) peak, Svolværgeita (the Svolvær goat), is the town's most distinctive feature. It appears to rise from the town centre and presents a challenge for all climbers. Located a 30-minute drive to the east is the fishing village of Henningsvær where you can find a series of islets that have examples of Norwegian architecture, particularly *rorbuer*, the traditional red fishermen's huts.

From Svolvær, it is possible to get a bus or ferry and head for the picturesque villages of Stamsund and Ballstad on the island of Vestvågøya; the well-preserved village of Nusfjord on Flakstadøya; plus the beautiful Reine and charming Å on Moskenesøya. The islands of Vesterälen are also reachable (p234).

1 The stunning Lofoten Islands, an archipelago in the Arctic waters of the Norwegian Sea, where islands are peppered with small villages.

2 The villages of Lofoten hold a long tradition of fishing. Here, cod fish are drying in Nusfjord.

3 The clear, calm waters around Lofoten make for excellent kayaking.

> INSIDER TIP
> **Relax in *rorbuer***
>
> Iconic to Norway, the red cabins - or *rorbuer* - were lived in by fishermen in the early 20th century. Few survive, but modernized versions are available to stay in and can sleep up to six people. Visit www.lofoten.info for details.

↑ The picture-postcard village of Reine, suspended over the water in Lofoten

# EAT

**Børsen Spiseri**
Enjoy the speciality stockfish under the wooden beams of this historic quayside warehouse on Svolvær.

🏠 Gunnar Bergs Vei 2, 8300 Svolvær 📞 76 06 99 31 🕐 Dinner

Ⓚ Ⓚ Ⓚ

**Brygga Restaurant**
Suspended on stilts above the waters of Å, this light and airy restaurant is a reliable choice for top seafood.

🏠 8392 Å 🕐 Oct-May 🌐 bryggarestaurant.no

Ⓚ Ⓚ Ⓚ

**2**

# VESTERÅLEN

🅐 E4 🅰 Counties of Nordland and Troms ✈ Andenes 🚌🚢 🅹 Rådhusgata 11, 8400 Sortland; www.visitvesteralen.com

The Vesterålen archipelago is often over-shadowed by its sister, Lofoten, but boasts the same beauty, wildlife and more. Here, jagged coastline segues into white sand beaches and, thanks to Lofoten's fame, fewer crowds descend on the charming fishing villages that pepper the scene.

Northeast of Lofoten is Vesterålen, which shares the island of Hadseløya with its sister archipelago, and includes three other large islands: Langøya, Andøya and Hinnøya. Vesterålen's hotchpotch of islands are largely greener, sandier and less dramatic than Lofoten's.

Charming fishing villages reign supreme, and the wild waters of the Norwegian Sea are home to herds of whales.

### Harstad

Hinnøya is Vesterålen's largest and most populated island. Its main town is Harstad, which developed around 1870 as a result of the abundance of herring. The Northern Norway culture festival is held here each year, around the summer solstice. Andenes, on the island of Andøya, is another popular destination.

←

A lighthouse in Andenes, on the island of Andøya

↑ A snowy scene in Nykvåg, Langøya island

Andenes is good for whale watching. Guided summer safaris offer glimpses of sperm whales *(inset)*, or orcas and humpbacks in winter. ↓

## TOP 6 VESTERÅLEN TOWNS

**Sortland**
Capital of Vesterålen, with many buildings painted blue.

**Harstad**
This town offers more buzz than others.

**Stokmarknes**
The home of Hurtigruten *(p245)* is otherwise a sleepy spot.

**Nyksund**
Abandoned for years following a storm, life is slowly returning here.

**Andenes**
A good spot for whale watching.

**Nykvåg**
A fishing community with rich bird life.

↑ A viewing point above Tromsø, with spectacular views across the city

**3** 🎨 🍴 ☕ 🛍️

# TROMSØ

🅰 E3 🏛 County of Troms ✈🚌 Prostneset 🚢 Prostneset
ℹ Samuel Arnesens Gate 5; www.visittromso.no

Known as the "Paris of the North" for its lively spirit, Tromsø is the largest city in the polar region of Scandinavia. It is located 300 km (186 miles) inside the Arctic Circle, on the same latitude as northern Alaska. There was a farming estate here in early Viking times, but during the Hanseatic period, trade and commerce boomed; Tromsø officially became a market town in 1794. The 19th century saw the town develop as a thriving port for sea traffic in the Arctic Ocean and Nansen and Amundsen started their polar expeditions from here. Today it's a popular choice for witnessing the breathtaking Northern Lights.

**①** 🎨 ☕ 🛍️

## Polaria

🏛 Hjalmar Johansens Gate 12 🕐 Daily 🚫 Some public hols 🌐 polaria.no

This national centre for research relates to the polar regions and is a great place to experience the Arctic landscape. A panoramic film allows the viewer to wander in Svalbard and experience the epic Arctic wilderness beneath the Northern Lights. There is also an aquarium featuring exhibits on fish found in the Barents Sea, including Arctic species, and a glass-bottomed seal pool.

**②** 🎨 ☕ 🛍️

## Nordnorsk Kunstmuseum

🏛 Sjøgata 1 🕐 Daily 🚫 Some public hols 🌐 nnkm.no

The regional art museum for Northern Norway, Nordnorsk Kunstmuseum, was established in 1985 primarily to show painting and handicrafts from the northern regions, including sculpture and textile art. The museum also arranges temporary exhibitions of work both past and present.

**③** 🎨 🎨 🛍️

## Polarmuseet

🏛 Søndre Tollbugata 11 🕐 Daily 🌐 uit.no

In the harbour area of old Tromsø, this museum studies polar hunting and research expeditions. Exhibits span the very first hunters on Svalbard, who trapped polar bears and seals, Fridtjof Nansen's journey to the North Pole in his ship *Fram* (1893–6), the life of Antarctic explorer Roald Amundsen (1872–1928) and Salomon Andrée's attempted balloon flight to the North Pole (1897).

### Did You Know?

Tromsø prides itself on having more pubs per capita than any other Norwegian town.

### (4)
## Nordnorsk Vitensenter

📍 3 km (2 miles) N of city centre ⏰ 11am–4pm daily 🌐 nordnorsk.vitensenter.no

On the university campus of Tromsø, the Nordnorsk Vitensenter (North Norwegian Knowledge Centre) features interactive exhibits that focus on Arctic conditions, from energy, climate and weather to the Northern Lights. The planetarium forms part of the complex, screening daily films about the Northern Lights, solar system and the earth.

---

### (5) 🎖️ 🖥️ 🏛️
## Tromsø Museum, Universitetsmuseet

📍 Lars Thøringsvei 10 ⏰ Daily 🌐 uit.no

Tromsø Museum is the regional museum for Northern Norway, and part of the university. It holds considerable collections from the Stone Age, Viking era and early Middle Ages. Sami history has a prominent place and there are comprehensive displays devoted to aspects of Sami life.

---

### (6) 🎖️
## Perspektivet Museum

📍 Storgata 95 ⏰ 10am–4pm Tue–Fri, 11am–5pm Sat & Sun 🌐 perspektivet.no

Tromsø's living history is told through photography and film. Social issues, modernity and diversity are a few of the themes explored, alongside more historical ideas.

---

### (7) 🖥️
## Botanical Garden

📍 Stakkevollvegen 200 ⏰ Daily 🌐 uit.no

This small but unique garden is packed with colourful species of plants from the Arctic region. It is open all day every day, and free to enter, but May to October are the best months to visit as the flowers should be in bloom and undisturbed by snow.

↑ Stunning stained-glass window at Ishavskatedralen

### (8)
## Ishavskatedralen

📍 2 km (1 mile) E of city centre ⏰ Daily 🌐 ishavskatedralen.no

Consecrated in 1965, the striking Arctic Ocean Cathedral was designed by Jan Inge Hovig, who intended its triangular roof to brighten up Tromsø's dark winter months. A 23-m- (75-ft-) high stained-glass window by Victor Sparre fills the east wall, showing the Second Coming of Christ.

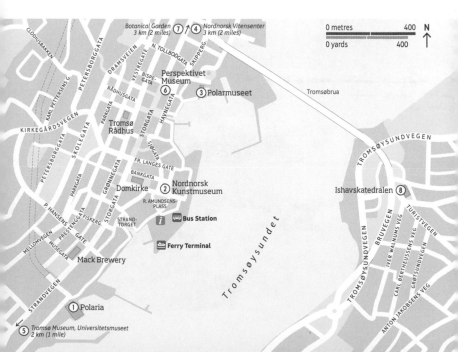

4

# SVALBARD

Longyearbyen Næringsbygget, Longyearbyen; 79 02 55 50 visitsvalbard.com

**Dramatic and elemental, this archipelago cast far away in the Arctic North is like nowhere else. Svalbard comprises colossal icebergs and endless icefields, and yet this hostile hinterland is home to some of the most rare and remarkable wildlife.**

From the Old Norse for "Cold Coasts", Svalbard consists of the Arctic Ocean islands of Spitsbergen (the largest), Nordaustlandet, Edgeøya, Barentsøya, Prins Karls Forland and several smaller ones. The archipelago lies 640 km (400 miles) north of the mainland, about one hour by plane from Tromsø. From April through to August, Svalbard sees endless daylight and milder temperatures, which means snow generally disappears by July. From October to mid-February the archipelago is in constant darkness, and temperatures plummet to -20°C. The main area of population is Longyearbyen, which has shops, cafés, banks and guesthouses in spite of its small size. Locals share their homeland with arctic foxes, reindeer, polar bears, and their waters with seals, walruses and whales.

## STAY

**Basecamp Hotel**

Centrally located in Longyearbyen, this mocktrapper's cabin promises a cosy retreat after a day exploring the icy wilderness. Traditional wooden interiors meets modern heating facilities, with vintage maps and textured fabrics running throughout. The hotel also organizes a number of expeditions.

**Hilmar Rekstens vei**

**basecampexplorer.com**

Kr Kr Kr

**Did You Know?**

Svalbard is home to approximately 2,700 people and 3,800 polar bears.

① Svalbard is home to a large number of polar bears, who sleep and hunt for seals on ice sheets. Sadly, glaciers throughout the Arctic are melting, putting the bears at risk and causing them confusion when hunting.

② Countless boat expeditions and animal safaris await in Svalbard.

③ Painted houses amid the snow in Longyearbyen, the most northern settlement in the world.

The icy, Arctic land-scape of Spitsbergen, in Svalbard

*Timeline*

### 1194

An Icelandic document mentions Norse seamen finding a place called 'Svalbarði' after sailing for four days from Iceland. This discovery hasn't been proved but has formed the basis for the modern name of the archipelago.

### 1596

Dutch explorer Willem Barents arrived in 1596 when looking for the Northeast Passage to China. He spotted Bjørnøya on 10 June and the tip of Spitsbergen a week later. Maps made following the expedition included Svalbard.

### 1920

The archipelago was placed under Norwegian sovereignty under the Svalbard Treaty, with two limitations: all nine parties to the treaty had equal rights to economic resources and Svalbard was not to be used for military activity.

### 1942

With German troops occupying Longyearbyen, a Norwegian expedition was launched to liberate the island. A garrison was successfully established in spite of attacking Germans.

Black-legged kittiwakes soaring in Svalbard

# EXPERIENCE MORE

**5**

## Helgelandskysten

🅰 E6 🅰 County of Nordland
➕🅰🛏🚌 ℹ Skippergata 1,
Sandnessjøen; 75 01 80 00
🆆 visithelgeland.com

The shipping channel along the coast of Helgelandskysten passes through a stunning landscape of islands and mountains. Whether seen from aboard the Hurtigruten (*p245*), or from the RV17 as it winds along the coast, this region never fails to delight.

Helgelandskysten is also known as the Realm of the Nessekonge, the wealthy merchants who held power over northern Norway until the early 1900s.

On the island of Torget is the unusual Torghatten mountain, which has a 160-m (525-ft) passage running right through it, formed when the land was lower than it is now.

On the island of Alsten is the Norse homestead of Tjøtta. The estate has several ruined houses and Viking burial mounds. The majestic mountain range De Syv Søstre (the Seven Sisters), which rises to 1,072 m (3,517 ft), towers above the island. There is also a 12th-century stone church, Alstadhaugkirke, where writer Petter Dass was a clergyman.

The island of Dønna is home to an aristocratic estate, Dønnes, and a stone church from 1200. Among the other islands, Lovunden is known for its large colony of puffins.

### Did You Know?

Røst, across the water from Bodø, holds an annual puffin festival in honour of their local bird population.

Hestemona, situated on the Arctic Circle, is dominated by the 568-m (1,863-ft) mountain of Hestmannen, named after a troll who, according to legend, turned to stone. Rødøy island marks the furthest point north on the Helgeland coast.

**6**

## Saltfjellet-Svartisen National Park

🅰 E5 🅰 County of Nordland
🅰ℹ Mo i Rana Tourist
Information; 07 800

Gloriously untouched landscapes typify the national park of Saltfjellet and Svartisen. In the east the undulating terrain is punctuated by peaks rising to 1,700 m (5,577 ft). Further west there are wide mountain plateaus and forested valleys.

Between here and the coast lies the Svartisen ice cap, Norway's second-largest glacier. It is made up of two glaciers, Østisen and Vestisen. **Polarsirkelsenteret** (the Arctic Circle Centre) is located in Saltfjellet, just by the Arctic Circle. It has a tourist office and slide shows. Nearby are three Sami sacrificial stones and a memorial to Yugoslav prisoners of war who were killed while working on the railway during World War II.

### Polarsirkelsenteret

♿🔈🅿 🅰 84 km (52 miles)
N of Mo i Rana 📞 91 85 38 33
🕐 May–5 Oct: daily 🗓 17 May
🆆 polarsirkelsenteret.no

## 7
# Mo i Rana

**🗺 F5** 🏛 **County of Nordland**
➕🖼📧 **ⓘ O T Olsens Gate 3;**
**75 13 92 00**

Little is known about the
origins of Mo i Rana – today
an industrial town – except
that it had a church and a
Sami market before 1860.
It was bought by L A Meyer,
who started a guesthouse and
initiated trade with Sweden.
Today central Mo is dominated
by Meyergården, a hotel and
shopping complex.

The museum, Rana Bygde-
museum, features the
collections of Hans A Meyer,
with sections on geology,
mining and rural culture.
Friluftsmuseet, an open-air
museum about 9 km (6 miles)
from Mo town centre, is also
part of Rana Bygdemuseum.

From Mo, the E6 runs southwards along Ranfjord, eventually reaching Mosjøen, with
its beautiful Vefsn Museum,
showing works by contemporary Nordland artists. The
Sjøgata street is lined with
timber buildings and warehouses dating from the early
19th century.

North of Mo is Grønligrotten,
a deep limestone cave with
a gushing stream that re-
emerges in nearby Seter-
grotten. Helmets must be
worn in the caves, and a
miner's lamp is needed to
explore Setergrotten.

## 8
# Bodø

**🗺 E5** 🏛 **County of Nordland**
➕🖼📧🚌 **ⓘ Tollbugata 13;**
**www.visitbodo.com**

Nordland's capital, Bodø,
occupies a wonderful setting
with Saltfjorden and its

←

The austerely beautiful
landscape of Saltfjellet-
Svartisen National Park

## WHALE WATCHING

There's nothing that compares with witnessing 20 m
(60 ft) of sperm whale breach the waves and sink back
into the sea with a hefty splash. Both Vesterålen and
Tysfjord, the deepest fjord in Norway, are year-round
whale-watching destinations. Guided safaris from
Andøya offer glimpses of the tremendous sperm whale
in summer, while orcas and humpbacks can be seen in
winter. Whale spotting in Tysfjord is especially good
between October and January, when orcas arrive to
feast on herring. A fully grown orca male can measure
up to 9 m (30 ft).

islands and nesting cliffs to
the west, the mountain
ranges of Børvasstindene
across the fjord to the south
and the island of Landegode
to the north. The midnight
sun can be seen here from
1 June to 12 July.

Domkirken, Bodø's
cathedral, is a modern, three-
aisle basilica, designed by
G Blakstad and H Munthe-Kaas,
and consecrated in 1956. The
stained-glass painting above
the altar is by Aage Storstein.

**Norsk Luftfartsmuseum**
is Norway's national aviation
museum, and it's one of
Bodø's biggest attractions.
The museum's exhibits sprawl
across around 10,000 sq m
(2.5 acres), and illustrate
Norwegian civil and military
history. Of particular interest
are Catalina seaplanes,
Mosquito fighter aircraft, the
US spy plane U2 and Junkers
52. Aviation enthusiasts will
also enjoy the on-site simu-
lator, which mimics a flight in
a Red Arrows jet.

Kjerringøy, 40 km (25 miles)
north of Bodø, was Nordland's
richest trading post in the
19th century. It is now part of
Nordland's county museum

and has 15 historic buildings
complete with interiors.
Nyfjøset (New Barn), which
houses a tourist information
office and a café, is a careful
replica of a barn that was
demolished in 1892. The main
museum building is located
near the cathedral.

A past owner of Kjerringøy
was Erasmus Zahl (1826–1900),
who helped Knut Hamsun
(p35) when he wanted to
become a writer. In his books,
Hamsun referred to the place
as Sirilund.

Saltstraumen is a natural
phenomenon taking place
33 km (21 miles) southeast
of Bodø. This is one of the
world's strongest tidal
currents. The water is forced
through a 3-km- (2-mile-)
long, 150-m- (492-ft-) wide
strait at speeds of up to 20
knots, which creates vast
whirlpools. The current
changes direction every 6
hours. At Opplevelsessentret,
a multimedia show explains
the mighty tide. There is also
an aquarium and a seal pool.

**Norsk Luftfartsmuseum**
🅰🅱🅲🅳 🏛 Olav V Gata
📞 75 50 78 50 🕐 Daily

## ⑨
# Narvik

🅰 E4 🄰 County of Nordland
➤🄿🚌 𝒊 Kongens Gate 39;
www.visitnarvik.com

Narvik developed as a shipping port for iron ore from Kiruna in Sweden. The Ofotbanen train line to Kiruna was completed in 1902, after which Narvik was given town status. Heavy bombardment by the Germans in 1940 destroyed most of the town.

After World War II, Narvik rose again to become Norway's second-largest shipping town. Activities connected with iron ore still form its economic base. The Ofotbanen passes below the mountains high above Rombaksfjorden, offering stunning views.

From Oscarsborg a cable car, Fjellheisen, climbs up to 700 m (2,296 ft). In summer it operates until 2am (the midnight sun occurs in Narvik from 31 May to 14 Jul).

**Krigsminnemuseet**, the War Memorial Museum near the main square, focuses on military campaigns that were fought here in 1940. Both Allied and German soldiers are buried in the cemetery near Fredskapellet (the Peace Chapel).

From Narvik, the E6 runs southwards, crossing a number of fjords either by ferry or bridges, including the impressive 525-m- (1,722-ft-) long bridge spanning the beautiful Skjomenfjorden. On Hamarøy, around 100 km (60 miles) south of Narvik, is the strangely shaped mountain of Hamarøyskaftet

> **In winter, try dog sledding or set out on a snowmobile safari by the brilliant blue light that is distinctive to winter in Finnmark.**

and the childhood home of Nobel Prize-winning novelist Knut Hamsun (1859–1952).

The scenic E10 road, Bjørnfjellveien, starts at Rombaksfjorden and ascends 520 m (1,706 ft) through the wild mountains of Ofoten to the Swedish border.

### Krigsminnemuseet
♿♿ 🄰 Torvhallen 📞 76 94 44 26 ⏲ Daily 🚫 Public hols

---

## ⑩
# Senja

🅰 E3 🄰 County of Troms
➤🚌 𝒊 Ringveien 2, Finnsnes; 77 85 07 30

Norway's second-largest island, Senja, can be reached by road (E6) from Bardufoss, across the bridge at Finnsnes. The landscape is green and welcoming on the mainland side, becoming harsher towards the sea coast. **Ånderdalen Nasjonalpark**, located on the southern part of the island, has an unspoilt landscape inhabited by elk and eagles.

Back on the mainland, in the south of Troms county large areas of wilderness,

including Øvre Dividal National Park, are home to bears. The lake-dotted park is also home to many other species of wildlife, including one of the densest populations of wolverines in Europe.

From Skibotn, about 100 km (60 miles) east of Senja, the E8 passes near the point where Finland, Sweden and Norway meet: the Treriksrøysa (Three-Country Cairn).

### Ånderdalen Nasjonalpark
🄰 35 km (22 miles) S of Finnsnes 𝒊 Sør-Senja Museum; 48 15 22 90

---

## ⑪
# Alta

🅰 F2 🄰 County of Finnmark
➤🚌 𝒊 Bjørn Wirkolas Vei 11; 99 10 00 22 🆆 visitalta. no

The largest town in Norway's northernmost county, Alta lies at the inner reaches of the Altafjord. At 70°N, the town is lucky to have a relatively mild climate amid the otherwise-frigid north. Alta is the gateway to Finnmark and the starting point for onward

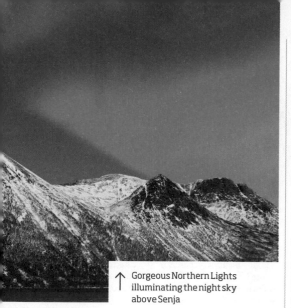

↑ Gorgeous Northern Lights illuminating the night sky above Senja

travel to places such as Kautokeino and the North Cape. Although the town is sprawling and not particularly attractive, the cultural and nature experiences on offer are exceptional.

The landscapes are also spectacular, with dense forest, mountain plateaus and northern Europe's largest canyon. Outdoor activities abound, including hiking, biking and fishing. The Altaelva, one of the longest rivers in the county, is one of the world's best salmon rivers (though visitors must apply for a permit in order to fish). Midnight sun occurs between May and August in Alta, with the extra hours of daylight allowing plenty of time to explore this fascinating region. Visit the rock carvings in Hjemmeluft, a UNESCO World Heritage site that contains traces of a prehistoric settlement. The **Alta Museum** is also located here, and features interesting exhibits relating to the Alta River from the Stone Age Komsa culture (7000–2000 BC) through to the latest hydroelectric project.

In winter, try dog sledding or set out on a snowmobile safari by the brilliant blue light that is distinctive to winter in Finnmark. At night, the *aurora borealis* often illuminates the skies. The Cathedral of the Northern Lights (Europe's northernmost cathedral) is an architectural icon, with a coiled titanium pyramid structure designed to look its finest when the natural light show swirls behind it.

**Alta Museum**

⊛⊛⊛⊛ ⬛Altaveien 19, Hjemmeluft ☎41 75 63 30
⬤Daily ⬛Some public hols

## THE WORLD'S MOST BEAUTIFUL VOYAGE

"The World's Most Beautiful Voyage" has earned its moniker. What began in 1893 as a means of mail delivery and transport has matured into an awe-inspiring coastal journey. The iconic Hurtigruten cruise takes 6 days, calling at 35 ports, to travel from Bergen to the far north Kirkenes. It sails through gorgeous emerald fjords, past contrasts of rugged mountain scenery and minuscule island villages. Halfway through the voyage, Hurtigruten passes the Arctic Circle, accomplishing by sea what it would take weeks to travel on land. A round trip takes 11 days to cover 5,200 km (3,230 miles). In summer, the expedition can feel like a Mediterranean cruise with endless midnight sun. In winter, you're likely to see the Northern Lights across the night sky; if you do not, Hurtigruten will book you another cruise for free.

The sun dips below the horizon at Nordkapp, Norway's most northern point

12

## Hammerfest

**F2 County of Finnmark Hamnegata 3; www.visithammerfest.net**

The polar bear on this town's coat of arms recalls the days when Hammerfest was a hunting and trapping centre. A settlement by the 9th century, Hammerfest was given town status in 1789.

It is the world's most northerly town at 70° 39' 48"N, as recorded on Meridianstøtten (the Meridian Pillar), which marks the first international measurement of the earth in the 19th century.

The town has endured many catastrophes, including being destroyed by a hurricane in 1856 and being razed to the ground in World War II. Each time it has been rebuilt in true pioneer spirit. In 1890 it was one of the first towns in Europe to install electric street lighting.

GREAT VIEW
**Summit Salen**

For an unforgettable vista of Hammerfest, scale the 86-m (282 ft) Salen Hill. Start the 15-minute, zig-zagging trek upwards from the Rådhus. At the top, take in views using the free binoculars available, check out the Sami turf huts and refuel in the Turista restaurant.

Hammerfest church is unusual in that it has no altar. Instead, the back wall is covered by a monumental abstract painting in glowing colours.

The Polar Bear Club, **Isbjørnklubben**, is a unique society that can only be joined by visiting Hammerfest in person. It has a museum illustrating the town's Arctic traditions. The invocation of a polar bear symbolizes the willpower and survival skills necessary to live so far north.

**Isbjørnklubben**

Havnegata 3 78 41 21 85 Daily

13

## Nordkapp

**F1 County of Finnmark Summer Fiskeriveien 4, Honningsvåg; www.nordkapp.no**

It was the English sailor Richard Chancellor who named Nordkapp (the North Cape) in 1533, during his attempt to find the Northeast Passage to China. Various important people travelled to view the North Cape, including the French king, Louis Philippe of Orleans, in 1795, and Oscar II in 1873. The latter was responsible for encouraging tourist ships to include the North Cape on their itineraries, and tourism grew rapidly. An impressive road – part of it below the sound of Magerøy – links the cape to the mainland. Every year, more than 200,000 people make the journey to this clifftop. **Nordkapphallen** (the North Cape Hall), inside the mountain, offers a panoramic view of the coast. A video showing Finnmark's changing seasons plays on a 225°-wide screen. Visitors also have the chance to become a member of the Royal North Cape Club.

From the top of the North Cape there is a sign-posted path to the promontory of Knivskjellodden, which is Europe's most northerly point, at 71°11'08"N. Honningsvåg, 35 km (22 miles) southeast of the cape, is where the Hurtigruten *(p245)* ships calls. It also has a Nordkapp museum.

**Nordkapphallen**

35 km (22 miles) N of Honningsvåg 78 47 68 60 Daily

14

## Vardø

**G1 County of Finnmark Kaigata 18; 78 98 69 07**

Two events at the beginning of the 14th century were to enforce Vardø's position as a bastion against incursions from the east: Håkon V built a fortress here and Archbishop Jørund consecrated the first church. The fortress, **Vardøhus Festning**, was rebuilt in the 18th century as a star-shaped fortification with parapets of earth and peat, eight cannons and a mortar. The last time the fortress was on active anti-invasion duty was during World War I; in World War II the site was used as a POW camp before the German invasion. There are tours of the commanding officer's residence, the old depots and the barracks. Four kings have written their names on a beam from the original fortress. The fort is now under the Royal Norwegian Navy's command. Vardø is connected to the mainland by a tunnel below the sound of Bussesundet, constructed in 1982. Fishing and fish processing are the basis of the local economy.

The fishing village of Kiberg, to the south, was known as "Little Moscow" because of partisan activity during World War II.

### Vardøhus Festning
⊗⊗ 🏛Festningsgata
📞46 87 04 00 🕐Daily

---

### ⓯
# Karasjok

🅰G2 🏛County of Finnmark
➕🚌 ℹLeavnnjageaidnu 1;
78 46 88 00

Karasjok (*Karásjohka* in Sámi) is the Sámi capital and the seat of the Sámi Parliament, **Sametinget**, which opened in 1989. Around 90 per cent of the local population speak Sámi, and the area is further home to approximately 60,000 reindeer. They can be seen grazing in autumn and winter.

The parliament building is well worth a visit. Its exterior is constructed with silvered oak, pine and birch, its conical shape reflecting cultural tradition. The main assembly hall is shaped like a Sami tent. The building also houses the Sami library, which contains over 35,000 volumes.

**De Samiske Samlinger** museum features Sámi handicrafts and exhibits on the Sámi way of life in an open-air venue, which includes housing and trapping pits.

The climate in these parts can be extreme. The record low temperature is –51.4° C (–60.5° F), and the highest temperature 32.4° C (90° F). With the right gear, however, outdoor activities are a must; dog and reindeer sledding are both popular (ensure those leading such activities are reputable before taking part).

### Sametinget
⊗ 🏛Kautokeinoveien 50
📞78 47 40 00 🕐Mon–Fri

### De Samiske Samlinger
⊗⊗🕐 🏛Museumsgate 17
📞78 46 99 50 🕐Daily
🚫Public hols

Herds of migrating reindeer in Karasjok, the Sámi capital ↑

**16**

## Kautokeino

**A F3** **County of Finnmark**

The name "Kautokeino" is a Norwegianized form of the Sami word *Guovdageaidnu*. Kautokeino is a mountain town surrounded by barren plateaus where reindeer husbandry is the most important economic activity.

Nine out of ten people here are Sami. Most locals have Sami as their first language, and the area is officially bilingual. Nomadic reindeer herders have lived here for hundreds of years, and the traditional lifestyle is still very much alive. Indeed, reindeer husbandry is a course on the Sami High School curriculum.

Easter is a time of transition for the Sami, just before they set off with their reindeer for summer pastures on the coast. It is marked by colourful, busy celebrations, with weddings, a *joik* (Sami chanting song) festival and reindeer racing.

For a deeper experience of Sami culture, the **Kautokeino Museum** is home to an open-air traditional settlement, with homes and lavoo tents, as well as outbuildings for storing reindeer food. Inside, the museum exhibits traditional handicrafts, from clothing to reindeer herding gear.

**Kautokeino Museum**

📍 Boaronjarga 23 🕙 9am-6pm Mon-Sat, noon-6pm Sun 🌐 rdm.no

---

**17**

## Vadsø

**A G1** **County of Finnmark** **i** Kirkegata 15; 78 94 04 44

Originally situated on the island of Vadsøya, the town of Vadsø moved to the mainland around 1600. Its fjord-side position gives this town a special charm, and brightly painted clapboard houses line the waterfront.

Over the centuries many Finns have settled in Vadsø,

leaving attractive examples of Finnish architecture, including Tuomainengården, a Finnish farmhouse that dates from 1840. Inside, the **Ruija Kvenmuseum** expands on the theme of the Kvænene (as the Finnish were known).

Vadsø is also known for its interesting bird life. Nearby Ekkerøy is a bird reserve with an easily accessible bird cliff, best known for tens of thousands of kittiwakes that return here every March.

An airship mooring mast, used by Amundsen's expedition to the North Pole in the airship *Norge* in 1926, still stands on Vadsøya.

**Ruija Kvenmuseum**

📍 Hvistendahlsgate 31 📞 78 94 28 90 🕙 Mon-Fri (20 Jun-20 Aug: daily) 🚫 Public hols

---

**18**

## Kirkenes

**A G1** **County of Finnmark** **i** Presteveien 1; 78 97 74 00 🌐 visitkirkenes.no

About 400 km (250 miles) north of the Arctic Circle, Kirkenes is known as the capital of the Barents Region and the gateway to the east. It is also the last port of call for Hurtigruten. Because of its spot on the Norwegian frontier, 10 per cent of the people in Kirkenes are Russian.

Iron ore was once the cornerstone of the local economy. Kirkenes supplied artillery materials during WWII, and was one of Norway's most bombed towns as a result. When the town was destroyed by retreating Germans in 1944, its 2,000 inhabitants were able to flee to nearby mineshafts.

The wilderness here is immensely appealing. Dense pine forests extend to the Treriksrøya monument, where Norway, Finland and Russia meet, and wholesome outdoor activities such as sledding or ice-fishing are very popular.

### MIDNIGHT SUN

In the "land of the midnight sun", the sun stays above the horizon permanently in summer. The further north of the Arctic Circle you venture, the more endless, rose-gold sunshine you get. Svalbard gets the longest period of midnight sun, with constant daylight between 20 April and 22 August. The liquid red light has the qualities of a simultaneous sunrise and sunset, and is caused by the tilt of the earth's axis and its rotation around the sun during the northern hemisphere's summer. Correspondingly, there is a period of winter darkness in this region when the sun never rises during the day, although it can be somewhat alleviated by the blazing Northern Lights.

# EAT

### Restaurant Nyt
Chefs at this restaurant are impressing with their reinterpretation of Northern Norwegian culinary tradition.

🅰E5 🏠Dronningens Gate 26, 8006 Bodø 🌐restaurant-nyt.no

---

### Hundholmen Brygghus
This buzzing waterfront gastro-pub offers hearty home-cooked meals and over 75 beers by the bottle.

🅰E5 🏠Tollbugata 13, 8005 Bodø 🌐hund holmenbrygghus.no

Ⓚ Ⓚ Ⓚ

---

### Sorrisniva
Savour Arctic flavours at the extraordinary Igloo Hotel's restaurant. Choose between three- to nine-course tasting menus.

🅰F2 🏠Sorrisniva 20, Alta 🌐sorrisniva.no

Ⓚ Ⓚ Ⓚ

---

### Storgammen
A Sami cultural experience, where guests sit on fur rugs around an open fire. Closed in winter except with advance booking.

🅰G2 🏠Leavnnjageaidnu 49, Karasjok 📞78 46 88 60

Ⓚ Ⓚ Ⓚ

←

Colourful, snow-covered houses in the small town of Kirkenes

# NEED TO KNOW

Flåm line train nearing snowy Myrdal

# BEFORE YOU GO

Forward planning is essential to any successful trip. Be prepared for all eventualities by considering the following points before you travel.

## AT A GLANCE

### CURRENCY
Norwegian Krone (NOK)

### AVERAGE DAILY SPEND

| SAVE | SPEND | SPLURGE |
|---|---|---|
| **750Kr** | **1,500Kr** | **2,750+Kr** |

| BOTTLED WATER | COFFEE | BEER | DINNER FOR TWO |
|---|---|---|---|
| **25Kr** | **30Kr** | **70Kr** | **750Kr** |

### ESSENTIAL PHRASES

| | |
|---|---|
| Hello | Hei |
| Goodbye | Ha det bra |
| Please | Vær så snill |
| Thank you | Takk |
| Do you speak English? | Snakker du engelsk |
| I don't understand | Jeg forstår ikke |

### ELECTRICITY SUPPLY

Power sockets are type F, also accommodating two-prong type C and E plugs. Standard voltage is 220–230v.

## Passports and Visas

Passports are required for everyone, except citizens of Nordic countries and EU nationals with ID cards from the states that are part of the Schengen Area. North Americans, Britons and Australians do not need visas for visits lasting up to 90 days. Check with your own government or with the **Norway Directorate of Immigration** if uncertain of your status.
**Schengen visas**
⬡ schengenvisainfo.com/norway-visa
**Norway Directorate of Immigration**
⬡ udi.no

## Travel Safety Advice

Visitors can get up-to-date travel safety information from the UK Foreign and Commonwealth Office, the US State Department and the Australian Department of Foreign Affairs and Trade.
**Australia**
⬡ smartraveller.gov.au
**UK**
⬡ gov.uk/foreign-travel-advice
**US**
⬡ travel.state.gov

## Customs Information

Norway is not a member of the EU, and so customs regulations on alcohol and tobacco are stricter than other European nations. An individual is permitted to carry the following for personal use:
**Tobacco** 200 cigarettes, or 250 grams of tobacco and 200 sheets of cigarette paper, or 50 cigars.
**Alcohol** 1 litre of spirits along with 1 litre of wine and 2 litres of beer; if no spirits, 2 litres of wine.
**Currency** No more than 25,000Kr in Norwegian currency can be carried in or out of the country without declaration.
It is possible to have another 27 litres of alcohol and an additional 500 grams of tobacco if the items are declared and customs duties paid upon arrival.

## Insurance

It is wise to take out an insurance policy covering theft, loss of belongings, medical problems, cancellation and delays.

Norway does not have a free national health service. Visitors from EU countries should secure a European Health Insurance (**EHIC**) card, which covers visitors from the European Economic Area (EEA). Australians should register at home with **Medicare** to ensure coverage in Norway. North Americans should arrange personal cover.

**EHIC**
W gov.uk/european-health-insurance-card
**Medicare**
W humanservices.gov.au

## Vaccinations

No inoculations are needed for Norway, but bring insect repellent if you are visiting the fjords.

## Money

Credit cards, debit cards and prepaid currency cards are accepted in almost all shops and restaurants. Contactless payments are also common. Cash is used only for small purchases – Norway is increasingly becoming a cashless society. Not every bank provides money exchange services involving cash.

## Booking Accommodation

Norway offers a range of accommodation options, from luxury five-star hotels to simple, remote cabins. Online booking is prevalent but tourist offices can also help locate inexpensive and private-home accommodation not otherwise advertised. In remote areas, it is essential to book ahead. Wilderness camping is allowed in Norway as long as campers are sensible and respectful.

## Travellers with Specific Needs

Few countries are better equipped for wheelchair access. However, some rural parts of the country and older transport systems, such as trams and ferry boats, can pose problems. Note that guide dogs can be denied access to buses if there are passengers with allergies. **Visit Norway** provides useful information on travelling around Norway. Otherwise check ahead for access information at specific sights.

**Visit Norway**
W visitnorway.com/plan-your-trip

## Language

There are three official languages (Norwegian, Bokmål and Nyorsk), plus several protected languages of the Sámi people to the north. Norwegian is spoken by 95 per cent of the country but English is understood everywhere, and most signs have English translations.

## Closures

**Lunchtime** A few shops and museums close for lunch during the working week.
**Monday** Museums are sometimes closed.
**Saturday and Sunday** Most shops and offices close on Sunday with exemptions in tourist resorts. Museums and restaurants tend to stay open, but banks are always closed on weekends. Many shops close at 2pm on Saturday.
**Public holidays** All offices and banks are closed but many museums and attractions remain open. It is best to check with individual venues for specific closures ahead of your visit. Transport services may be reduced.

| PUBLIC HOLIDAYS | |
| --- | --- |
| New Year's Day | 1 Jan |
| Good Friday | 19 Apr (2019) |
| | 10 Apr (2020) |
| Easter Sunday | 21 Apr (2019) |
| | 12 Apr (2020) |
| Labour Day | 1 May |
| Constitution Day | 17 May |
| Ascension Day | 30 May (2019) |
| | 21 May (2020) |
| Whit Sunday | 9 Jun (2019) |
| | 31 May (2020) |
| Christmas Day | 25 Dec |

# GETTING
# AROUND

Whether you are visiting for a short city break or for a tour of the fjords and far north, discover how best to reach your destinations and travel like a pro.

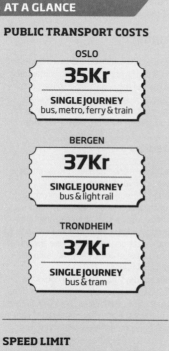

## AT A GLANCE

### PUBLIC TRANSPORT COSTS

**OSLO**

**35Kr**

**SINGLE JOURNEY**
bus, metro, ferry & train

**BERGEN**

**37Kr**

**SINGLE JOURNEY**
bus & light rail

**TRONDHEIM**

**37Kr**

**SINGLE JOURNEY**
bus & tram

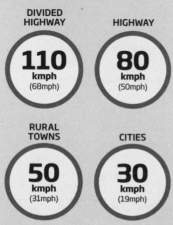

### SPEED LIMIT

**DIVIDED HIGHWAY**

**110** kmph (68mph)

**HIGHWAY**

**80** kmph (50mph)

**RURAL TOWNS**

**50** kmph (31mph)

**CITIES**

**30** kmph (19mph)

## Arriving by Air

Norway has 50 airports handling domestic flights, ensuring access to every island and Arctic settlement. Oslo airport (OSL) at Gardermoen is the second busiest in Scandinavia, with flights arriving from 151 international destinations. Bergen airport (BGO) at Flesland is popular for cruise-ship tourists, and Stavanger airport (SVG) at Sola sees commercial activity. Budget airlines from around Europe use some of the smaller airports, like Sandefjord (TRF) and Kristiansand (KRS). For information on getting to and from Norway's airports, see the table opposite.

## Train Travel

### International Train Travel

Norway is integrated with other European networks via Sweden. There are no high-speed trains. The standard of comfort and service on board is high. Students and budget travellers with **Eurail** or **Interrail** multi-country passes have access to the entire Norwegian network. Eurail has a pass limited only to Norway. Note that all such passes must be purchased outside Norway prior to arrival.
**Eurail**
W eurail.com
**Interrail**
W interrail.eu

### Domestic Train Travel

All areas of Norway are served by the state-owned company, **NSB** (Norwegian State Railways). Intercity trains provide frequent service between the main cities, such as Oslo, Bergen, Stavanger and Trondheim. As with costs in general, the price of train travel is more expensive here than the European average. Seniors over 67 years can get a 50 per cent discount with proof of age. Minipris e-tickets offer discounted fares on intercity trains. These are made available on NSB's website a month in advance. There are a limited number available so purchase online well in advance.
**NSB**
W nsb.no

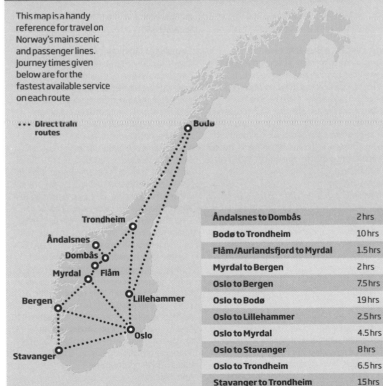

## GETTING TO AND FROM THE AIRPORT

| Airport | Distance to city | Taxi fare | Public transport | Journey time |
|---|---|---|---|---|
| Bergen (Flesland) | 15 km (9 miles) | 500Kr | bus/rail | 30 mins |
| Kristiansand | 16 km (10 miles) | 250Kr | bus | 20 mins |
| Molde Årø | 5 km (3 miles) | 275Kr | bus | 20 mins |
| Oslo (Gardermoen) | 45 km (28 miles) | 600Kr | bus/rail | 20 mins |
| Oslo Torp (Sandefjord) | 110 km (69 miles) | 2,000Kr | bus/rail | 80 mins |
| Stavanger (Sola) | 14km (9 miles) | 400Kr | bus | 20 mins |
| Tromsø | 5 km (3 miles) | 200Kr | bus | 15 mins |
| Trondheim | 35 km (22 miles) | 600Kr | bus/rail | 25 mins |

## RAIL JOURNEY PLANNER

This map is a handy reference for travel on Norway's main scenic and passenger lines. Journey times given below are for the fastest available service on each route

••• Direct train routes

Bodø

Trondheim

Åndalsnes

Dombås

Myrdal   Flåm

Bergen

Lillehammer

Oslo

Stavanger

| Åndalsnes to Dombås | 2 hrs |
|---|---|
| Bodø to Trondheim | 10 hrs |
| Flåm/Aurlandsfjord to Myrdal | 1.5 hrs |
| Myrdal to Bergen | 2 hrs |
| Oslo to Bergen | 7.5 hrs |
| Oslo to Bodø | 19 hrs |
| Oslo to Lillehammer | 2.5 hrs |
| Oslo to Myrdal | 4.5 hrs |
| Oslo to Stavanger | 8 hrs |
| Oslo to Trondheim | 6.5 hrs |
| Stavanger to Trondheim | 15 hrs |

## Public Transport

Norwegians are enthusiastic supporters of public transport, though in smaller cities outside Oslo it is often more practical to walk or cycle rather than negotiate buses and trams.

### Public Transport Operators
**Ruter (Oslo)**
🆆 ruter.no
**Skyss (Bergen)**
🆆 skyss.no
**AtB (Trondheim)**
🆆 atb.no
**Kolumbus (Stavanger)**
🆆 kolumbus.no

### Buses and Trams
Bus tickets should be purchased online or from kiosks and ticket machines. Buying on board incurs a hefty surcharge. Passengers are required to validate their tickets using card scanners on the platform or on board. In Oslo, the best method is to buy online and flash the QR symbol on your smartphone at the electronic scanners. Tickets can be bought for a single journey to specific zones or for unlimited travel for periods of a day or longer. Oslo and Bergen offer discounted city passes for tourists.

### Long-Distance Bus Travel
In comparison to trains and planes, buses in Norway are a considerably cheaper option for long-distance journeys. Cities and airports are well-served by coaches, and have free Wi-Fi. **Nettbus** is the biggest operator, with routes to Lillehammer and Bergen, but not to the north. For the west coast, the best choice of routes is with **Kystbussen**. In the Stavangar region, **Boreal** operates express lines to Oslo airport and Bergen.
🆆 nettbus.no
🆆 kystbussen.no
🆆 boreal.no

### Metro
Oslo has T-banen, the only rapid transit system in Norway. With 101 stations along tracks extending 85 km (53 miles), the city is well served by this network. T-banen tickets are also valid for buses and ferries.

### Taxis
Official taxis are clearly identified. They are not hailed in passing but booked by phone or found at designated ranks outside hotels or stations. Taxis can be scheduled in advance for specific time pick-ups, at no extra cost, but beware of phoning for an immediate pick-up, as billing begins the moment you make the order. Rates increase significantly at night and at weekends and holidays. Uber exists only in Oslo.

## Driving

Norway has clean and safe roads with well-mannered drivers. Instead of multi-laned roads of concrete, as seen elsewhere in Europe, the roads here are modest and often attractively lined with trees. In rural areas, moose and other wandering animals pose serious hazards.

### Driving to Norway
It is possible to drive from London to Oslo in under 24 hours using the Hirtshals Kristiansand ferry route, connecting Denmark and Norway. Drivers approaching from other points in Europe are likely to use the E6 motorway which runs through Malmö, Helsingborg and Gothenburg in Sweden, before crossing the border at Svinesund in the southeast of Norway.

### Car Hire
Valid driving licences from any country are accepted in Norway, although drivers must be at least 19 years of age and have held a licence for a minimum of a year. Note that drivers under 25 years incur daily surcharges of up to 160Kr. There is no upper age limit. Hire rates are more expensive than elsewhere in Europe. Cars generally must be returned to the point of original hire.

### Driving in Norway
Over 100 public roadways require cars to board ferry boats as part of the journey. These crossings are marked as dotted lines on road maps and are always the shortest routes. Booking ahead is not possible and drivers should allow extra time for such crossings when planning long journeys.

Norway is one of the top three most expensive nations in the world for both diesel and petrol. Owners of electric vehicles (EV) are rewarded and all 8,000 public charging stations are free. Furthermore, EV cars pay no road tolls and can park free in some cities, Oslo for one. They also have the right to drive in bus lanes.

Norway has 237 tollbooths, all of which can be driven through without stopping if you register your number plates online before travelling, with **AutoPASS**. This is also used to pay for congestion charges automatically. Bergen and Oslo both have Low Emission Zones, where fees vary according to the type of vehicle. As these regulations are subject to change, it is best to consult the **Urban Access** website for up-to-date information. Be aware that Oslo may announce temporary bans on all diesel cars at times of high pollution levels.
**AutoPASS**
🆆 autopass.no
**Urban Access Regulations in Europe**
🆆 urbanaccessregulations.eu

## Rules of the Road

Dipped headlights are mandatory at all times when driving. Drivers must carry a reflective safety vest and emergency triangle. Snow tyres or chains are required in mountainous areas in winter. Cars descending a hill always have priority on narrow mountain roads. Some roads are only wide enough for one vehicle but there are areas to pull over to allow other vehicles to pass.

Child seats and seatbelts are mandatory, and driving while holding a phone is prohibited. Penalties for speeding and for driving over the alcohol limit (p258) are more severe than elsewhere in Europe and may result in prison sentences. On roads that do not display a yellow diamond sign (indicating a through road), you must give way to drivers coming from the right. Aggressive overtaking is an offence. Illegal parking invariably results in a swift penalty in urban areas.

In case of breakdown, **Falck** and **NAF** will provide emergency assistance 24 hours a day.

**Falck**

☎ 02 222

**NAF**

☎ 23 21 31 00

## Hitchhiking

Hitchhiking is not uncommon in Norway, but the weather and distances add to the risks. As a result, hitchhiking in the far north is not advised. On ferries, payment is per passenger rather than by vehicle.

# Bicycle and Motorbike Hire

Bikes are a popular way of seeing Norway and you'll see many Norwegians cycling, particularly in cities. Avoid congestion in Oslo with blue **Bysykkel** bikes. Pay a subscription then pick any bike at the 200 stands, swapping it for another within 45 minutes. The scheme is intended for getting from one spot to another, rather than for sightseeing. In Bergen, meanwhile, you can hire **BimBimBikes**. **Eagle Rider** in Lyngdal, near Kristiansand, supplies Harley Davidson bikes for touring the fjords.

**Bysykkel**

🅆 oslobysykkel.no

**BimBimBikes**

🅆 bimbimbikes.com

**Eagle Rider**

🅆 eaglerider.com/norway

# Boats and Ferries

Sea voyages are both spectacular and practical. Car ferries from Kiel in Germany, Hirtshals in Denmark and Strømstad in Sweden arrive in four Norwegian ports: Oslo, Larvik, Kristiansand and Sandefjord. **Color Line** is Norway's biggest car ferry operator, and operates the world's largest cruise ferry vessel. Ferries even provide city transport. In Oslo, Bygdøy and its maritime museums are serviced by the Bygdøyfergene **Boat Sightseeing** ferry.

**Color Line**

🅆 colorline.no

**Boat Sightseeing**

🅆 boatsightseeing.com

## Luxury Cruises

Luxury cruises through the fjords are fabulous. A more ambitious option is a voyage all the way up the coast into the Arctic, taking in Tromsø, Svalbard and the Lofoten Islands. Fjord cruises normally last for one or two weeks, and Arctic cruises for longer. The longest coastal route is Bergen to Kirkenes, in Finnmark. Some of Norway's most scenic ports include Stavanger for Lysefjord, Flåm for Aurlandsfjord and Geiranger for the wild Geirangerfjord.

**Hurtigruten** is the traditional operating company, with daily sailings and working cargo vessels. **Silversea** has a number of Arctic cruises, including one that travels from Alaska to Norway. **Fjord Travel** is a Bergen-based company and offers some of the longest coastal tours.

**Hurtigruten**

🅆 hurtigruten.no

**Silversea**

🅆 silversea.com

**Fjord Travel**

🅆 fjordtravel.no

---

### TRAVELLING THE FJORDS

Even if you don't have time or money for a week-long cruise on a luxury liner, it is possible to experience the famous Norwegian fjords by other means of transport.

**Aeroplane**
Grab a window seat on any flight into Bergen for views of Vestlandet.

**Ferry Boat**
A ferry from Bergen to Flåm takes five hours. Making eleven stops, it negotiates the longest and deepest of the fjords, Sogneford.

**Mini-Cruise**
In only three hours a catamaran can do the round-trip tour of Osterfjord from Bergen to Mostraumen.

**Railway**
Starting or ending on Aurlandsfjord, the Flåm-Myrdal Railway is one of the most spectacular rail journeys, from sea to mountain in under two hours.

# PRACTICAL
# INFORMATION

A little local know-how goes a long way in Norway. Here you will find all the essential advice and information you will need during your stay.

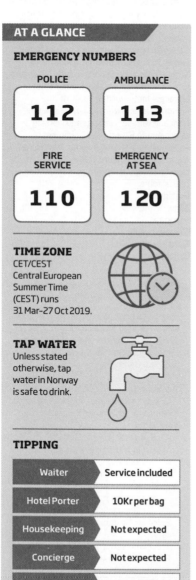

## AT A GLANCE

### EMERGENCY NUMBERS

| POLICE | AMBULANCE |
|--------|-----------|
| **112** | **113** |

| FIRE SERVICE | EMERGENCY AT SEA |
|--------------|------------------|
| **110** | **120** |

### TIME ZONE
CET/CEST
Central European
Summer Time
(CEST) runs
31 Mar–27 Oct 2019.

### TAP WATER
Unless stated
otherwise, tap
water in Norway
is safe to drink.

### TIPPING

| Waiter | Service included |
|--------|------------------|
| Hotel Porter | 10Kr per bag |
| Housekeeping | Not expected |
| Concierge | Not expected |
| Taxi Driver | 10Kr per bag |

## Personal Security

Norway has a low level of violent crime. Stealing and pickpocketing are, however, reported to be on the increase, particularly in cities like Oslo and Bergen, with statistics higher than in other Nordic countries. Reasonable care should be taken not to leave bags and cameras on tables or benches, for example. Any incidents of theft or otherwise should be reported to the police and an official crime report obtained for insurance claims.

## Health

In case of accident or emergency, treatment is swift in Norway's excellent hospitals. European visitors with an EHIC card *(p253)* are considered of equal status with Norwegian citizens. Note that treatment and medicines are not free and tourists are advised to secure personal travel insurance. Each town has one pharmacy *(apotek)* that is always open or 'on call'.

## Smoking, Alcohol and Drugs

Tobacco smoking is outlawed indoors in all public buildings. The blood alcohol limit for drivers is less than half the EU average, at 0.02%, and routine roadside checks are common. This makes even the smallest glass of wine or beer problematic. Marijuana remains illegal, except when medically prescribed. Penalties for both drink-driving and use of narcotics are severe.

## ID

Visitors are not required to carry passports or ID cards on their person but, in the case of an incident, you must be able to produce suitable identification at a local police station within 12 hours.

## Local Customs

Unlike many other European customs, lunches are brief and dinners are early in Norway; a lunch typically entails a quick sandwich and dinner is often eaten before 6pm. Handshakes are frequent while cheek kissing and hugging are rare. The dress code throughout the country is informal. Shoes should be removed when entering a Norwegian home.

## LGBT+ Safety

Like their Scandinavian neighbours, Norwegians are enthusiastic supporters of LGTB+ rights and laws prohibit discrimination and hate speech. Oslo hosts a number of LGTB+ events annually, and the Gay Happiness Index ranks Norway second only to Iceland. As a result, LGBT+ travellers should not face any issues when visting Norway.

## Visiting Churches and Cathedrals

Norway does not have any dress codes or head covering rules for visiting its churches. That being said, show respect when visiting churches and cathedrals.

## Mobile Phones and Wi-Fi

Phone signal is strong, even along the fjords and in Arctic towns, although 3G and 4G coverage can be patchy in more remote parts. European travellers can use up to 15GB of their data allowance without being charged an additional fee. Most businesses and institutions have Wi-Fi open to everyone, so there is no need to request a password.

## Post

Every village has a post office, open until 5pm on weekdays and 3pm on Saturdays. Stamps can be bought in hotels and small shops. Yellow post boxes are reserved for local letters within the same postal code and red boxes are for everything else. Courier services like DHL exist but most packages are delivered by the government mail service.

## Taxes and Refunds

Norway's VAT rate is Europe's highest, at 25 per cent. Refunds are possible, if the proper papers are stamped and the goods presented unused

to Customs upon departure from the country. Items under 315Kr (290Kr for food) do not qualify. Visit **Premier Tax Free** or **Global Blue Tax Free** for more information about taxes and refunds.

**Premier Tax Free**
🆆 premiertaxfree.com
**Global Blue Tax Free**
🆆 globalblue.com

## Discount Cards

Many destinations offer a visitor's pass or discount card for events, museum entry, guided tours, activities and even transport. Consider how many of these offers you are likely to take advantage of before purchasing, as this might not be the most cost-effective purchase. The following cards, available online and from participating tourist offices, offer some of the best deals:

**Oslo Pass**
🆆 visitoslo.com
**Bergen Pass**
🆆 visitbergen.com
**Fjord Pass**
🆆 fjordtours.com

### WEBSITES AND APPS

**Norway Tourist Board**
The most comprehensive guide for tourists is www.visitnorway.com. There is also an associated app.

**Ruter**
For train and bus information in Norway, visit www.ruter.no. The affiliated RuterReise and RuterBillet apps can be used to plan routes and purchase tickets.

**Norway Lights**
This site and its downloadable app show when and where the *aurora borealis* will be visible. Visit www. norway-lights.com.

**Visit Norway VR**
This all-platform app means you can swoop over the fjords in 3D with 360-degree panoramas–handy if you don't plan on visiting the fjords.

# INDEX

# M

# PHRASE BOOK

When reading the imitated pronunciation, stress that part which is underlined. Pronounce each syllable as if it formed part of an English word and you will be understood sufficiently well. A few sounds, particular to Norwegian, are represented by small capitals in the pronunciation guide. Below is an explanation of these.

| | |
|---|---|
| ew | try to say 'ee' with your lips rounded (or the French 'u') |
| h | the 'h' sound as in 'huge' |
| i | the 'i' sound as in 'high' |
| ur | the 'u' sound as in 'fur' |

## NORWEGIAN ALPHABETICAL ORDER

In the list below we have followed Norwegian alphabetical order. The following letters are listed after z: æ, ø, å.

## 'YOU'

There are two words for 'you': du (addressing one person) and dere (addressing two or more people). The polite form, de, is seldom used.

## IN AN EMERGENCY

| | | |
|---|---|---|
| Help! | Hjelp! | yelp |
| Stop! | Stopp! | stop |
| Call a doctor! | Ring etter lege! | Ring etter lege |
| Call an ambulance! | Ring etter ambulanse! | Ring etter ambool_a_ngsseh |
| Call the police! | Ring til politiet! | Ring til pohlit_ee_at |
| Call the fire brigade! | Ring til brann-vesenet! | Ring til br_o_nnvesenet |
| Where is the nearest telephone? | Hvor er nærmeste telefon? | vohr er nairmeste telef_aw_n? |
| Where is the nearest hospital? | Hvor er nærmeste sykehus? | vohr er nairmeste s_ew_keh-hooss? |

## COMMUNICATION ESSENTIALS

| | | |
|---|---|---|
| Yes/no | Ja/nei | yah/ni |
| Thank you | Takk | takk |
| No, thank you | Nei takk | ni takk |
| Yes, please | Ja takk | yah takk |
| Please (offering) | Vær så god | varshawgo |
| Excuse me, please | Unnskyld | oonshewl |
| Good morning | Mor'n | mawrn |
| Good afternoon | God dag | go-dahg |
| Good evening | God kveld | go-kvell |
| Good night | God natt | go-natt |
| Goodbye | Morn'a; (informal) ha det | morna; hah-deh |
| Sorry! | Om forlatelse! | om forlahdelseh |

## USEFUL PHRASES

| | | |
|---|---|---|
| I don't understand | Jeg forstår ikke | yi forsht_aw_r ikkeh |
| Please speak more slowly | Kan du snakke langsommere | kan doo snakkeh lang-sawmereh |
| Please write it down for me | Kan du skrive det opp for meg? | deh op for mi |
| My name is ... | Jeg heter ... | yi h_ay_ter |
| Can you tell me ...? | Kan du si meg ...? | kan doo see mi |
| I would like a ... | Jeg vil gjerne ha en/et ... | yi vil yarneh hah ayn/et |
| Where can I get ...? | Hvor kan jeg få ...? | vohr kan yi faw |
| What time is it? | Hvor mange er klokken? | vohr mang-eh ar klokken |
| I must go now | Jeg må gå nå | yi maw gaw naw |
| I've lost my way (on foot) | Jeg har gått meg bort | yi hahr gawt mi bohrt |
| Cheers! | Skål! | skawl |
| Where is the toilet? | Hvor er toalettet? | vohr ar toh-a-letteh |

## SHOPPING

| | | |
|---|---|---|
| I'd like ... | Jeg skal ha ... | yi skal hah |
| Do you have ...? | Har du ...? | hahr doo |
| How much is this? | Hvor mye koster denne/dette? | vohr m_ew_-eh koster denneh/dehtteh |
| I'd like to change this, please | Kan jeg få bytte denne (dette)? | kan yi faw b_ew_teh denneh (dehtteh) |
| Can I have a receipt? | Kan jeg få en kvittering? | kan yi faw ayn kvitt_oy_ring |
| Can I try it/them on? | Kan jeg prøve den/dem? | kan yi pr_uv_eh den/dem |
| I'm just looking | Jeg bare kikker | yi b_ah_reh Heekker |
| Do you take credit cards? | Tar du kredittkort? | tahr doo kred_i_ttkort |

| | | |
|---|---|---|
| antique shop | antikvitetshandel | antikvit_ets_handel |
| baker | bakeri | bak-er_ee_ |
| bookshop | bokhandel | b_oh_khandel |
| butcher | slakter | sl_a_kter |
| cake shop | konditori | kohnditohr_ee_ |
| cheap | billig | b_i_lli |
| chemist | apotek | apoht_oy_k |
| craft shop | husflidsforret-ning | hoosfleeds-forretning |
| department store | varemagasin | v_ah_remaga-seen |
| expensive | dyrt | dewrt |
| fashion | mote | m_oh_teh |
| fishmonger | fiskebutikk | fiskehboote_e_kk |
| florist | blomsterbutikk | blomsterboote_e_kk |
| gift shop | gavebutikk | g_ah_vehboote_e_kk |
| grocer | dagligvarebutikk | d_ah_glivahreboote_e_kk |
| hairdresser | frisør | frees_ur_ |
| market | marked | m_a_rked |
| newsagent | avis-og tobakks-butikk | av_ee_ss aw tohb_a_ksboote_e_k |
| post office | postkontor | p_aw_stkontoor |
| sale | salg | salg |
| shoe shop | skobutikk | sk_oh_boote_e_kk |
| supermarket | supermarked | s_oo_permarked |
| toy shop | leketøysbutikk | l_oy_ketoys-boote_e_kk |
| travel agent | reisebyrå | r_ai_ssehbewraw |

## SIGHTSEEING

| | | |
|---|---|---|
| art gallery | kunstgalleri | kunnstgaller_ee_ |
| church | kirke | Heerke |
| fjord | fjord | fjord |
| garden | hage | h_ah_ge |
| house | hus | hews |
| mountain | fjell | fye_a_ll |
| museum | museum | mews_eu_m |
| square | plass | plahss |
| street | gate | g_ah_te |
| tourist office | turistkontor | tur_ee_stkont_oo_r |
| town hall | rådhus | rawdh_ew_s |
| closed | stengt på grunn | stengt paw grewnn |
| for holiday | av ferie | ahw f_e_reeh |
| bus station | busstasjon | bewss-stash_oh_n |
| railway station | jernbanestasjon | jairnbanestash_oh_n |

## STAYING IN A HOTEL

| | | |
|---|---|---|
| Have you any vacancies? | Har dere ledige rom? | hahr dereh laydi-eh rohm |
| I have a reservation | Jeg har reservert rom | yi hahr ressarv_oy_rt rohm |
| double room | dobbeltrom | d_o_bbeltrohm |
| twin room | tomannsrom | t_oh_mannsrohm |
| single room | enkeltrom | _e_ngkeltrohm |
| room with a bath | rom med bad | rohm med bahd |
| shower | dusj | doosh |
| toilet | toalett | toh-a-l_e_tt |
| key | nøkkel | n_u_kkel |

## EATING OUT

| | | |
|---|---|---|
| Have you got a table for ...? | Kan jeg få et bord til...? | kan yi faw et bohr til... |
| Can I see the menu? | Kan jeg få se menyen? | kan yi faw say men_ew_en |
| Can I see the wine list? | Kan jeg få se vinkartet? | kan yi faw say v_ee_nkarteh |
| I'm a vegetarian | Jeg er vegetarianer | yi ar veggetahreeghnehr |
| Waiter/waitress! | Hallo! Unnskyld | hall_o_ _oo_nsk_ew_l |
| The bill, please | Regningen, takk. | r_i_ning-en takk |
| beer | øl | url |
| bottle | flaske | fl_a_skeh |
| buffet | koldtbord | k_a_wltb_oh_r |
| cake | kake | k_a_hkeh |
| children's portion | barneporsjon | barneporsh_oh_n |
| coffee | kaffe | k_a_ffeh |
| cup | kopp | kopp |
| fork | gaffel | g_a_ffel |
| glass | glass | glass |
| knife | kniv | k-neev |
| menu | meny | men_ew_ |
| milk | melk | melk |
| open sandwich | smørbrød | sm_u_rhn_i_r |
| plate | tallerk | tal-_a_rk |
| receipt | kvittering | kvitt_oy_ring |
| schnapps | akevitt | _a_kevitt |

| | | |
|---|---|---|
| serviette | **serviett** | *sarvi-ett* |
| snack | **smårett** | *smoawrett* |
| soup | **suppe** | *sooppeh* |
| spoon | **skje** | *shay* |
| sugar | **sukker** | *sookker* |
| tea | **te** | *tay* |
| tip | **tips** | *tips* |
| waiter | **kelner** | *kelner* |
| waitress | **serveringsdame** | *sarvayringssdahmeh* |
| water | **vann** | *vann* |
| wine | **vin** | *veen* |
| wine list | **vinkart** | *veenkart* |

## MENU DECODER

| | | |
|---|---|---|
| ansjos | **anshoos** | *anchovies* |
| baguette | **bagaitt** | *French stick* |
| blåskjell | **blaw-shayll** | *mussels* |
| bringebær | **brjnge-bair** | *raspberries* |
| brød | **brur** | *bread* |
| dyrestek | **dewrestek** | *roast reindeer* |
| eddik | **eddikk** | *vinegar* |
| elg | **ailk** | *elk* |
| fenalår | **fehna-lawr** | *cured leg of mutton* |
| fisk | **feesk** | *fish* |
| flatbrød | **flaht-brur** | *'flat bread' (leaf-thin crispbread)* |
| flyndre | **flewndre** | *sole* |
| fløte | **flurteh** | *cream* |
| fårikål | **fawreekawl** | *lamb and cabbage stew* |
| gaffelbiter | **gahffel-beeter** | *small fillets of herring soaked in marinade* |
| geitost | **geytost** | *sweet, brown goat's cheese* |
| gravlaks | **grahv-lahks** | *cured salmon* |
| grovbrød | **grurv-brur** | *wholemeal bread* |
| grønnsaker | **grurnn-sahker** | *vegetables* |
| hellefisk | **hellefisk** | *halibut* |
| hummer | **hummer** | *lobster* |
| hvalbiff | **vahlbiff** | *whale steak* |
| hvitvin | **veetveen** | *white wine* |
| høns | **hurns** | *chicken, poultry* |
| is | **ees** | *ice cream, ice* |
| jordbær | **joordbair** | *strawberries* |
| kalv | **kallv** | *veal* |
| karbonade | **karbonahdeh** | *minced beef steak* |
| kjøtt | **HURtt** | *meat* |
| kjøttkaker | **HURttkahker** | *minced beef balls* |
| kneipbrød | **k-neyp-brur** | *crusty wheaten bread* |
| knekkebrød | **k-nekke-brur** | *crispbread* |
| kokt | **kookt** | *boiled, poached* |
| koldtbord | **kawltbohr** | *cold buffet* |
| krabbe | **crahbbe** | *crab* |
| kreps | **krepss** | *crayfish* |
| kveite | **kvaiyteh** | *halibut* |
| kylling | **HEWlling** | *chicken* |
| laks | **lahks** | *salmon* |
| lam | **lamm** | *lamb* |
| makrell | **mahkrel** | *mackerel* |
| melk | **mailk** | *milk* |
| mineralvann | **mineralvann** | *mineral water* |
| multer | **mewlter** | *cloudberries* |
| mørbrad | **murbrur** | *sirloin* |
| okse | **ookseh** | *beef* |
| oksestek | **ookseh-steek** | *roast beef* |
| ost | **oost** | *cheese* |
| pannekaker | **pannekahker** | *large thin pancakes* |
| pariserloff | **pareewser-loff** | *French stick* |
| pinnekjøtt | **pinne-HURtt** | *salted, dried side of lamb* |
| pisket krem | **piskett kraim** | *whipped cream* |
| poteter | **pootaiter** | *potatoes* |
| pølser | **pURlser** | *frankfurter sausages* |
| rakørret | **rahk-URret** | *fermented trout* |
| reinsdyr | **rainsdewr** | *reindeer* |
| reke(r) | **rehker** | *prawns* |
| ris | **rees** | *rice* |
| rogn | **rogn** | *roe* |
| rugbrød | **rewgbrur** | *rye bread* |
| rødspette | **rURdspetteh** | *plaice* |
| rødvin | **rURveen** | *red wine* |
| røkelaks | **rURkelaks** | *smoked salmon* |
| rømme | **rURmmeh** | *soured cream* |
| rå | **raw** | *raw* |
| saus | **saws** | *sauce* |
| sei | **saiy** | *coley* |
| sild | **seell** | *herring* |
| sjokolade | **shokolahde** | *chocolate* |
| skalldyr | **skall-dewr** | *shellfish* |

| | | |
|---|---|---|
| skinke | **shinkeh** | *ham* |
| skjell | **shayll** | *shells* |
| smør | **smURR** | *butter* |
| smørbrød | **smURRbrUR** | *open sandwich* |
| saus | **saws** | *sauce* |
| stekt | **stehkt** | *fried, roasted* |
| sukker | **sookker** | *sugar* |
| suppe | **sooppeh** | *soup* |
| surkål | **sewkall** | *sauerkraut* |
| svin | **sween** | *pork* |
| syltetøy | **sewlte-tURj** | *jam* |
| søt | **sURt** | *sweet* |
| torsk | **tawshk** | *cod* |
| tyttebær | **tewtte-bair** | *cowberries or lingonberries* |
| tørr | **tURr** | *dry* |
| vafler | **vahfler** | *waffles* |
| vann | **vann** | *tap water* |
| varm | **vahrm** | *warm, hot* |
| vilt | **veellt** | *game* |
| vin | **veen** | *wine* |
| øl | **URl** | *beer* |
| ørret | **URrett** | *trout* |
| østers | **URsters** | *oysters* |

## NUMBERS

| | | |
|---|---|---|
| 0 | **null** | *nooll* |
| 1 | **en/ett** | *ayn/ett* |
| 2 | **to** | *toh* |
| 3 | **tre** | *tray* |
| 4 | **fire** | *feereh* |
| 5 | **fem** | *fem* |
| 6 | **seks** | *seks* |
| 7 | **sju/syv** | *shoo/sewv* |
| 8 | **åtte** | *awtteh* |
| 9 | **ni** | *nee* |
| 10 | **ti** | *tee* |
| 11 | **elleve** | *elveh* |
| 12 | **tolv** | *tawll* |
| 13 | **tretten** | *tretten* |
| 14 | **fjorten** | *fyohrten* |
| 15 | **femten** | *femten* |
| 16 | **seksten** | *sisten* |
| 17 | **sytten** | *sutten* |
| 18 | **atten** | *atten* |
| 19 | **nitten** | *neetten* |
| 20 | **tjue/tyve** | *Hoo-eh/tewveh* |
| 21 | **tjueen/enogtyve** | *Hoo-eh-ayn/ ayn-aw-tewveh* |
| 22 | **tjueto/toogtyve** | *Hoo-eh-toh/ toh-aw-tewveh* |
| 30 | **tretti/tredve** | *tretti/tredveh* |
| 40 | **førti/førr** | *fURti/fURr* |
| 50 | **femti** | *femti* |
| 60 | **seksti** | *seksti* |
| 70 | **sytti** | *sUrtti* |
| 80 | **åtti** | *awtti* |
| 90 | **nitti** | *neetti* |
| 100 | **(ett) hundre** | *hoondreh* |
| 110 | **hundre og ti** | *hoondreh aw tee* |
| 200 | **to hundre** | *toh hoondreh* |
| 300 | **tre hundre** | *tray hoondreh* |
| 400 | **fire hundre** | *feereh hoondreh* |
| 1,000 | **(ett) tusen** | *toossen* |
| 10,000 | **ti tusen** | *tee toossen* |

## TIME

| | | |
|---|---|---|
| today | **i dag** | *ee-dahg* |
| yesterday | **i går** | *ee-gawr* |
| tomorrow | **i morgen** | *ee-mawern* |
| this morning | **i morges** | *ee-morges* |
| this afternoon | **i ettermiddag** | *ee-ettermiddag* |
| this evening/tonight | **i kveld** | *ee-kvell* |
| late | **sent** | *saynt* |
| early | **tidlig** | *teeli* |
| soon | **snart** | *snahrt* |
| later on | **senere** | *saynereh* |
| one minute | **et minutt** | *et minoott* |
| two minutes | **to minutter** | *toh minootter* |
| quarter of an hour | **et kvarter** | *et kvartayr* |
| half an hour | **en halv time** | *ayn hal teemeh* |
| Sunday | **søndag** | *sURndag* |
| Monday | **mandag** | *mandag* |
| Tuesday | **tirsdag** | *teerssdag* |
| Wednesday | **onsdag** | *ohnssdag* |
| Thursday | **torsdag** | *tawrssdag* |
| Friday | **fredag** | *fraydag* |
| Saturday | **lørdag** | *lURrdag* |

# ACKNOWLEDGMENTS

The publisher would like to thank the following for their kind permission to reproduce their photographs:

Key: a-above; b-below/bottom; c-centre; f-far; l-left; r-right; t-top

**123RF.com:** Lutsenko Alexander 239ca; Drepicter 184–5t; Stefan Holm 19t, 212; lightboxx 233ca; Andrey Omelyanchuk 78–9b.

**4Corners:** Massimo Borchi 116–7b, 126tl.

**Ægir BrewPub:** 12clb, 44bl.

**Alamy Stock Photo:** 914 collection 51crb; AB Forces News Collection 95cra; AF archive 190br; AGE fotostock 28bl; Fadi Al-barghouthy 190–191t; AM Stock 30tl; Ange 138–9t; ATW Photography / *Henrik Ibsen* by Nina Sundbye ©DACS, 2018 35cl; Avalon / Picture Nature 169br; Guillermo Avello 203br; BeautifulArctic 238–9b; Steve Bly 210bl; Lasse Bolstad 157tl; Ian Bottle 219tr, 224b; Mary Cárdenas 110–111t; Carefordolphins 243cra; Chronicle 49clb, 50bl; Classic Image 52cb; Luis Dafos 60crb, 101tr; Ian Dagnall 125t; Janna Danilova 27b; David Bleeker Photography 43cl; Gabriele Dessì 72cra, 80–81t, 89tl, 102tl; Oscar Dominguez 76–7t; dpa picture alliance 76br, 144bl; Stale Edstrom 156b; Øystein Engan 46cra; Europe/ Peter Forsberg / *Peer Gynt* by Dyra Vick © DACS 2018 126bc; Everett Collection Historical 76clb; Everst 194–5b, 202tr; FLHC 61.77br; Folio Images 84–5; Paul Gapper 142tl; Jeff Gilbert 65cl; GL Archive 49cla; Glasshouse Images 52t; Gonzales Photo 47cr; Hemis 33cla, 39bl, 74bl, 131b, 153tl, / Caviglia Denis 247b, / Bertrand Gardel 58br, / Ludovic Maisant 64–5t, 65cb; History and Art Collection 95cla; Robert Hollingworth 111crb; Hufton+Crow-VIEW 120; Gordon Hulmes 36bl; imageBROKER 36–7b, 163tl, 172br, 174br, 178t; Interfoto 226tc; Ivoha 172–3, 209tl; Ivy Close Images 49bc; Roger Johansen 222br; Johner Images 38–9t; Marcin Kadziolka 143br; Ivan Kmit 30–31b; Albert Knapp 83b; Wojciech Kruczynski 43tr; Line 245br; LOOK Die Bildagentur der Fotografen GmbH 248clb; De Luan 48bc; mauritius images GmbH 19bl, 228, 235bl, 242br, 244–5t; Minkimo 140–141t; Graham Mulrooney 104bl; Andy Myatt / *fountain* by Wenche Gulbransen © DACS 2018 97b; National Geographic Image Collection 42tl; Nature Picture Library 39cr; Alexander Nitzsche 118bl; Norphoto 29cb; North Wind Picture Archives 49tl, 51cb;

Novarc Images 234–5t; Andrey Omelyanchuk 96tl; Jackietraveller Oslo 87tr; Panther Media GmbH 138cb; parkerphotography 32–3t; PearlBucknall 138bc; The Picture Art Collection 48crb, 50tr, 50cra, 50crb; The Print Collector 50cr; Prisma Archivo 50tl; Alex Ramsay 106; Realimage 198clb; Rolf Richardson 119tc; robertharding 206br, 207t, 222t, 225tr, 236t; Jose Francisco Sanchez 198bc; Eugene Sergeev 227b; Keith Shuttlewood 176tr; Adelheid Smitt 23cla; Jon Sparks 115t; Dave Stamboulis 36tl; Stockimo / Arthur Gebuys 38bl; Parinya Suwanitch 88bl; Jochen Tack 249l; Steve Taylor ARPS 161br; Glyn Thomas 111bc; Nikolay Tsuguliev 246tl; Grethe Ulgjell 82bc, 100tc, 127crb; / Grethe Ulgjell /*Marilyn Monroe* (2009) by Richard Hudson: Polished Mirrored Steel/H:250cms/ Ed:3/3 + 2AP's, Exhibited by Sotheby's at Chatsworth "Beyond Limits Exhibition" 2009., Web:<www.richardhudsonsculptor.com>, Location: Ekebergparken Sculpture Park, Kongsveien 130tc; Utterström Photography 160–161t; Lucas Vallecillos 21tr, 29br, 188t, 197cra; Rob Watkins 45crb; Jan Wlodarczyk 176–7b, 200–201b, 211t; WS Collection 95tc; Xinhua 47cl; Yegorovnick 31cl, 99crb; Anna Yu / *Heptakord* by Turid Angell Eng © DACS 2018 82tr; Zoonar GmbH 100b.

**AWL Images:** Ludovic Maisant 90; Doug Pearson 13cr.

**Bass Oslo:** 62–3t, 63cla.

**Bergen Fest:** courtesy of DawBell / Jarle H. Moe 46cr.

**Bridgeman Images:** New York Public Library, USA 49tr; The Sorting Building, Norway / Photo © O. Vaering 51t.

**Depositphotos Inc:** Nanisimova_sell 127b.

**Dorling Kindersley:** Frits Solvang 116t.

**Dreamstime.com:** Valentin Armianu 16c, 54–5, 102–3b; Andrey Armyagov 195ca; Balipadma 170–171t; Helena Bilkova 37t; Bragearonsen 144–5t; Ivan Kmit 199; Sergii Krynytsia 196; Kyolshin 232–3b; Lubastock 169crb; Michael Müller 76cl; Mariabk 195tr; Mariuszks 47crb; Julie Mayfeng 123bl, 187tl; Nanisimova 98–9b; Nenad Nedomacki 124bc; Nightman1965